THE SUBSTITUTE ASSHOLE

THE SUBSTITUTE ASSHOLE

How a rogue suburban kid's escape from
conformity collided with a cultural revolution,
drug smuggling, psychedelics, and federal prison

A memoir by
Dean Quarnstrom
1943-2021

Compiled and edited by Evan Quarnstrom

Copyright © 2024 by Dean Quarnstrom and Evan Quarnstrom.

All rights reserved.

No part of this publication may be reproduced, distributed, or transmitted in any form or by any means, including photocopying, recording, or other electronic or mechanical methods, without the prior written permission of the publisher, except as permitted by U.S. copyright law.

For permission requests, contact Evan Quarnstrom [evanquarnstrom@gmail.com].

For privacy reasons, individuals names and potentially identifying details have been altered in most cases.

Editing, compilation, and cover design by Evan Quarnstrom.

ISBN: 979-8-218-33991-3

Acknowledgements

I'd like to give a heartfelt thanks to those who contributed to helping me finish my father's memoir, namely, my stepmother, Jeanie, and all those who helped edit, such as David, Nate, Shelley, and Lars. Thanks to my siblings, Anne, Erin, and Nik, for sticking together during difficult times.

And, of course, thanks to my father, Dean, for sharing his stories and trusting me to be a part of this project.

-*Evan Quarnstrom*

Contents

Acknowledgements   v
Prologue   ix
Introduction   x
Preface   xiv

Part I: Rockets

1   *In the Beginning, the Circus*   2
2   *Growing Up Fast: Chicago in the '50s*   11
3   *Cattle Truck Hits Overturned Vehicle*   25
4   *Love and Mercy, San Francisco, April 1964*   28

Part II: The Outlaw Years

5   *Weed's Early Days in the Haight*   35
6   *Ram Dass Retreat*   45
7   *Letter to Ram Dass*   47
8   *Ignore Alien Orders*   49
9   *One Brave Beauty*   51
10   *Never Trust a Prankster*   53
11   *The Acid King*   57
12   *The Dead and Cassady*   64
13   *The Lab*   68
14   *Yamananda, Bliss of Death*   73
15   *Hassler and Lee*   77
16   *The Outlaws*   80
17   *The World Smoke Ring Champion, '67*   84
18   *The Second Hell's Angels Acid Test at Kesey's*   88
19   *The King of Lompico*   91
20   *Funny Money*   93

21	The First Smuggling Adventure	95
22	Chez Ray and Sleazy Dean	102
23	Teenie Weenie Deenie	112
24	Rockets and the Gopher	114
25	Maybe You Use Your Mouth Too Much	116
26	Seventeen Strangers, 1972	130
27	Easy Money	139
28	Word Is Bond	147
29	Waiting for the Load	153
	Photos	162
30	The Stash Houses	174
31	El Jefe	182
32	Butter and Woodstock Gail	185
33	Colombian Gold	192
34	Pulling Off the Big One	194
35	Bart the Fart	199
36	Abandon Ship or Save the Load	201
37	Awakening 1963	210

Part III: Boron

38	How Did I Ever End Up Here?	215
39	Journaling in Boron	220
40	Boron Stories	261
41	Hollywood Halfway House	267

Part IV: A Fresh Start

42	Mary's Gifts	284
43	Victims by Our Own Hands	287
44	Tales to Tell You	289
45	Letters to Big Ben	293
46	Hey Nik, Let's Talk About Money	298
47	Worlds Away	300
	Obituary	302
	Epilogue	304

Prologue

Who was behind this new earth-shaking rock 'n roll lifestyle? The outlaw pirates. We had many faces: We were writers, poets, musicians, diggers, explorers, students, smugglers, chemists, risk-takers, dealers, the counterculture, the kids who suddenly woke up and knew they could make it happen, and were learning how to enjoy the process of driving the rising waves higher and higher.

I was a founding participant in the first wave, and unfortunately, the last group of a well-intended, honest, and trustworthy breed of pot smugglers. 'The Man' called us criminals, but we were honored and respected as homegrown, in-the-flesh folk heroes by our own generation, the customers we serviced. Our group risked it all to stay living on the outside, a small bunch of rogues who took great pride in beating the law to earn a living. And man, what a great living it was.

- Dean Quarnstrom, Chapter 16 , 'The Outlaws'

Introduction

My dad, Dean Quarnstrom, was born on January 13, 1943 and died 78 years later on August 13, 2021. He was a lot of things to a lot of people. I can confidently tell you that Dean was a brother, a writer, an adventurer, a photographer, a fatal car crash survivor, a hippie, a smuggler, a salesman, a classic car enthusiast, a six-time husband, a convicted felon, a father, and always an iconoclast. Dean reinvented himself many times, leading lives that ranged from a sly kid who cut his teeth on the streets of 1950s Chicago, to a partner of the Harvard psychology professor Richard Alpert (later to be dismissed for LSD experiments and become spiritual guru Ram Dass), to the right-hand man of famed LSD chemist Owsley Stanley. He eventually settled down as a family man, becoming a father of three in Santa Cruz, California, of which I am one. Despite my father's decades of adventures and tribulations, for much of my life I knew very little about who he truly was.

Yet I still find myself pondering the same question: Who was my father?

My parents split in 1997, when I was five years old. I spent most of my time at my mother's, visiting my dad every other weekend and spending one week of summer together – usually at Lake Tahoe. As a result, I didn't have the traditional father-son relationship with my dad. The familial environment didn't allow for a profoundly deep connection to grow and flourish. That said, it's not that we didn't try. We took advantage of the time that we had together – watching basketball games, going on day trips around Santa Cruz, and eating burritos around the dinner table from our favorite local taquerias.

It wasn't until I left home that I began to discover who my father was. When I moved away to San Diego for college in 2010 and the physical distance between us grew, we found a way to connect through a shared passion for writing. Writing runs in our family. My paternal grandparents, Gordon and Leonore, were writers. They ran a travel publication for many years. My late uncle, Lee, Dean's brother, was a journalist and wrote a memoir of his own. My father worked at the high school newspaper in Winnetka, Illinois and continued to write throughout his whole life. That's where his passion for communicating via written word began, which then transitioned into writing screenplays, journaling in prison, and penning letters to his kids to be read in the future. These events all, directly or indirectly, led to the creation of this memoir.

Dean and I used to correspond over email, sometimes sending thousands of words at a time. We were both able to more freely express our feelings and thoughts through the meticulous, yet creative, exercise of turning them into written words. Through this process I realized that I was much more like my father than I ever thought. I could relate to his advice, experience, and the stories that I read – things that I had never heard about when we were living in the same town. I began to see myself in him, something that I had previously been conditioned to believe was not true. As the onset of Parkinson's disease exacerbated his inability to hold long conversations, writing was our tool to circumvent the challenges and continue to let our relationship bloom.

When Dean started compiling all of his lifetime stories into a memoir, he came to me for help. We both loved writing and genuinely enjoyed working on this project together. He would send me excerpts and ask for my opinion, bouncing ideas off me of how to connect a common thread through the story. We organized and sifted through thousands of photos, each one capable of spurring an hour-long story about events that occurred long before my birth. This was when I really began to know my father.

However, as Parkinson's, and a new diagnosis of Chronic

Lymphocytic Leukemia, took control of his body and mind, our communication became more difficult and infrequent. On Friday, June 11, 2021, Dean sent me an email with the subject line "Worlds Away." He was asking for some technical help converting file types of images and for feedback on some memoir passages. I responded the next day, June 12. In that email I gave some advice and apologized that I wasn't going to be in town for Father's Day. But I didn't know it would be his last. I never got a response.

Dean's condition worsened much faster than we could have foreseen. I drove up to Santa Cruz from San Diego in August of 2021 after he had received a diagnosis of terminal cancer. I knew this was the end – the end of the emails, our late-blooming relationship, and of the man responsible for my birth – but I thought we had months to say goodbye, not days. My siblings, Nik and Anne, my stepmother, Jeanie, and I were holding Dean as he took his last breath on Friday, August 13th, 2021, just five days after my arrival.

In Dean's final days, he never asked me to finish his memoir for him. It didn't need to be said. But he must have had this moment in mind when he recruited me to join the project. He knew this day would come. You can't expect to live too long with Parkinson's. There was an unspoken understanding that this was the next step in a project that had been decades in the making. After his passing I scoured his computer files, hard drives, and discs, rummaging for anything that I deemed valuable for the memoir. I found the stories that he had purposefully written to be in this memoir, but also old letters, journals, and poems that helped answer my original question: Who was my dad?

Even after his death, the process of getting to know him has not stopped. I compiled hundreds and hundreds of pages of his writings, reading each and every word. I am still getting to know him through his words, just as if he were still at his office desk, typing away emails and stories to me. That is the story of how this memoir came to be.

Dean was a conflicted, complex man, constantly searching for the purpose of his life and for ways to reconcile his pursuit of too much of life's pleasures with the traumatic

Introduction

events that seemed to fall on him from nowhere. In his final years he was frequently concerned about the legacy that he would leave in this world. Just like everyone, he was imperfect. But he was full of love, a love that he learned to channel into his relationships and his three children.

Putting together this memoir has been a crucial part of the healing process for me. Sometimes I am in awe of the unassuming man that my father was and the adventures he lived when he was my age. Other times the stories bring back painful memories and tears flow as I mull over the words. I don't care if this memoir is read by five people, or five million. This memoir marks the completion of a project that my father and I had been working on together. It allowed me to grow closer to and better know my father than most children can ever hope for.

There hasn't been a day that I don't think about you, Dad. I miss you.

- Evan Quarnstrom
19 March 2023

Preface

A triggering event? Which one?

Here we go. It's happening again, another triggering event? And just when I'd taken a first giant step on the road to liberation from a life-long craving for more of all of it.

I'd begun living into my own aging while holding close Buddha's wise words that connect desire to the causes of all human suffering. I was no longer daydreaming about future promiscuous encounters or worrying about the cessation of a whole production of glorious sexual adventures.

Only after exhausting all available avenues of worldly distractions – the potential, the present, the imaginary – only then did I find that I had no options left but to accept the unavoidable: I'd reached old age, still very much alive and with no immediate life-threatening emergencies. Well, except maybe for those medications that my heart depends on to maintain a steady blood pressure, medications that had, unexpectedly, one mind-bending side-effect: the complete loss of my life-long, unflinching need for intimate sexual contact.

At first, I couldn't understand what had happened to me. The one worldly and consistent goal that I'd long held so dear, the one desire I'd never refused had simply disappeared. My thoroughly enjoyable sexual appetite, my hopes and drive to find more of it, had vanished.

At the same time I was coming to see that I could embrace the meaning of Buddha's teachings on suffering: Life is all about suffering. Freedom from suffering comes only with the absence of desire, including, unfortunately, sexual desire. I finally got it. I was experiencing a radically new and unfamiliar sense of inner-peace in my life.

Accepting this truth produced a mental and physical lightness in my whole body and soul, an overall sense of well-being. I was actually enjoying the lack of mental pressures.

But in 2013 everything changed. I was diagnosed with Parkinson's Disease.

But wait...what's this......? I mean, you're kidding, right? Hey, slow down a little. You're saying wha......Parkinson's? Hold on...you're telling me I have Parkinson's Disease...? No way...

Silly me, hoping I was on some path to real self-awareness.

Well, fuck me now for real, the old Puppet Master has really done it this time, shifted the whole goddamned-paradigm-thingie on me once again.

I'll have to admit, witnessing the invasive onslaught of the Parkinson's Disease bulldozer slowly moving in, taking control, revealing the devastating power of its non-stop move into my life – similar to what the sexual thing had once done, but this time promising no pleasurable, rewarding outcome – certainly got my full attention.

I'd recently begun editing my still-unfinished memoir, sorting through the many years of scattered, random notes, the stories of memorable people and events I'd been part of in my past. I'd typed and hand-scribbled these stories onto notecards, yellow sticky-note pads, scraps of paper, and in spiral-bound notebooks as I'd experienced them, and had done so over the past six decades. I had boxes and drawers full of notes and stories to organize. I was engaged, really enjoying the process, reassembling a timeline of people and events I was able to recall in detail, personal tales of my earlier lives and my former wives.

And I'd definitely been savoring a certain, ironic sense of self-satisfaction, having survived intact into my '70s after so many years of living on the edge through exotic, erotic, grand, and often dangerous adventures and people. Yet now, in retrospect, it all just seems not so important, almost normal when compared to what I'm hearing will soon be coming my way.

One of the possible titles I'm considering for these memoirs is "The Substitute Asshole," a good example of the kind of life some of us had during the late 1960s. So much was happening to those in my generation who could see it, all in a very short, condensed period of time.

I delivered the U.S. mail to the largest number of rural mailboxes on a single route in the entire U.S.A., in Felton, California. One postal driver delivered the daily mail to over 1,000 rural households. After many years of delivering this route's daily mail, the one regular driver had developed a serious hemorrhoid problem from the long hours sitting in his car. I lived at the furthest box on that route. We became friendly, chatty acquaintances and whenever I'd bump into him we got along. When his hemorrhoids really started flaring up, I just happened to be available when he asked me if I could deliver the mail to his route, just until his irritated butthole got some rest and healed up a little.

The idea of working for the U.S. government appealed to me; it could be a beautiful cover story if I ever needed one. An easy gig, I'd earn some legitimate income, and keep supplying my weed customers at the same time. Why not? I was living in paradise, caretaker of a beautiful, remote redwood forested estate. So, right up until the regular driver passed away from butthole complications many months later, I was known by him, by a few friends, and within the local post office as "The Substitute Asshole." Shortly after the worn-out driver passed on, my postal rural route was eliminated, then divided up and re-awarded to four Vietnam vets.

I'd skated through decades of fast times, hard living, psychedelic adventures, and numerous outlaw escapades. After years of great times, some difficult times, and numerous love affairs, in 1989 I settled down into the confines of a real job in the technology industry, to raise my new family and in good time to help support my three lovely children's efforts to get accepted to, then make it through, college. I had spent the last 20 years employed in a variety of above-board, Silicon Valley high-tech, high-income positions, staying healthy long enough to retire, old enough to enroll in Medicare.

What's so amazing to me right now is how all of these grand memories suddenly paled in comparison to the unforgettable flash of real fear and uncertainty that engulfed me when the doctor informed me that I had Parkinson's Disease. I was unprepared for and devastated by this news. My knees went all-wobbly and I had to sit down to keep from losing my balance.

I felt as if I'd been banished to a barren desert world, ruled over by unseen monsters, magnitudes more powerful than anything I'd ever imagined, let alone confronted. I've named my illness "Parkys," as shorter words are easier to deal with when living with this disease. What the fuck!

Since being cast into the thick of this Parkinson's gambit, knowing I've been handed a death sentence, most of my past life's uniqueness and fleeting escapades are useful only for their entertaining memories. Parkys' bold, raw power, the swiftness of its full-on physical and mental assault on my life, is mind-boggling and relentless, with no relief anywhere in sight.

So I asked myself, am I supposed to just roll over and surrender to a numbing, downhill decline, the physical and mental deterioration of everything that's me? To accept this absolute, meaningless end to an otherwise great American story, and leave it at that?

No-fucking-way! See, I do know one thing that's certain about life: When nothing is ventured, nothing is gained.

I turned to the Internet to start personal research and quickly discovered that little-to-no applicable medical or pharmaceutical information exists on Parkys. Ten million sufferers worldwide, yet almost no cutting-edge research exists or is being planned.

There has to be something, someone who can help me, maybe a healer in the Brazilian jungles, a sadhu in Madras. What about Don Juan? I'm really not ready to sit back and wait to suffer excruciating pain in a couple of years, lose muscle control or my immune system, knowing these lovely symptoms are only the precursors to what comes last, but certainly not the least of Parkys' living hells: full-on dementia, a bug on the wall waiting for another time to attack. Then you finally die from this invasion.

No fucking way, not quite yet, thank you very much!

So I dug a little deeper, talked to friends of friends, and learned that there is an experimental drug called Ibogaine that might be effective in helping stop the gradual physical and mental slide that's unavoidable with PD (Parkinson's Disease).

But no one can say for sure if this drug works or not because the drug was banned in the U.S. over 40 years ago for all the wrong reasons. No research or studies have been run to test this drug. There are no funds available to study it on rats, let alone humans, because this drug, when taken in very large doses, is a hallucinogen, similar to LSD. It has "no known medical uses" and is considered by the DEA to be as bad as heroin and LSD. So, even though some research has been performed in other countries on how the drug works in the brain, no human has ever tried this drug in tiny dosages over time to see if it has any effects on PD. The drug is legal in most countries on Earth, including Canada and Mexico, where it is currently utilized to wean people off heroin addictions.

I've got an incurable illness. What do I have to lose? I volunteered to be the first human guinea pig to test this drug in an official, controlled study. I spent 60 days in a Parkinson's research study in Mexico using the drug and it worked its magic on me. The drug reversed Parkinson's unrelenting takeover of my physical body, mental capacity, and best of all, my soul.

I regained use of facial muscles and expressions that were frozen, or immobile before. I regained vocal strength and use of my right hand. I could stand erect, having regained my sense of balance, and no longer feared that I might easily fall down. My right arm contracted and expanded without ratcheting. I could carry on a conversation for more than a minute. And best of all I regained a sense of myself in space and time. I felt the re-emergence of my creative edge, which was slowly diminishing over time.

I was told that what I was experiencing was a first in medical history, that this resurgence of physical and mental capacity had never happened before to a sufferer of PD (no one had ever microdosed for PD) and that news alone made my eyes tear up. It seemed to be a cure, at least for now.

Most of what I need in order to feel human is still functioning quite well. I've brushed up against the Death Beast a few times in my life before Parkys and it's never stopped me. So, maybe there's another adventure in store ahead for me.

My neurologist's response when I asked, "Why me?" wasn't helpful. "No one really knows what causes Parkinson's; some medical researchers believe it's hereditary, others feel it's the result of past trauma, a major 'triggering event' that happened earlier in life, and there's new research that's pointing to the microbes found in one's gut," he explained.

A triggering event? I thought, "Which one? I mean, there have been so many."

Maybe it was that life-changing, deadly car accident on the I-5 that changed my life's trajectory? Or the amount of LSD that I'd consumed? Or maybe that shattering moment when the judge in Southern Georgia sentenced me to 15 years[1] in federal prison? Or when I'd learned that my smuggling partners actually considered the Colombians' offer to toss me out of our DC-6 during its next flight north from Colombia? I'll never know, and it really doesn't matter anyway.

Hadn't I been the one who sought out all those unpredictable thrills and chills? Hadn't I loved the rush and excitement of those many potential "triggering" events? My life's littered with the consequences of my past adventures; the earth-shaking highs and awesome successes, and the terrible losses and failures. I'd be hard-pressed to pick

---

1   Three sentences of five years that were to be served simultaneously.

which one had unleashed this berserk Parkys attack on my mind and body. There were so many to choose from.

~ ~ ~

Listen up, kids

My three young children, if you only knew. If only you could sit down and show some interest for a few minutes, I'd clue you in to some stories of my personal history, which is yours, too, and tell you about what's really been going on in our little world and in your lives. If only even one of you were interested enough in your dad to just listen, you'd hear some damn good stories about who I might be.

Not gonna happen. So instead, I'm writing down my stories here, as a letter to you and maybe someday you'll want to read it. It's good stuff, filled with grand adventures that are worth knowing if you're ever wanting to know and understand where you came from and who your dad really was.

Today, there's an incredibly large and powerful hole in my heart touching every minute of my life, everything I see or do or think about, and it's caused by a gnawing sense of loss that fills me, all because I haven't spent enough time with you guys while you're growing up. I've missed out on so much of your life, from infancy to whatever comes next. I've done everything possible except have your mother jailed to get more time with you, but nothing works in my favor.

Yesterday you were in third grade, tomorrow, high school and, as I read this again, today is April 13, 2012, now it's college. Nothing's really changed for the better for me as far as spending more time with my kids, and now it's time you're on your own.

I'd like to tell you about the meaning of life, but I'd be lying to you because I don't know it. I can say that everything I'm telling you in this letter is the truth as I understand it. And I'll bet by the time you read this, you're already seeing that the truth is damn hard to understand or figure out.

Preface

I know how little the written word appeals to your Millennial Generation, but if you'd like to know something about who your dad is, and where I've been, just try to hang in here, read my words for a while, and imagine...once upon a time long before texting and cell phones...it's June, 1977...way 'back in the day...'

Part I:
Rockets

Given that my father passed before he could complete this memoir, there are some gaps and holes in his timeline that could make it difficult to follow the story. Thus, I've interjected my own voice to attempt to fill in those gaps at the start of each of the book's four sections. So, let's go back to the very beginning...

My father had a peculiar childhood. It certainly set him on the path in life that he would follow as an adult. Growing up, he bounced around schools, from Washington state to the suburbs of Chicago, Illinois. His parents, Leonore and Gordon Quarnstrom, clearly loved him, but the family dynamics were dysfunctional. Between being forced to attend Catholic schools and always being the 'uncool' younger brother who never fit in, Dean always knew that his future was somewhere far away from the small world he lived in. He didn't want the same old boring life that everyone else had. There had to be adventure elsewhere.

-Evan

Chapter 1

In the Beginning, the Circus

I'm already an old man: 63, 68, 70 years have flashed on by while I put my life into words, but I have no idea of how old I really feel. I don't have the energy that just came naturally to me until a few years ago. In fact, I had so much energy in my hippie days that everyone called me "Rockets." Yet I feel now almost the same in my mind as I did when I first ran away from home, before I was in kindergarten in Longview, Washington.

I knew at that early age I needed to be moving on if I hoped to take it all in, get laid one day too. When the first opportunity to take off appeared, I just up and left home to join the traveling circus that stopped briefly in Longview, Washington every summer. Both times I asked to join, the circus hired me on the spot to help raise its huge tents. I knew they were always moving on to new places, and I was joining it for real. I was ready to leave my parents and brother with no regrets, ready for new adventures everywhere the circus would take me. Boy was I naive.

The first time I asked for a job, some guy set me up pounding wood stakes in the ground. He told me it was very important work, which I loved doing until the cops showed up and took me home. The following summer I tried to join up again, and the same thing happened. I just wasn't smart enough to figure out that the circus manager was ratting me out, was calling the cops and turning me in. I wanted to go and I trusted the circus to be my ticket out. But I've always trusted people more than most deserved, and, as I've always stood by my beliefs, I've had my share of bad troubles for being such a trusting, foolish young soul.

My childhood was important. The love I felt lacking from my parents was important. The relationship I had with my older brother was important.

As far back as I can enter and explore memories from my youth, I was leaving home hoping to get somewhere that felt better, and I knew it was out there. My childhood memories are so vivid. I can remember getting nothing I wanted or needed from my parents; their understanding of love was meaningless, unaffectionate, almost non-existent and not what I knew I needed. My relationship with my brother was based on fear and competition. He was never a friend for me, never there when things got rough, and was always out only for himself. Your family should be the bottom line, the last ray of hope, but in my family, I had to make a life on my own.

The parents, the family love situation, or lack thereof, drove me away. I had a dominant, remote father and a neurotic mother, and I searched for a better love, more fun, as far back as I can remember. I tried to hang with the older guys, felt their search was more defined than mine, and would follow them into secret tunnels they dug, hideouts, or on adventures far away from my house.

I just knew there was something more important to do with my life than what I was doing at the time, hopefully more fun, and all I had to do to find it was start looking. And, of course, the first and best place to look was in what moved me the most: girls, sex or the idea of it, what it might make happen, the promise of what it would bring to the game.

My next-door teenage neighbor told me all about fucking girls when I was four years old. "Ya stick your weenie in her pee hole, see..." Now, this was some really important information, and I started looking around all the time for couples really doing it. In fact, it became the most exciting of potential options that I could imagine for myself, to stick my rock-hard boner into a girl's funny little slit, not that I often got to see one. I had wet dreams from as far back as anything else I can remember. Surely sex must have been the impetus driving my young need to hit the road because it wasn't happening for me at home. Man, did I dream of seeing and touching a real, live naked girl. I mean *all the time*. Even in kindergarten, I thought about this girl named PJ being all naked and my girlfriend, at least I remember the rush I got from just thinking about the possibility of her and me. I really liked my wet dreams, but even then I knew to keep my sexual desires safely hidden inside. Already in kindergarten, I feared any authority that might want to control my sex thoughts.

If I'd ever told my Catholicized parents about my wonderful sexual feelings, or even something as simple as how some kids on our street always threatened to hurt me whenever they saw me, they wouldn't have believed me. They were so sure about their righteous morals and civility, so rooted in their religion. Mom would see one of those bullies bicycling by our house and always say nice things about all the "wonderful" kids living just down the street, especially those "nice young boys" I was terrified of. Even at the age of four or five, I knew deep down inside what was as obvious as dog shit on the grass: Telling the truth would only bring me grief and trouble. Lesson number one: Don't tell anyone what you're really thinking or doing.

Somehow I'd figured out very early on how to find adult association and stay safe whenever necessity demanded, but never to trust sharing my inner thoughts and fantasies with most of them. I just knew at age five how this worked, how easily adults would jump to the wrong conclusion and subsequently be misled, and I used what I'd learned about them to my advantage.

Sometimes a few of the older Longview kids would tolerate me hanging out with them, as I was really interested in the chance of actually seeing one of them having live, technicolor, real sex. They were always bragging about what they did with girls whose names I knew in the underground rooms and caves they'd dug and fixed up in many nearby vacant lots and backyards. Maybe we'd smoke cigarettes, someone would pass a lit one around along with a few sorta-dirty girly pictures. I never saw any live sex shows, and I'd never tell another soul what I was up to.

One cave was outfitted with a lamp and couch, and I was sure that the kid who built it was fucking girls whenever I wasn't there to be a witness. He was probably 10 or 11 years old at the time, and I had a vivid imagination for a seven-year-old. I was sure people were screwing everywhere my brain could see it possibly happening.

~ ~ ~

I started the second half of my third grade in Silver Springs, Maryland, at the local Catholic school. Every morning before class, rain or shine, all eight grades lined up outside the school, and, like the good little uniformed soldiers for Jesus the adults thought us to be, all of us standing at strict attention, we would greet the Big Boss Nun as she passed by, reviewing her troops before anyone could enter school. "Good morning, Mother Aaa-Maaa-Daaa," everyone chanted in unison as she strode by. I only pretended to comply to keep a low profile and stay out of trouble. I mean, I was an outsider already, doing whatever it took not to get noticed while knowing inside that this was truly stupid stuff that I was doing. Here I am, getting to be an old man, and I still remember the ridiculous madness of my Catholic education.

My family shared a two-unit townhouse with a real southern white racist, my first encounter with someone who hated blacks. My father, a liberal Democrat, was forced to "draw the line" about her racial outbursts, and as soon as the school year reached Christmas vacation, we up and moved again a few miles further west to Bethesda. The nun who taught my fourth-grade class there was the worst yet, a bossy mean older lady who seemed out of control and went way beyond the scope of behavior that my youthful sensibilities could tolerate. I committed my first conscious act of righteous rebellion. I decided to simply withdraw and go catatonic when sitting at my desk, not moving a muscle or saying a word until the class went home or until I got transferred to the other fourth-grade class. So I sat frozen at my desk for days, refusing to speak, answer her direct questions, or react in any way to her vicious threats, which included being told that my refusal to obey meant I was going straight to hell.

After a week of speechless and fearless non-violent inaction, my parents were finally informed and the unexpected actually happened: They helped solve the dilemma. I got transferred to the other class with a nice-looking lady lay teacher. I marvel that I was so sure of my humanity and so unafraid of authority at such a young age.

The Bethesda neighborhood kids formed the Chestnut Street gang. The leader, Billy, who lived in a military household, named me number two in command of six or seven adolescents. Our big thing was patrolling the main entrance to a vast network of rain drainage tunnels running under Bethesda, just big enough for small kids on kids' bicycles to ride under the city in the dark for miles. The large circular opening to the tunnels was on the edge of our turf, near the Naval Hospital, completely hidden in a dense urban forest. Unexplored caverns led to grand adventures and daring escapes in our youthful minds. Actually, it was a good place to begin a serious exploration of the art of petting with the girls in our gang. That's what I was thinking about, fuck the spelunking.

~ ~ ~

Then we moved back to Longview, Washington and that was the end of Billy telling me about feeling up his girl's naked nipples while they kissed in the tunnel. To finish out fourth grade I had another sadistic nun teacher who punished any disobedience by beating the kid's knuckles with a 12-inch metal ruler until one time she broke Tommy's finger. Tommy's dad put a stop to that. He pinned her against a wall by the neck, screaming threatening profanities in her face.

My father was mysterious to me. I knew he wasn't happy with his work. He wanted something bigger than some nine-to-five office job, just like I always have. His small locked home office was upstairs in our house in Longview, but I knew where he hid the key and would sneak in to look through his cluttered desk and drawers, letting my imagination fly in the small dark space. He kept clippings of everything he ever wrote, and had a special thin pair of scissors, very long and shiny, like a short sword, that he used to clip a story from newspapers in one fell swoop. His locked office was a powerful spot for me; it was his escape room, and I enjoyed breaking in and exploring it.

We moved to Wilmette, Illinois, 20 minutes north of Chicago on Lake Michigan, when I was in fifth grade at yet another Catholic grade school. I had been in six schools before fifth grade. Music in the '50s was really bland, but suddenly, just after we moved, there was Elvis. Elvis was the man, rock 'n roll was really big time, and by seventh grade the nuns at St. Joseph's were horrified. Good Catholic boys came to grade school emulating The King. I had a greased-back DA[1], undid my top shirt buttons, and did my best to have the Elvis attitude.

Somehow I knew in my soul that getting good grades in school was one of the secrets to getting away with being a bad boy. But in my mind I questioned or flat out rejected everything I was told to believe in. From as far back as I can remember the hypocritical values and moral teachings of the Catholic Church seemed hollow, a total sham meant only to scare me away from the good stuff. But I learned early to keep up appearances and avoid making waves about religion with older folks. My mom was a devout Catholic, convinced that our time on Earth was all black and white, good and bad, heaven and hell. Telling how I felt wouldn't develop her trust. Parents simply had to be handled, that was it, plain and simple.

Boy Scouts was a nice place for any boy to experience positive values and social obedience. Dad, who rarely let

---

1   The DA was a popular haircut worn by Elvis Presley and Little Richard, among others. The hair was slicked back at the sides, with somewhat of a pompadour in front. The slicked-back sides came together in the back and looked like a duck's tail or ass, shortened to DA. It took a lot of combing to keep it in shape.

on what he believed in outside of politics, believed Scouts were a good thing for children so Scouts would be good for me, his youngest son. He even participated in an occasional Scout overnight. Man, did the adults have it totally backwards. Scouts were a major influence and catalyst for future juvenile delinquent forays into crime and the mayhem that young boys, whether secretly or openly, so enjoyed. I learned how to hot-wire a car in Scouts, and a few of us car lovers took late night country thrill rides in whichever parents' car was the easiest to get started. Very few in our troop of good Catholic boys could be found doing actual Scout business sitting around the Scout campfire.

Turns out my dad had his own reasons for getting me to play Boy Scout. He was a wily coyote himself and used the Scouts to sneak around himself on the overnights. His ruse was to tell his wife that he was assisting with the Scouts, but I'd only see him for a few hours at the start of an event, and then he'd take off to see his girlfriends, just like I did in the years to come. I could've facilitated his trysts if he'd known anything about who I really was and asked for my help.

Then there was Tommy. The Scouts pried open his sexual closet door big time. One of my Scout classmates figured out that he could force Tommy to suck his cock any time, anywhere: at school in the bathroom, after school in the bushes, and on Scouting events in a tent. Tommy didn't like doing it in public, but a small group of the meaner Scouts started forcing him to suck anyone's dick who wanted to try it out. Big fun for a small group on those Scouting overnights out in the woods. I didn't want this weird kid sucking me off, but I was there, watching, laughing along with these sick little mean fucks in the tent or the bathroom or wherever they gave the order.

Then at lunch one day the meanest bully, Bobby, a big kid whom everyone feared, gave Tommy two options or get beat up. Bobby wanted to shit and watch Tommy eat it, so the choice was: either eat Bobby's shit off the ground, or Bobby would shit directly into Tommy's mouth. It was hard to believe what I was hearing, let alone that it was actually happening in eighth grade Catholic school, but Tommy got down and took it directly in the mouth. I never knew if he liked it or just didn't want to get beat up.

I didn't stay around this group much longer. It all seemed really out of control, crazy, but I sure wasn't going to rat anyone off. That was the only rule: no telling. Ever. Or else. What did Tommy tell his parents when he went home, covered with that smell? Man, I could never figure it out. All I knew was that telling the truth wouldn't fly at home; no way my parents would ever believe me if I told them any of this stuff.

While most kids in grade school were into sports, I was always more interested in girl-hustling than getting roughed up by a bunch of boys. Somehow I became an altar boy for two years after they told us that God would be closer to us if we just got closer to him. I don't know why but I'd always get a boner when the priest gave his sermon.

There'd be times when I'd try to reignite some belief in the Catholic gods, embrace some higher god-ness within my young, lost soul, but whatever inquiry I attempted always ended up hitting the same old wall: "It's one of God's mysteries and must be accepted without question, believed without proof." I got no answers to my bigger questions.

My first steady girlfriend was Sandy in sixth grade, and I recall the after school dance sessions in her basement, slow dancing to ballads or fast rocking to Elvis. Sandy had actual tits and I loved pressing against them while moving slow and holding her so close. One day the swelling buds disappeared; she'd strapped them into a thick bra. No more nipple-dance action.

I finally got my hand wrapped around a fleshy live breast just before entering eighth grade. Its owner had just finished grade school, lived next to a large, wooded cemetery, and one day she had me follow her past her backyard and into the trees, then into an open space surrounded by evergreens, and let me feel her up. She pulled down the right half of her bra so I could see the whole baby standing there on its own. Man, I was squeezing and rubbing her nipple while we were standing on someone's grave. I loved it, just kept rubbing and pulling and trying to understand what I had a hold of, and the incredible hard-on I was carrying.

My thinking was pretty confused by this point because most of what I wanted to do in life would send me straight to hell. I'd quit going to confession in seventh grade, right after the priest told me I had to stop masturbating. Man, first they told me I couldn't be intimate with girls and then I couldn't even be intimate with myself. Jacking off was a pleasure, as were smoking cigarettes, fast cars, and the high I got from alcohol, all big sins in the church.

Chapter 2
Growing Up Fast: Chicago in the '50s

My mother encouraged me to attend Catholic high school, but I refused. I chose the local public high school, New Trier, which was ranked in the top five public high schools in the nation in the late fifties. From that moment on, attending public high school, everything changed for the better for me.

I was already smoking Camels and drinking. I was never held accountable for my actions, and believed I knew how to escape all detection. Were my parents really that deaf, dumb, blind, and stupid? I had to reek of tobacco smoke all the time.

My freshman year was a carryover from the hoodlum years. I followed my image of the bad boy: a duck's ass Elvis haircut and hood boots to walk with a swagger. My first real friend outside of the Catholic group, Dick, was a lot like me. He was a fighter, and we looked to get into trouble. Together we got interested in hotrods, cars, girls, and sex. Meeting up with Dick set my life in forward motion.

Dick's uncle owned a specialty store in Wilmette. It turned out he was the local pornographer, the same nice guy selling rolls of film to my unsuspecting mother. He gave Dick a deck of French porno playing cards, which were the first pictures of real sex I'd ever seen.

Then he asked Dick if he and his friend (me) might like to romp around naked on a bed while he shot some photos...priming his pump with hard core excitement for the kiddies, I guess. I loved the dirty deck of cards, but knew enough about sexual weirdness to refuse his uncle's desire to photograph naked children.

Dick would let me borrow the deck. They hid well in a pants pocket and were responsible for my first, really great masturbation session, fantasizing about those lovely French babes. And the result of my thorough examination of this wondrous deck of porn was that the cards were the catalyst that finally uncorked the bottle holding back my Sex Genie, which had been lying there in wait to emerge, pushing at the edges of my forming psyche. Oh Yeah!

I was working at the corner drugstore, a whiz kid behind the counter and cash register at Porter's Pharmacy. I was a salesperson, an apprentice to the pharmacist, a stock boy, and, when I was 16, the delivery boy. I loved the variety of responsibilities and selling condoms to the needy. I took great joy in helping people to get it on.

Ron was a year ahead of me at New Trier and lived just up the block from my house. He asked me to get him some rubbers because he didn't want to get his girlfriend pregnant. I was happy to help a friend in need, but both of us were too young to buy rubbers at the time. You had to be 18 in Illinois, so I stole a box for him from the stock in the basement, then a second and a third. I was happy knowing my buddy was out there actually getting laid and that I was assisting with his sexual fulfillment.

It turned out he lied to me, resulting in my first brush with the law. Ron was selling the rubbers to his older schoolmates, all still minors, and got busted when one kid ratted him out. And just as quickly, to save himself, he immediately sold me out, telling The Man[1] that I was his source, the kingpin supplier behind a contraband condom ring. The biggest bummer for me was that Ron was a rat, and that he wasn't sharing any of the profits with me.

Poor Mom couldn't believe it when the cop called her to come to the police station to pick up her son. She didn't

---

[1] Dean mentions "The Man" throughout the book. He is referring to various forms of authority – usually the police or government.

know what "prophylactics" were – maybe a cop term for some kind of stolen goods, but not a word in common usage by her Catholic friends.

I bought my first hotrod in 1957, my freshman year. I couldn't legally drive a car yet, but man, it sure looked good sitting there in my driveway. It was a Canary-yellow '51 Ford convertible with a chromed continental kit added to the rear. By the time I was old enough to drive, I'd already moved on from cool appeal to real speed – the much faster GM cars. My souped-up '49 Olds coupe, with a '53 J-2 engine and '37 LaSalle floor shift, 3-speed transmission, was quite the hit with the high school crowd.

Dick's friend, Woody, had a '53 Fordillac, a '54 Ford coupe with a tricked-out Cadillac engine. One cold, wintry night four of us guys arranged to stay at each other's house, or in other words, to stay up all night. Our parents would think we were staying at Dick's, or Woody's. This car was the fastest thing I'd ever been in, and we were joy-riding all over the North Shore, up and down Eden's Highway, going 120 mph in the freezing winter night, doing roadside spins in the shopping center parking lot at 60 mph, sliding 'round and 'round on ice. There were lots of laughs and no fear.

My car was very fast off the line and very few could win a zero to 60 mph race against me. Cruising late one night, I stopped at a red light on Green Bay Road as a teen stopped next to me, driving Daddy's hot new Chrysler 300 convertible. We each made moves indicating we wanted to race, which involved badass glaring at each other when stopped side by side at a red light. When the light turned green, we each shot out real fast, me grinding my '37 LaSalle floor stick into second, staying neck and neck up to 80 mph and still climbing, the force pinning me against the front seat. Suddenly, the Chrysler disappeared. It wasn't in the lane next to me nor in my rearview mirror. I made a quick U-turn and headed back south. Oops, the kid hit a parked car, shearing off the right side of Daddy's new Chrysler. He was climbing out the driver's door so I just kept going, no sense in getting both of us in trouble.

I started driving frequently into Chicago during my

sophomore year. It was a different country, edgy, exotic, unfamiliar, and totally fascinating to a few of us suburban kids. Chicago had definite physical boundaries for different races, ethnic cultures, and income levels. Blacks on the south side, Jews to the north side in Rogers Park, Poles to the north and west, and Irish with a slice of the close-in south. The wealthy had the three or four blocks running north and next to Lake Michigan. God help any black male caught walking along north Lake Michigan – if you were black and even driving close to the lake, watch out. I knew this, but didn't understand how deep the racial river ran.

Dick introduced me to some kids from the north side of Chicago, just south of the border with Evanston, Howard Street. No one I knew before ever actually lived in Chicago; for most upper middle class whites it was all way too scary.

That's how I met Benny, the first blue-collar-roots white kid I'd met who carried a gun. It was legal to buy guns if you could walk into a store, so I visited a sporting goods store in an out-of-the-way area of Chicago one day and bought myself a sweet .32 automatic for reasons I don't recall. I thought I was bad.

Benny was short and mean, liked to fight, and was always accompanied by this huge Polack kid, Birdbrain, who was his bodyguard. Birdbrain was really big, a giant at 6 feet 4 inches, 225 pounds. He followed Benny everywhere and did whatever he was told to do, or, as we often said, was dumb as a rock.

I had wheels and most Chicago kids didn't. My car was our ticket to share in some big-time city adventures. We'd all cruise the north side Chicago streets at night, looking for chicks, for people to hassle, for trouble. Benny was the instigator and Birdbrain was the answer to any situation.

One night Benny wanted to crash a black party in Evanston, only a few blocks north of his home. When we arrived, I saw that it was a real all-black party, in a small, crowded apartment, with everyone about the same age. It was a first for me. There were so many hot, beautiful black teenagers, dancing to great Chess Records sounds, and I got really interested in having some fun. I could Dirty Boogie dance with the best of them, and things were hopping between me and this one very lovely young lady for a while, up until Benny grabbed my arm, yelling, "I'm gonna kill who stole my piece..." He hadn't mentioned before the party the 12-gauge sawed-off shotgun he'd hidden in his trousers, its two pieces secured out of sight, one half hidden in each pant leg. When Benny figured out that the barrel half was missing, he got pissed.

Now, before the party, Benny had coerced Birdbrain into chugging most of a fifth of whiskey, and by the time we hit the party, Birdbrain was dead drunk and passed out in the back of my '49 Olds. Benny just happened to have left his small blank-firing starter pistol, used to start races, in my glove box. It was useless, but scary looking, just enough to get someone killed. It looked like a palm-sized, .22 caliber Saturday Night Special, without the real bullets. So sure enough, Benny was suddenly waving his little black blank pistol around the party, screaming, "I'm gonna find out who stole my gun." Shit, the party screeched to a halt with Benny's drunk ranting and threats. My fun stopped cold.

I finally got Benny to move himself first through the door outside, thinking we'd better get the fuck out of there real soon. Outside, we were met by a phalanx of pissed-off black dudes who started beating the shit out of Benny. Two turned and started hammering on me too, but somehow Benny and I struggled free and ran to my car.

"Birdbrain's gonna clean up you fuckers," Benny yelled back as we ran.

"Fuck, I'm gonna die right here, tonight," I thought.

Birdbrain was still puking in my back seat. I got the car moving and Benny hopped in the passenger side, screaming, "I know those niggers, they're gonna pay for stealing my piece," and was still raving about it when I dropped him and Birdbrain at his house. That was the last time I ever saw the two of them. I'd never seen anyone express such pure, unmitigated racism so up-close and personal before that night. And I never wanted to see him again.

When I finally got home, the parents were waiting up for me. Until that eventful evening, I'd tried to fit my love of night driving and chasing girls into their parental time expectations, except my concept of keeping track of time limits often didn't meet theirs. They asked me for my excuse for being so late this time, as all trust in their youngest son had disappeared when my mother caught me pushing the family Chrysler out of the driveway well before I was 16. Since that night, anything I told them was suspect, even the truth.

For the first time, I decided to tell them some of the ugly truth. I told them about the party in Evanston where me and some friends had been cornered and attacked by some party-goers, and I'd been hit and pushed around pretty good, and that was why I was late. They didn't believe me.

I suppose I could have led them outside to smell the puke covering my back seat, but knew it wouldn't have made things any better, as I'd skipped explaining the drinking angle.

So I next did what I always found myself doing. I told them whatever might minimize the damage, the aftershocks, the consequences of having pushed my parents into strange and unfamiliar parenting territory yet again. I'd learned to tell them just enough to ease their concerns, hoping they wouldn't bother me anymore. They were totally square, and I was quickly becoming the hippest of the hip.

In my opinion, this is how the whole beatnik[2] craze, followed by the hippie craze, in fact, the whole culture of the '60s, got up and started across this country. Kids knew way more about the streets, about life, about their culture, than their parents would ever begin to understand. I saw my parents' values and goals as worthless pursuits. The parents weren't having any fun, when I was learning that life could actually be quite a giggle.

~ ~ ~

---

2 A subculture in the 1950s and early 1960s that subscribed to a non-conformist, anti-war, minimalistic lifestyle, often using literature or poetry as means of self expression; a precursor to the 'hippie' movement of the '60s and '70s.

New Trier tested and placed new students in classes of peers based on learning ability and I.Q., ranging from the very smart to the average student or below. A few new students were also placed in special first-period homerooms with the other 'problem' students, so an on-hand school psychologist could monitor these misfits. Some were lacking social skills, some were testing for potential behavior problems. Sure enough, I got placed in the fuckups homeroom with a psychologist as my advisor. Some were bright, some were mentally challenged, and some were just plain dull. A few were real nutcases – my kind of people.

My parents were also getting reports from unknown sources that I was smoking, ditched a class, and was up to other mischievous stuff. The advisor must have been secretly ratting me off to Mom and Dad.

One time I ditched school to go fishing with the older next-door neighbor. We drove to Wisconsin on the first hot, sunny day of spring after the usual long, dismal winter. We actually fished and I got terribly sunburned. Again, I felt the truth just wouldn't cut it, so I made up a story to explain the sunburn. I told old Mom I got sick at school, came home, and fell asleep in the backyard, hence my beet-red face.

Little did I know that Mom had had a meeting with my advisor at school that day. She knew I'd never made it to my homeroom and caught me in another lie. Oh well.

I never invited friends to my house. It was No Funsville there with Mom hovering about. I was always gone, looking for something that was never found at home. If I tried to talk to the folks, it always came off to them as weird. I had no goals, no Catholic friends, no focus, and, in fact, I probably sounded like a bad teenage hoodlum.

I chose to avoid the path of parental wrath instead of seeking their approval, which was much too difficult to achieve. I quit the Catholic Church, but I didn't tell them. They wouldn't ever understand. I couldn't verbalize, or even joke about, anything sexual; my fantasies alone were salvation-stopping sins to a God-fearing Catholic.

The first time I fell in love was with Jeanie. I saw her one night at a school basketball game before Christmas sophomore year. She was really cute and shy, smiled at me, and had what seemed to be giant tits. By age 15, I was definitely a tit man. I started going to her house after school where we started making out in front of the TV. Her folks were kind enough to disappear upstairs for an hour or so and our passions flowered. We were hot, but as soon as I tried to touch those lovely giant tits, Jeanie would stop me. She was moral and it wasn't right. But the kissing and heat was there and I didn't give up.

Finally, after a long and strenuous struggle while making out, I broke down her first line of defense, one hand made it through at last. I felt a hard nipple from the outside of her large-cupped bra. It was little reward for the countless hours of making out I'd invested in this project over a few months.

The real problem came when she finally gave in to our passion and let me get one hand inside the bra to the prize. My reward for such success? A new obstacle, one that finally did me in: a nightly, very painful case of the 'blue balls,' my reward for the thrills without ejaculation. Night after night I got up to head home feeling only pain in my balls. I'd reached the outer limit of her love, and it wasn't enough.

Jeanie remained a virgin throughout college. I visited her a couple of times while driving through Boulder where she attended undergraduate school. We would hang out and make out, but no sex. But then she came to visit in San Francisco after Ruby's[3] parents had rescued me by taking her home. At last, I became Jeanie's first lover. It was very exciting. It had been six years since I'd started trying to get into her pants. And when I finally succeeded, that's all it was. Love didn't exist within me anymore. Everything was now pure lust. I think Jeanie would have stayed with me if I had asked, but all I wanted from a lover was the physical sex.

Love, it turned out, I associated with what my parents had with each other, which wasn't love, but something

---

3   Dean's first wife, soon to be introduced in the story.

much uglier. I didn't want any part of that bullshit. Love's always been a big problem, but not like it was then. I'd work hard to get the girls to fall in love with me, and as soon as they did, I'd leave. I wanted the sex, the friendship, but not the exclusivity of one.

Jeanie is still a good friend, still beautiful. Finally in 1999, we hooked back up and both fell madly in love. Years later, it's still as good as it ever was.

~ ~ ~

During high school, I planned a bold, nighttime robbery of the corner drugstore where I worked. I knew my way around the basement between adjoining businesses and it was a very interesting activity, mentally putting everything into place. I wasn't really going to rob the store. It was a macho fantasy, but I had a detailed plan and it would have worked. I even got some lock picks and taught myself the basics. I went so far as to pick the store's rear door one day, proof of concept, but didn't go in. I had larceny in my heart, but I wasn't really bad. I just liked the fantasy of being bad.

Mom found my burglar kit, cotton gloves, lock picks, cutter, and tape for breaking glass. I was too stupid to hide it well enough, and, instantly, I became an arch-criminal in her mind, along with being a deadbeat juvenile delinquent. She actually believed I was some kind of big-time burglar, when really I was just a weird kid with gangster dreams. If she had found the .32 automatic pistol and the .22 rifle I'd hidden in the garage, that would have pushed her over the edge. She probably would have turned me in to the cops.

I was armed and ready. For what, I don't know. I would practice shooting in the open farm country just inland from our town. I bought the guns from a sporting goods store when I was 14, so it was probably legal, even considering at 14 I looked like I was ten. I've never looked as old as my real age.

By the time I was 16, I had an official ID that said I was 28, and it worked for getting into music clubs in Chicago, and also for ordering drinks. They'd let you do anything if you were smart enough to cover their asses, as well as your own. Chicago street rules: Pay attention, always cover your ass, never snitch, and always pay any debts. Then you can have a really good time.

By the end of my sophomore year, I was leaving one friend group and moving on to another with greener fields. Music was the beat, and Chicago had the very best live be-bop jazz in the world. The first time I had to be dragged to downtown Chicago to see live jazz at the Birdhouse. After that, I went on my own. I loved this music.

By my junior year, I was following Coltrane whenever he played Chicago, north side, south side, wherever. At the Sutherland Hotel, 47th and Drexel, he played on a small stage floating in the middle of a few black drinkers, junkies, jazz fans, and my group, a few white kids from the north shore. Pam had baked Coltrane some birthday cookies and tried to give the treats to him during a break. He looked down from the small stage at her, then over at the rest of us white kids, and muttered, "Fuck off..." We were big fans and it hurt to hear that we weren't his brothers and sisters.

Between Miles Davis, Charlie Mingus, Cannonball Adderly, Thelonious Monk, Lambert, Hendricks and Ross, and Horace Silver, music became the medium and it got my new group of friends together for the good times. Folk music was important too, just not as groovy as jazz. We would have real singing parties. Everyone learned Judy Collins' and Joan Baez's songs, the Kingston Trio's, plus all the standards from Woody Guthrie, and the Delta bluesmen.

Then came the first time I ever got laid. Al Funk and I were at the Gate of Horn music club. It was getting late, and he told me about this whorehouse he knew in Braidwood, way south of Chicago. I was a bit drunk and really ready for some first-hand and up-close pussy. Al drove his daddy's brand-new Roadmonster Buick and we made it there in an hour, driving over 100 mph most of the way on a brand-new, empty freeway. Ten bucks got me my first 'half and half' – half blow job, half real fuck.

It was incredible; electric doors buzzed open at the rear of a tiny roadside bar that didn't serve liquor, complete with six or seven funny-looking women dressed only in bras and panties. I picked one, followed her into a tiny cubicle, and didn't know what to do. I just took off my pants. Then she grabbed my dick to check it for something, unhooked her well-stuffed bra, and her tits sank to her stomach. I wondered what was really going on, but before I knew it I was fucking a real woman and I came like I had never come before. My god, it was great and I couldn't stop humping. It was the start of something big for this young laddie, that's for sure.

At this same time we discovered some of the illegal drugs floating around the music scene. Our gang hooked up one night with a young musician, Sammy, and he offered to get me a lid of grass. I was to pick him up the next day at his house in northwest Chicago, which I did. I was in my dad's Chrysler, and the first thing he said I had to do was help him get high. We drove to seven drug stores, where I ran in to buy four-ounce bottles of legal terpin hydrate and codeine cough syrup, as Sammy needed his opiates before we got my grass. I knew that pot was a soft drug and I was willing to try it, but I wasn't into anything harder and refused to start drinking a quart of sweet codeine syrup to get a high.

For my very first pot score, I was told to park behind Sammy's friend's car when it had stopped ahead of us at some park in the middle of nowhere Chicago. He had made the arrangements, and we started driving around looking for his friend. He spotted his friend's car parked at the curb in the next block and told me to pull up behind it. Just as I started to make my move, another car sped by my car and screeched to a stop, blocking the parked car just ahead. Plainclothes cops jumped out and surrounded the dealer's car.

I, of course, just about shit in my pants, but I kept driving and we got away. I almost got busted on my very first run to score some drugs.

~ ~ ~

China Pryce was one of many unusual classmates at New

Trier. Her family must have been super rich because she lived in a mansion with maids and cooks. She was quite the avant-garde girl and started supplying pot to our gang. China was weird, but really smart and somewhat homely. She was interested in our new world of 'anything goes.'

The newspaper/artist/musician crowd that I found myself in the middle of was smoking pot, drinking frequently, and having a wonderful time of it all. We had incredible parties, folk music group singing, beach parties, and jazz parties, usually at some member of the group's fabulous mansion on Chicago's North Shore.

China somehow got busted during our senior year. She was buying from her maid, who was busted scoring for her and the rest of us. China, when faced with the real ultimate authorities, became the first 'rat' in my life experience whose actions affected a lot of people's lives. She turned in her closest friends, five or six people, everyone but me. I still don't know how I got passed over, but many of my party friends had a rough first taste of the law in action. I was sure I was next and the paranoia ran supreme in my meager little world of Wilmette. No one went to jail, but the bust put a big cramp on my attempt to run in the new world of non-stop fun.

I met Ruby Hammond the summer before senior year. We eyed each other from our separate cars at Richard's Drive-in, the best burger carhop hangout in our vicinity. She was with another beauty, Audie Hornby, and the two of them encouraged my advances. Ruby invited me to her house for a party, so I followed her in my car, and what a party it was. I married Ruby three years later.

From the first moment I entered Ruby's home and met her parents, brothers, and all the crowd that had the good fortune to find this house, I felt like I was finally in the presence of adults with children who loved life and lived to the max. Dolores and Roland Hammond invited me into their home, encouraged me to discover the love they knew I could share with their daughter, and I soaked up their world like a dry sponge. Finding Ruby and her house was the start of some affirmation in my life that changed in a truly wonderful way just about everything I thought I knew.

At Ruby's house I found an alternative to the kind of life I had known for the past 17 years. Here was a family, four children, a grandmother living on the third floor, dogs, and neighbors, who communicated with each other, who actively loved each other, and loved the life they were living.

Ruby and I started seeing each other daily. Our passions were growing and it was obvious that I was going to have my second sexual encounter.

I was invited to stay for dinner early on in the new relationship, the first clue I had earned an open invitation to the Hammond house. There were quite a few friends of Ruby's older brother Nick at the house, too. They almost lived there, playing music, drinking beer, and emanating lots of great youthful happiness. I was falling in love with Ruby, the house, the parents, the whole scene.

After dinner one night, Roland had had a few bourbons, was smoking his Kool unfiltered, and asked me to have a talk with him. He got real serious, stared at me, frowned, then asked point blank if I was planning on sleeping with his daughter. Ruby was sitting right next to me. I felt like I was on the edge of a black pit. I didn't answer and probably turned bright red. I already was sleeping with her, but I didn't plan on discussing my passions with her father.

"Dean, there's only a few rules around this house. One, no hard liquor for those under 21. Two, you will always use a condom or birth control if you sleep with Ruby. It's obvious to me that this will happen soon, so no babies. Do you understand? Three, Grandma Cully, on the third-floor, isn't to know any of this."

Something leapt to the skies from my heart. I was being given the first set of truly important rules in my life. Roland laughed out loud, welcomed me into his house, and told me I was a great young man. He asked Ruby if she had thought about birth control yet. Then Dolores appeared, and they decided mom and daughter would get Ruby fitted for a diaphragm immediately.

Unbelievably, I decided at that moment I was going to marry Ruby, and asked her shortly after. She said "yes." We waited three years, and there you have it.

The Hammond family welcomed me as a son. I almost moved in during my senior year. I would go there immediately after school, stay for dinner, do my homework, dance and drink beer with all our friends, and sometimes even stay overnight. Even though the third Roland Rule was to never let Granny from the third floor catch Ruby and me having sex, we still did it on the living room couch after everyone else had left, or in Ruby's bed when things were safe. We had sex day in and day out.

One time, Roland and Dolores left for the weekend, and Ruby and I locked ourselves in their bedroom and had loud and passionate sex in their bed. Suddenly, someone was pounding on the locked bedroom door.

"Ruby, I know you're in there with a man! Open up the door right this minute!"

We freaked out. Granny had busted us at last and I saw that a good thing was about to end. I would be banished from the house. I jumped out of bed, and did the classic 'hide behind the clothes in the closet,' away from Granny's inspection.

Ruby finally let Granny in, acting angry, asking why her grandmother woke her up. But Granny barged in right by her, searching the room. She looked in the adjoining bathroom, behind the shower curtain, peeked under the bed, and then opened the closet's sliding door. I froze. She poked around, moved some clothes, and looked right into my face. It was very dark and she didn't see me. I was laughing by this time, so was Ruby, but not so loud as to catch her attention. Granny knew in her heart she had heard Ruby and me fucking our brains out, but she couldn't prove a thing.

Chapter 3
Cattle Truck Hits Overturned Vehicle

"Coed Killed In Collision. 3 Hurt As Cattle Truck Hits Overturned Vehicle," was the front-page headline in The Longview Daily News in Longview, Washington, on January 25, 1964.

"Three young people injured in a traffic accident on the Pacific Highway south of the Longview interchange early Saturday morning remained in hospitals today as treatment of their injuries continued. A fourth person in the car, Miss Lynee Pennekamp, 18, of Oakland, Calif., died in the accident. Dean Quarnstrom, 21, a former Longview resident, is in St. John's Hospital under treatment for a broken nose and a compression fracture of his lower spine. He will spend at least two weeks in the local hospital, then will remain in a body cast for an indefinite period to follow."

"Mrs. Ruby Quarnstrom, 20, Dean's wife, is in Providence Hospital at Portland, where she was rushed following the accident for treatment of head injuries. She has been unconscious since the accident, suffering a brain contusion. Miss Nancy Pinney, 19, Los Angeles, who was driving young Quarnstrom's car at the time of the accident, is in St. John's Hospital suffering from lung, shoulder, arm and facial injuries."

"All that is known concerning the mishap is that the northbound car went out of control, veered across the median strip into the southbound lane and rolled on its side. A loaded cattle truck, driven by Donald Lee Bennett, 30, Rt. 1, Oakville, smashed into the Volkswagen bus. Bennett was not injured."

~ ~ ~

I can barely hear the pained voice calling out through the raging wind and rainstorm. I turn towards it as another lightning flash illuminates the driver, Nancy, in the front of the van. She's dangling upside-down from her seatbelt, struggling, suspended beneath the van's steering wheel. I remember that she was driving. She's pleading, begging for someone to help her. I can't, not yet.

People, faces I don't recognize, appear in bright flashes of lightning. Some people are moving about, while others are just standing there, staring, all looking very ghost-like when lit by the flashing, intensely white light through the sheets of rain. Are they helping her?

Now I'm stumbling through chunks of sharp metal and broken glass debris scattered across the wet pavement, trying to get to the rear of the van. Two men have crawled inside and are blocking the rear hatch, saying something about getting the girl safely outside. Fuck! That's Ruby! That's my wife! She's moaning, so she's not dead. Who are these men?

As soon as they've got her out, I crawl back inside the van. I've got to find the pound of weed I'm bringing to sell in Seattle. I can't remember where we've hidden it, and I frantically rummage through the bags and suitcases I pull free from the chaos inside the van. My only thought is that the weed means years in jail in Washington State if the cops find it before I do.

I can't find it. Shit! Now I can't even move my legs.

Two strangers manage to lift me from the van, set me down on a rolling gurney, and take me to a nearby waiting ambulance. I really can't move. Next thing, I'm looking up at strips of fluorescent lights flickering overhead as I roll by. I'm being pushed along on a quiet, smooth gurney inside a hospital. I remember now, we're in Longview. I was born in this hospital, and I start asking for Dr. Johnson, remembering my childhood doctor.

~ ~ ~

It was a difficult experience for this 21-year-old man-child to live through, physically, let alone to digest emotionally, being so young at the time. This dramatic twist of fate popped open an unknown door into my mind, revealing knowledge previously hidden from my consciousness. Once revealed, it has guided me along the paths I've followed or searched for ever since. It took the blunt force of a tragic moment to wake me up enough to see that much more than I'd previously imagined is possible in this life and that it can all be taken away, or just disappear, in the blink of an eye.

I saw how nothing in life is ever promised or owed to anyone. No one escapes suffering in their life. I wasn't immortal, not above the fray of all humanity. Likewise, I'd never know or attain anything during my life by waiting for it to come to me unless I made the personal effort to get it or to make it happen. Nothing ventured, nothing gained. I felt these truths about my life coming from the depths of my being. It was the only meaningful explanation for the undeserved pain and suffering in the world, in my life, that made any sense to me, spoke to my gut-level inner feelings.

I saw how completely foolish it would be to waste even a minute of my life doing something I didn't want to be doing. In the same breath, what could possibly be so important in this life to cause anyone unhappiness or worry? Nothing is ever that important. Life is what it is, and nothing more.

Chapter 4
Love and Mercy, San Francisco, April 1964

The Sixties was a time when my generation believed we had the power and the will to wrestle control of our own futures from the insane forces then in charge of America. Why get excited about the challenges we'd been taught to embrace, like careers, families, or the truth in politics, when most were built on lies and deception? I'd come of age thinking that the world would be destroyed by Russian or American A-bombs at any moment. Nothing was worth the effort when the future was fucked-up far beyond any reasonable understanding. Honest respect for humanity had all but disappeared. The world I awoke to was truly bent, that's what I believed, and with a new sense of being.

I was a confirmed existentialist long before I knew what the word meant. With the auto accident came death, suffering, and a list of critical life concerns that should have tossed my young mind into emotional confusion, or so the medical and religious professionals all believed, but it didn't. This tragedy just happened. It steamrolled into and over many lives without meaning or cause. My previous life's ambitions and inhibitions were rendered meaningless and disappeared. My moral compass was wiped clean of any old rules that had held me back. I realized that only I held the keys to my life ahead. I could pursue whatever the fuck I wanted to, including fulfilling those hidden desires I'd suppressed in the shadows, the ones beckoning to me for as long as I could remember...SEX, DRUGS, and ROCK

Love and Mercy, San Francisco, April 1964

'N ROLL. Everything I'd been sublimating for over 20 years suddenly broke free, burst into existence after my auto accident, and it felt like I had been reborn into a new world, without past concerns or a need to consider the future's outcomes. I was, for the very first time in my life, absolutely free to choose whatever I felt might work.

Two months after the deadly accident, my wife's parents took their brain-rattled daughter back to their home in Chicago. I was unprepared to deal with the revised version of my former wife. The person who had returned to me after many weeks in a Portland hospital had survived our accident, still a very beautiful woman, but with the maturity and mind of a seven-year-old child, unable to understand or manage her own hormone-crazed, 20-year-old body. Her strongest desire was to have physical sex day and night. The nuns in Portland had tied her hands to the hospital bed to stop her incessant masturbation. On paper, this might sound almost too good to be true, but the reality proved quite the opposite. I couldn't deal with her, and her parents understood. This was the first of many enigmas I'd face regarding personal sexual issues: either not enough, or too much of a good thing.

~ ~ ~

After the accident, I returned to San Francisco. Marilyn picked me up in a North Beach bar, the first breath of sexually-freshened air I'd inhaled since the accident. She was beautiful, said she was a poet from Calgary, and was overtly coming on to me. I was ready. She took me to my Hugo Street apartment and fucked my brains out two ways: with her fine Buddhist mind and her openly senuous body. Marilyn! She took me out the window I'd yearned to open, and I never looked back.

Marilyn showed me how to extract the fuzzy fluff from dried peyote cactus buttons, the part of the hallucinogenic plant that makes people sick. She boiled the pulpy remains in water and asked me to drink the tea. Then we both drank more.

She knelt in front of me, stared deeply into my wide eyes, and whispered softly, "Aren't you pretty, like Easter eggs and robins and things."

She kissed my eyes, face, and ears, and sank her tongue into my mouth. The walls of my apartment vanished and I was standing alone at one end of a long, narrow bridge over a deep gorge, now and then barely-visible through a thick, swirling fog. Across the bridge, a man dressed like a court jester was dancing and laughing while beckoning me to cross over the deep chasm on either side of the now-swaying bridge. He seemed a very friendly, happy jester. All I had to do to join him was cross over the bridge. I was welcome in his world over there, and he was waiting for me to join him, but I couldn't do it. I was afraid. I must have been talking out loud, telling the vision that I couldn't make it across the chasm, that I was afraid to let go and cross over as Marilyn softly encouraged me, "Go with it, Dean, cross over the bridge. It's a safe bridge, nothing bad will happen, go on over…"

"No, nooooo, I can't do it, I don't know how to get back." I held my ground, resisting the vision's powerful appeal, afraid that if I crossed over I would never find my way back. Suddenly my living room reappeared. The jester had disappeared. I was overwhelmed, confused as to why I'd refused to taste the unknown. Next time, I told myself, I'll know better. I'll just do it. I've been waiting for that jester's beckoning call for over 50 years now.

We talked about the meaning of my vision. We were both still so high and I understood what had happened. Best of all was when she said she loved me.

We crossed the quiet streets outside the apartment and headed into Golden Gate Park. It was a weekday and we had the dense forests all to ourselves. Marilyn showed me the gracious forms of the trees and the giant overhead ferns, the intricate lace of vegetable matter that's so similar to our own body's structure. She taught me the meaning of dirt and of green.

"Take your clothes off and roll with me on the earth, let it all get inside your soul." I followed her instructions.

Love and Mercy, San Francisco, April 1964

"Taste my body. Have sex with me, Dean, then we can make love, my beautiful Dean, here, now, under this giant fan of ferns, really, we can do it here on the grass, now, Dean, under the open sky. Yes, that's it, that's right. Yes, yes!"

It was a first, the most wonderful experience of my life. I knew the sweetness of pure lust in the same breath as feeling an absolute pure love flowing between two hearts. We shared this psychedelic experience from the edges of a single consciousness.

Unanswered questions had been explained, revealed to me through this goddess. I wanted more, I was thirsting for more time with her, but she left as quickly as she had appeared. What she'd opened for me became the rock foundation for my life to come. I now understood that loneliness is the human condition, what all people experience. She showed me how to live and feel what is there for the taking, then left me turned inside-out. The only thing I knew for sure after my short time of being in love with this Marilyn was that love is real, and very little of our modern culture and society made any sense in light of knowing and tasting this truth.

Part II:
The Outlaw Years

As my dad was adapting to (and enjoying) the 1960s in San Francisco, he met many particularly interesting characters that would alter the trajectory of his life – the Merry Pranksters, Richard Alpert, and Owsley Stanley, to name a few.

His brother, Lee, who also made the 1960s pilgrimage to San Francisco, had hooked up with a group of counterculture hippies, social critics, and acid experimenters, the Merry Pranksters. While Dean had mixed feelings about the Pranksters and was never fully accepted into the group, they nonetheless had an impact on his life. Dean ended up leaving San Francisco for the backroads of the Palo Alto foothills to be closer to his brother and the Pranksters, living in a dead-end, dirt-road cottage on Homer Lane. It was the beginning of a new chapter for Dean, starting a chain reaction that would lead him straight to Richard Alpert and Owsley Stanley.

Alpert was a Harvard University professor studying the effects of LSD. When his controversial studies eventually led to his dismissal from the university, he headed out west to the Bay Area. His life intertwined with Dean's when Alpert appeared at Dean's Homer Lane residence. Alpert and Dean formed a friendship and a partnership. Dean would arrange the logistics and planning for Alpert's speaking tours and aid in the corresponding distribution of LSD. Alpert would later travel to India, study Hinduism, and return as 'Ram Dass,' an enlightened spiritual guru.

Through Alpert, Dean was introduced to the peculiar, mysterious acid chemist Owsley Stanley. Owsley, or 'Bear,' as he *liked to be called, was the Grateful Dead's original soundman, but would later become better known as the 'Acid King' – the first private party to mass produce LSD in the country. Dean and Owsley crossed paths at a time when they both had what the other was looking for. Owsley needed a right-hand man who hadn't yet lost his mind to drugs. And Dean's endless search for the next big adventure made him and Owsley the perfect match. Whether Dean knew it or not, destiny had presented him with a series of paths that would forever change his life.*

-Evan

Chapter 5
Weed's Early Days in the Haight

In 1964, living in San Francisco's Haight St. neighborhood while an undergrad at the San Francisco Art Institute, I learned that I'd never get much of a buzz from weed if I bought a five-dollar bag from friends or small-time dealers. More often than not, it was low-grade Mexican mixed with useless seeds and woody stems. It could also be Kansas Sativa found growing wild along the rural midwestern farm country roads every summer or Mexican mixed with dried oregano leaves, or something worse. It just didn't get you high.

In order to score any decent weed you had to buy an ounce or more, and you still risked getting some dicey shit. One older beatnik pot dealer living high on Twin Peaks sold me an ounce of purported Jamaican Gold through an intermediary, but by the time I got my hands on it, the pot had turned into a small baggie of nothing but seeds and stems. That was a valuable learning experience. First time, shame on you; second time, shame on me.

There was definitely a growing demand for decent weed, and if your word was trusted, you could do really well selling it.

During my last two years of college, I did photography for three major advertising agencies in San Francisco, testing out a career path. I also started dealing 'lids,' or ounces, of good pot to people I knew or to friends of friends, and this level of exposure felt too risky and dangerous to continue doing. But I liked the reward for the service, and decided

I needed to move up the pot food chain.

So whenever an opportunity arose, I'd buy better product from a supplier closer to the smuggling source. And I'd sell it only in larger quantities with fewer transactions so fewer people knew about me. Fairly quickly I had success within the emerging hippie enclave where I lived and among fellow students at my art school. Before long I was buying and selling pounds at a time, and then kilos of better grades from Mexico and countries to the south whenever I came across them for sale. I didn't yet see myself only as a pot dealer.

The '60s revolutionary culture was bursting to life all around the country, and it had all started in San Francisco, on the streets where I lived. Being alive in the middle of this culture was full of excitement and discovery, and I enjoyed my life as an art student, working photographer, and trusted pot dealer. I was studying with already-famous photographers and artists, including Ansel Adams, Imogene Cunningham, Blair Stapp, and Benno Friedman. Even after the accident, I found the San Francisco environment fueled my passion and drive to work with photography, and I even earned a Master of Fine Arts degree, all the while becoming a successful pot and psychedelic wholesaler.

I could see how my identity as an artist co-existed with my life as a drug dealer; I knew I could pursue my love of photography and manage my pot world at the same time, and wasn't confused with conflicting moral interpretations of which was better: Both were wonderful and fulfilling. I went so far as to use my MFA degree to land a straight job for the security I imagined a real job might provide in the event my smuggling gig died or landed me in trouble. I got a photojournalism teaching position at a respected community college in Santa Cruz; one day a week was manageable at the time and could help with my public image.

But I also understood that the photography gig was only a diversion, not a path to some prestigious career or teaching position. Teaching was meant to convince any investigating local or federal drug agent that I wasn't really a real drug dealer. No, in reality, I was a starving artist, an art teacher, and journalist just trying to get by. I figured that if something bad ever happened regarding the law, my legitimate employment might very well offset any illegal mistakes I might make regarding my outlaw criminal life. I always believed that a little worthy pre-planning would prove beneficial to my ultimate freedom if I was ever busted for drugs. And when it all came grinding to an end years later, my belief in the value of legitimacy in the eyes of the world was proven only partially correct.

The Master's degree was proof that I was a real member of my society who'd achieved a bona fide status; important information to anyone who might want to think otherwise. No matter what drugs I'd ingested, that Master's degree somehow ensured that I could still qualify as a normal person. Certainly, I'd experimented with altering my consciousness often enough to cause some to doubt that I'd ever make it through to the other side, but I did.

There was a saying in the '60s, "Can you pass the Acid Test?" and I knew all along that I could, and could live my private life in any manner that I felt was worthwhile. To this kid from Chicago, that meant keep your nose clean, keep whatever it is you like to do out of public sight, invisible to anyone who could hurt you, and never 'rat out' another person, even an enemy.

I always held some sort of legitimate gig, be it selling knitting yarn at the world's original, back-to-nature natural yarn and hand-crafts supply store in Berkeley, Dharma Trading Co. (a lovely place to meet interesting women), teaching photography/photojournalism at the community college in Santa Cruz, or working with Native American, Latino, and third-world groups on government-funded alcohol and drug abuse prevention training programs at the University of California, Santa Cruz. These looked good on my resume, and provided some source of legal income. I was convinced that The Man kept track of everyone's personal information in a big database somewhere in Washington, D.C. If the shit ever hit the fan regarding my dealing, a job history might help to mitigate any punishment meted out to me.

My markets expanded throughout the Bay Area, but life in the City was becoming too crowded and paranoid, filled with too many drug-crazed youth. My brother, who'd recently hooked up with Ken Kesey and his Merry Band of Pranksters and moved to a cabin in the mountains just west of Palo Alto to be closer to Kesey, mentioned an opportunity to rent a two-room cabin beside a secluded, wooded stream close to Palo Alto on a funky dirt road called Homer Lane just west of the Stanford campus. I jumped at the offer. I left my righteous Hayes Valley apartment with the classic curved-glass second-floor bay windows, sold my second-hand furniture, and moved. It was urban, rural, private, shielded from the hot summer sun by stands of giant live oak and bay laurel trees and cooled each night by breezes blowing inland from the Pacific Ocean.

Homer Lane dead-ended in a dirt parking lot, facing a row of eight small and rustic, clapboard cottages. The cottages housed a close-knit community of students, artists, educators, LSD enthusiasts, and well-known '60s characters, including Ken Kesey. Homer Lane brought on major changes to my life that I was ready to embrace. I took my first acid trip on Homer Lane early in 1965. It was a most remarkable time and place to trip, with new friends that I felt I'd known forever; a tiny spot on Earth so special and unique, happening at a time in history like none before.

I had a ready source for pure LSD from a new friend, Richard Alpert, the infamous ex-Harvard professor who'd just moved from Boston/New York to California to teach at Stanford. One day Manny and I returned to our Homer Lane cottage from a road trip to Mexico City to find that our unlocked front door opened not to the sparsely furnished crash pad we'd left only two weeks before, but to a transformed, unfamiliar world.

Our friendly next-door neighbor had offered her East Coast friend, Richard Alpert, the use of the cottage while we were away and he had moved himself right in, completely redecorating the entire interior with oriental rugs, Tibetan

Thangkas, enlarged photo posters of mystics and spiritual leaders. There was a six-foot poster close-up of Meher Baba's serenely happy-face, plus a variety of the latest swirling, eye-dazzling psychedelic posters. Gauzy rainbow-colored Indian-print bedspreads floated gracefully overhead, covering the bland plaster ceiling, billowing in the refreshing afternoon breeze pouring in through an open window. Large pillows were scattered around on the room-sized Oriental rug, and there was not a proper chair in sight. Sai Baba's powerful incense, Nag Champa, along with soft Indian raga background music, filled my senses.

A smiling thirties-something stranger was relaxing, spread across a few pillows, his balding scalp barely hidden by a thinning clump of dark hair pulled into a classic combover; his protruding, gumball-sized eyes seemed to float out from deep-set sockets, shaded by an enormous, protruding forehead. He introduced himself with a warm, "Hello, you must be Dean and Manny. I'm Richard. Jane said I could crash here if I took care of Howard (my cat). Hey, I'm just about to drop some really good acid, would you care to join in, take a trip?" I felt like I'd known the man forever.

This was the very same Richard Alpert that I'd heard and read so much about, a psychologist and renowned expert on psychedelic drugs. Newspaper reports claimed he'd turned on Boston, Harvard, and the East Coast. I owned a copy of his version of The Tibetan Book of the Dead, which I'd kept close at hand during my first LSD trip. Wow! This was far out. He's here, living in my house!

Without missing a beat, Manny and I both accepted his offer, "It'd be a real pleasure, it's great to finally meet you, too."

I popped the sugar cube he offered into my mouth, then he put a cube on his own tongue. Manny followed suit and off we went.

Our trip lasted for 48 hours, refueling with more cubes along the way. We traveled through a universe of places and spaces we'd each discovered and freely shared, both with and without spoken words, within one another's minds and dreams, fears and passions, a consciousness shared within the safety of this soft, peaceful environment. We each told stories from our lives, both spoken and without words; psychic interactions that I'd believed were impossible to feel and share freely with another human, another man, and especially with a gay man, as Richard revealed without fear or shame to anyone. No secrets were withheld. Intimate personal stories flowed from a fountain of knowledge within each of us, deep and powerful truths, simultaneously felt and understood by one another.

What passed between us was god-like, real communication without words; even the few moments of personal stress or fears were handled gently by our experienced guide and new friend, a fearless explorer of the consciousness of inner space. We traveled through forms of realities beyond the senses; truths about existence were revealed and shared, and this knowledge, in turn, opened my heart and soul to the grand potential hidden deep within every form of life. Every question was answered, no truth illuminated was left unexplored, and we, ever so softly, gently, revealed to one another our most-secret, darkest fears, which, for reasons rendered meaningless, had been hidden away from conscious awareness.

Richard and I developed a bond of friendship, of mutual trust and acceptance, and a deep and lasting love. The experience was a major lesson for me on friendship and trust that transcended our genders and sexual identities. Richard, who later changed his name to Ram Dass, remains a close friend today, over 50 short years later. Now, as I look back, I have to ask myself, how often in one's life does one make a friendship such as this, one that lasts forever? Rarely to never.

Richard asked me to work with him; he needed help arranging a series of lectures throughout the country on LSD and the spiritual experience that this mind-altering substance made available to man.

"Perfect, Richard! Yes, I'd love to work with you, in fact, it's exactly what I'd like to be doing right now," I responded.

As I wanted a place of my own to live, and I still was exploring this new San Francisco Bay Area world of free-thinking people, I naturally moved on to the next great frontier of cultural experimentation, Berkeley, to explore and to exploit. I rented a secluded, rustic cabin hidden behind a larger Victorian on Chandler Way and close to the university. So, on to Berkeley it was, on to its abundance of young women looking to discover the possibilities of living and being free. I began arranging lecture events along the West Coast for the rising cultural hero, Richard Alpert, who was spreading the good word about LSD from Canada to the beaches of Southern California. Things were turning out well; I continued this work, and continued to explore my inner self with acid as often as I could.

Richard mentioned that, at the same time I was setting up his lectures, and only if I was comfortable doing so, I could make some serious money for both of us by distributing his pure LSD to a few trusted people he knew in the cities I'd be visiting. He'd supply the LSD to me along the way.

Alpert, and his ex-partner at Harvard, Tim Leary, had become the public faces in the media in support of the "dangerous" illegal psychoactive drug, LSD, and Richard couldn't risk distributing it himself in the U.S. after its recent government classification as an illegal Class 1 substance, in the same category as heroin. But the '60s generation felt differently about its use and importance for mankind, and I was up for the offer and the income.

Taking a road trip with Alpert, now we're talking about some real fun! The gist of this gig was that I would start on the West Coast, rent a large auditorium or hall in major cities, place announcements in the local papers, and seed these markets with high-quality acid a few weeks before Alpert's speaking event, creating a new demand for acid as well as an opportunity for us. For the price of admission to his lectures, Richard would offer advice and give information to everyone who needed it or wanted to know what had just happened to them, and they'd become our new customers. I'd often deliver bottles of aspirin with 250 mcg of LSD dropped onto each pill. Best cure for headaches.

The plan worked, creating large audiences in every city we visited for Alpert's lectures on psychedelics. Building the attendance for each new lecture meant greater income from ticket sales for the lecture, "An Evening with Richard Alpert." The events were similar to today's social networking events, large gatherings of similarly-minded, curious people in each city who shared the LSD experience as their reason to attend. This was happening at the same time that Kesey's Merry Pranksters were on the road performing their own promotions for LSD and its mind-altering experiences, the Acid Test "happenings," that were being held throughout California.

Create a demand for acid, then fill it, and, if a few souls were driven out of their minds, hey, don't worry too much; someone will be dropping by real soon, maybe spend an evening explaining to all the lost souls how to find themselves again. This is what Alpert did best.

Pure genius, I said to myself. I mean, there were no guidebooks or ground rules yet established for exploring the mind's inner-spaces, and the '60s people were interested enough and willing to pay a small fee to learn more about their recent experiences.

I'd rent 2,000-seat auditoriums in Berkeley, or Vancouver, Santa Monica, Seattle, place advertising in local bookstores and in local fringe newspapers, set up radio interviews on the newly-hip underground FM stations, and sell quantities of pure LSD in each city where Alpert would soon be speaking.

When Richard showed up a month later, there were always a few unfortunates still suffering from their encounter with the psychedelics, known in some areas as the "acid casualties," those very few who hadn't passed the Acid Test while tripping. There were always a few waiting in line the night of the event, desperate to understand what had happened. With my LSD supplier's blessing, and a few trusted contacts in the important cities, I expanded, hitting the road early in 1965, spreading this seed of change across the land. In my own way, I helped fuel the '60s cultural revolution.

I was welcomed graciously everywhere I traveled, and delivered large quantities of LSD to Seattle, Portland, San

Diego, Laguna Beach, and Santa Barbara; I received an enthusiastic welcome in Chicago, selling "the good shit" to new friends and then to their friends, who spread it through Old Town, the Near Northside, Evanston's Northwestern U., the U. of Chicago's beatnik/hipster students, and outwards from there, in all directions. They were lined up and waiting for acid in Ann Arbor and in Akron, Ohio. New Yorkers welcomed me as well, although I was not the first person to deliver acid to the East Village crowd. Even so, they sure did love the pure product I brought to them, and they'd take as much of Owsley's finest, his infamous "White Lightning," as I could bring.

Every city provided a new magical adventure for me, each with its own variety of newly-hip, underground culture to explore, understand, embrace, and try to appreciate. In Chicago, my new "best friend," George, was so excited that I'd actually showed up with the pure acid that he just had to reciprocate with an equal, and to him 'Best of Chicago,' gesture. From the depths of his dark, Navy peacoat, he produced a cherished possession and presented it to me: his chrome-plated, .38 Colt Police Special pistol. He said he'd personally stolen it from a Chicago cop. "A real beauty, don'cha think, bud?" he said, grinning from ear to ear. "Take it, it's yours."

"Real groovy, man....ah, George, it's great." I'd met George at Big John's, on North Wells Street, where The Butterfield Blues Band was performing, and we were standing in plain sight along the side wall. Having grown up amongst this city's deep love of handguns, I wasn't freaked out by the sight of a pistol, but I'd left this cool, tough-guy lifestyle and attitude behind when I'd moved to the Bay Area, and without regret. I asked George, "Uh, dude, think maybe you could, uh, just mail it to me?"

This powerful, mind-altering new drug often turned many new business encounters into exciting opportunities for new sexual encounters as well. It was a total gas to open up new, hip markets with such a great product, providing a well-paid service and product to very appreciative customers. Johnny Appleseed was rewarded on many levels, but mainly with cash and sex in every part of the country. I didn't treat these respectfully offered sexual gifts with the same blasé attitude many rock musicians had toward their new groupies. I didn't take it all for granted, but I also didn't shy away from sexual invitations when the vibes and offerings felt right.

I was good at handling bulk sales. I was careful, honest, and not afraid to face and take the occasional risk, and quickly gained the trust and recognition of my suppliers. I was creating my own success.

Later, in 1969, after Richard had spent a year in India traveling, then sitting at the feet of his new guru, Neem Karoli Baba, he returned to his family estate in New Hampshire and continued working on his new book, "Be Here Now." In 1970, after a stint with his fellow spiritual seekers in Taos, New Mexico, he finished and published it.

My good friend, now known as Ram Dass, continued his post-India westward journey and ended up in Santa Cruz where he and a few followers of Neem Karoli moved into a house I'd acquired in Soquel just next door to my own home where we again picked up our relationship and I became the official tour manager for his upcoming nationwide speaking tour. This time we would be promoting the wonders of his recent journey, his discovering and living a spiritual life.

Chapter 6
Ram Dass Retreat

It was 1973, or so, and more than 100 devotees of Ram Dass had gathered for a meditation retreat I'd arranged. It was a week of silence at a dorm-style Boy Scout summer camp we rented in the Santa Cruz Mountains during the winter rainy season. Many well-known '60s movers and shakers came to sit with Ram Dass, their old friend and recent spiritual convert to Hinduism.

Ram Dass closed the week of guided meditations and vegetarian cuisine with a short lecture on his faith, followed by a period of silent meditation. My last remaining responsibility was to manage the cleanup and removal of everything we'd brought in to the site during the previous week: the PA system, food, and spiritual decorations. Finally, when the closing prayer was over and the close group of spiritual seekers were saying their final goodbyes, one last attendee, Norman, remained sitting in the large room, seemingly transfixed in some other world. Apparently, he was still meditating, and certainly not yet packed up and prepared to leave.

Norman's friend had pulled up and parked just outside in a panel truck, hoping to gather up Norman and his camping gear quickly before heading back to Los Angeles. But Norman was totally unaware of where he was or what was going on all around him, sitting still while the now boisterous group of hippies were preparing to leave. Norman didn't move a muscle. He sat absorbed in deep meditation, erect on the floor, his legs crossed in a perfect lotus meditation position.

Finally, after everyone had left the now-empty and very quiet hall, I went over and behind Norman, placed my hand on his upper back, and whispered in his ear, "Norman, your truck is here," then removed my hand and quietly walked away.

Norman suddenly seemed convulsive, his body jerking up, down, back and forth in all directions, shaking from head to foot. He was having a Kundalini whole body experience, like the 'whips and jingles' from alcohol withdrawal, like a dog shedding water after a swim.

When the thrashing around finally stopped, Norman jumped up and turned in a circle, asking who'd touched him on the back. I was the only person still in the room, so I put my hands together in a Hindu spiritual praying acknowledgement, and just smiled at him. He returned the greeting, his hands clasped together and body bent forward, bowing down in a thankful manner, and said, "Thank you for opening my heart and my soul. Namaste."

I smiled and Norman, almost ecstatic, explained what had just happened to him. For the entire week he'd been struggling in silence, locked within himself and feeling mentally blocked, unable to pull himself out of a profound spiritual suffering. That is, right up until the moment I'd touched his back while whispering in his ear that "Your BLOCK is here."

Wham Bam Thank You Mam Shazam! Everything changed for him in a flash; his mind and body had burst open. My touch and words had broken through and re-opened his being, filled his heart with bright light and love, and his energy was flowing again. In the blink of an eye Norman was back and ready to get moving and he left the gathering a very happy camper.

We hugged, both feeling his new joy. Norman gathered up his belongings, waltzed outside, and left in his truck. I hadn't said a word during this post-event happening, and later regretted not having asked him for some money in return for my magic. So you tell me. I say God works in funny ways.

Chapter 7

Letter to Ram Dass

Dearest Ram Dass,

I'm so glad to see that you're coming back to Santa Cruz. My house is a block from the Rio Theatre, and seeing your name in large red letters, "RAM DASS," hanging on the Rio's outside marquee, warmed my soul…you know, happy that I will be able to sit with you again, and then remembering some of the great road trips we've taken together, way back when…

…and, if today your damaged memory needs a jolt, we first met in 1965, on Homer Lane. When Manny Meyer and I returned from Mexico, Adrian told us that you'd taken over Manny's and my cabin up the hill. Thinking it was appropriate to get high before being introduced, I was loaded when I knocked on your front door.

"Come in!" was an invitation to enter your psychedelic den, and you made both of us as cozy as could be, having redecorated the room to ease and calm even the most seriously engaged tripping mind. You were taking care of my cat, Howard, if my memory isn't failing me.

"Hello, I'm Richard," you announced to the two of us, and, within minutes, you caught up to us and then we all took off on a wonderful, extended three-day trip into the innermost realms of the worlds each of us inhabited and were able to share with one another.

So, I'll see you at the Rio, for sure, and hope we can say

hello, once again.[1] As always, I love you.

- Dean Quarnstrom, 22 April 2006

---

[1] Before Dean passed, he did meet with Ram Dass once again while on vacation in Maui.

Chapter 8
Ignore Alien Orders

The real origin of "Ignore Alien Orders":

It must have been in the Spring of 1970 when I first visited Roy and Fred's new warehouse in North Oakland, where they could be found loitering about. One of their Berkeley, California crew had used family money to buy this former furniture factory in an estate sale; a lock, stock, and barrel, turnkey machine-shop operation.

Roy and Fred were friends from high school. After moving to San Francisco in 1964, I'd stayed in touch, and a few high school friends made their way to the West Coast. I had friends from three different groups of former Chicago-area transplants in the San Francisco Bay Area: the high-school crowd, former University of Chicago students who attended Stanford University in Palo Alto, and a number of hipsters, poets, journalists, and beatniks from Chicago's folk, blues, and beat scenes.

Fred was hard at work, shaping and drilling holes in a small metal plate, and Roy was engaged in some other project.

"What's happening?" I said (one of our 'hip' cultural greetings) when I was inside their workshop.

Fred looked up, smiling, and said, "Hey, Rockets, look at this!" He held out a beautifully-machined, very colorful, thick metal plate that read, "IGNORE ALIEN ORDERS." and continued, "Last weekend I dropped some righteous White Lightning and tripped in the hills above Berkeley. There I was, whipped outta my mind and really digging the walk in the woods and across bright green open meadows, when I bumped into a barbed-wire fence blocking my way. Really brought me down, and then I saw a metal sign, just the size of this one, (the one he was showing me) that said, "Government Property. Do Not Trespass!" Blew my mind, I mean, we are the people who make up the government, and I say to myself, I give you permission to enter, and I crawled under the fence. Right then the words just came to me. What I heard in my head, plain as day, was, IGNORE ALIEN ORDERS. When it's finished, I'm going back up there and mounting this sign right next to the No Trespassing sign. What'dya' think?"

"Right on!" I replied.

Chapter 9

One Brave Beauty

A few months before moving to Berkeley, I'd unexpectedly met a UC Berkeley student beauty. While visiting Berkeley with my Homer Lane buddy, Stanley, we dropped by the house of his student friend, Lester, who shared a rental with a number of Berkeley female students, all very involved in the ongoing free speech movement and student protests happening daily on campus.

That very morning's front-page story in the local newspaper, The Berkeley Gazette, detailed the previous day's student protests on UC Berkeley's campus. It included a photo of Mario Savio, the student protest ringleader, standing above a student crowd on a Berkeley Police car roof, speaking through a megaphone to hundreds of students crowded around the cop car next to Sproul Hall on the Berkeley campus. Two officers were trapped inside the vehicle and one courageous female sat against the police car's front bumper, blocking its forward movement.

Picture it: One beautiful student protester bravely blocked the police car, while Mario, the crowd's leader, stood on the car roof, shouting out the truth to the large crowd of angry protesters. What a wonderful picture of student dedication to personal beliefs. I'd immediately fallen in love with the lovely female student in the newspaper photo; she had it all. I was proud of her, for her fearless bravery and personal commitment to free speech, and I was awed by her beauty.

Well, the young woman who answered our knock on

Lester's front door was this same lovely woman in the morning newspaper photo, the beautiful student blocking the cop car, the same woman I already had fallen in love with, Laura Leonard. I'd met other potential lovers in similar, seemingly predestined fashions. Was it just a coincidence or was something grander happening all around us all? Another one of the many unanswered questions I've carried throughout my life.

Before the door had closed behind us, I'd quietly told Laura that I was madly in love with her, how I'd been struck through the heart with this wonderful desire to know her, somehow be with her, and here she was. And the love gods were shining brightly on both of us that fine evening. One thing led to another, and just a few days later, I made love to the second virgin of my still very young, but blossoming love life. Laura introduced me to yoga meditation and to the Maharishi Mahesh yogi well before he'd met the Beatles, and I've practiced his yoga exercise ever since. Laura and I remained on and off lovers for a few years to come. Every now and then we would spend a week or so together as companions and lovers, maybe hiking in a high-Sierra wilderness.

Chapter 10
Never Trust a Prankster

1965

After moving from Homer Lane to Berkeley I met, fell in love with, and accepted Terry's proposal to marry her within an hour of meeting her. I was struck by lightning, and like meeting Marilyn a year earlier, I was unprepared and blind-sided by the whole unfolding, magical evening. After a fruitful acid sales expedition away from the Bay Area on behalf of Alpert, I returned to my Berkeley cottage in great spirits and with our princely rewards safe in my pockets.

I unlocked and opened my hide-away cottage's only door to find a smiling woman, a stranger, welcoming me home. There was the lovely Terry, curled up and reading a book, lying on my bed, which pretty much filled the one-room plus kitchen and bath cabin hidden behind a large Victorian. She introduced herself and said that Len had put her up at my place for the past few days, somehow knowing that I had been on the road. Len lived with his long-time girlfriend, Toni, and they shared a house in San Francisco. Having his secret, former Chicago lover now shacked up in Berkeley had worked out really well for Len. But now I was back home, and Terry had other plans in mind besides time with Len.

"Hello Dean, I've been here for a few days. Len thought it would be OK with you if I stayed here. My job's just around the corner, so it's worked out well for me so far. So, I've gone through all of your stuff, your photography and writings, your clothes, and I like everything I've seen. And now I like how you look in person too, so if it's OK, I can tell you that I want to marry you. Do you have any acid?"

I was stunned, to say the least. And after a non-stop, ecstatic 20-hour drive home to my Berkeley cabin from Seattle, wired on dexies and horny as could be, I was blown away. Holy shit, there, relaxing on my bed, sat the very same fantasy dream-woman from Chicago who each of my new Stanford and former University of Chicago friends had, at some time or another, mentioned as being the woman of their dreams – a sexy beauty, so smart, and coming soon to California. I'd dreamt of meeting this Terry someday.

I'd heard wild tales of her brazen global adventures, seen pictures of this beautiful, voluptuous, blonde beatnik from Chicago, and had long ago decided that she was among the finest of the fine. I was in love with the idea of her, and told her how I'd loved her for a long time already. "Yes, of course, I'd love to marry you. Here's some fine LSD," producing a sealed baggie with my personal stash of prepared sugar cubes, each soaked with 250 mcgs of pure Sandoz self-realization.

We each ate a cube, then immediately undressed and crawled under the sheets to get close, then even closer, and then intimate as new, greedy lovers will do. The powerful drug began to emerge, and soon took control over the rest of the evening.

As our acid trip unfolded in all its glory, Terry suggested that we might want to drive to San Francisco to see Bob Dylan and his new rock band performing at the Masonic Auditorium that evening, the music that had set the mood for our taking LSD the night before. We each dropped another cube of acid and drove my '47 Caddy convertible (a most-lovely period in Post War II, American auto-body styling) over the Bay Bridge to the City where we found a parking space close to the theater, on California St. atop Nob Hill. The ticket office had only two, fourth-row, center seats remaining for sale, a perfect miracle. We floated inside to our seats, both ecstatic with such gifts from the gods, the tickets and our new-found love. We were totally blasted out of our gourds, but I knew I could pass the Acid Test, and act like a normal person on the social level while still enjoying the other dimensions and hallucinations that played with both of us. It seemed to me that Terry was glowing with an inner light and we held hands tightly as we made our way to our seats.

When we finally found our seats, to Terry's immediate left sat Joan Baez, and Dylan spent most of that evening singing directly to her. He introduced "Sad Eyed Lady of the Lowlands," looking directly at his folk-singer lover, while we sat only a few feet to the side; it felt like Dylan was singing his newest songs directly to Terry and me. It was an incredible experience, almost perfect. Both days unfolded for us in a sublime rhythm, a perfect first encounter with an incredibly beautiful woman.

On the trip home to Berkeley, Terry laid her head on my lap as I drove, top down in the chilly night air, and unzipped my bell-bottomed, ass-tight bright maroon cords as we moved through fog now hovering just above the road. We passed beneath the freeway street lights' orange glowing beacons, flashing on and off like strobe lights as we sped by, illuminating in still action her gift to me, my first-ever blow-job in this most-luxurious, purring Cadillac convertible, as the swirling cables and melting steel towers of the 11-mile bridge to Berkeley passed by overhead. Nothing could have been better, ever.

Unbelievable, I was going to marry the woman of my dreams.

We moved into a large apartment in North Oakland the following week. Within a month we'd traveled to Tijuana, where in 20 minutes I was divorced from Ruby and re-married to Terry. The marriage lasted for eight months, during which time we'd moved in with mutual Chicago friends living in a remote estate in the mountains above Palo Alto. These Homer Lane, Stanford friends had formed a rock band, "The Anonymous Artists of America." They needed some financial help with their living expenses, and Terry and I were just the right, known roommates with some cash to contribute.

In those too-few mid-Sixties years, it wasn't strange for everything to suddenly change overnight, in housing, in love affairs, in friends, and locations; it was happening in my life every few months. A few months of living with the band was enough, so we left Rancho Diablo, on Skyline Blvd., for the peace and quiet of an even more-remote cabin an hour South on Zayante Road in the Santa Cruz Mountains.

There, I processed thousands of aspirin tablets soaked in LSD which were distributed to all corners of the country. For me, the effort was as rewarding as I'd ever imagined it could be. I was in love, living close to a "Whole Earth Catalog" off-grid lifestyle, and still, with a short drive, I could be an active participant in the Bay Area's exploding rainbow of music, colors, and emerging hippie community. At the same time, I was building a functioning underground acid distribution channel throughout the hinterlands of America, managing a risky business, as out of sight of the public's eyes as was possible at the time. Yet I was totally naive and unprepared for what was to happen next.

Returning to our remote canyon cabin after being away for two days on out-of-state funny business, I opened the front door to an empty house. Quickly, I discovered that Terry had left me, had completely moved her stuff and herself out, without warning or even a 'Dear John,' note. What is going on? Soon I knew: Terry had run off to Mexico with her new lover, Zonker, who'd stepped in, as he often did, to woo a woman when the other partner was off making a living. Zonker was a notorious ladies' man, and a longtime Merry Prankster. I understood the saying, "Never trust a Prankster," and knew they'd headed south to Mexico, to join up with the Pranksters on Kesey's flight from the U.S.A. to avoid his jail sentence on a pot possession conviction. It was a more exciting lover and lifestyle than I offered, I guess. It took a while for my broken heart to mend, but my business was booming and kept me busy.

Chapter 11
The Acid King

Somewhere along the way, Richard Alpert met up with Augustus Owsley Stanley, the reputed 'acid king.' I guess Owsley made it his business to contact all the Jr. Mr. Bigs. He had the best acid and wanted to spread it around. Richard had been getting his acid from England, 100,000 microgram packages mailed in letters. But when the Englishman got discovered, Alpert hooked up with Owsley to supply me and other friends with good babies.

Soon I was really into it, traveling back to Ann Arbor, New York, Chicago, spreading good times and righteous White Lightning Owsley LSD. I would get the stuff in powder form or gram lots and spend a few days dividing it up and diluting it with methanol to drop it onto Bayer Aspirin, a good vehicle – cure your headache in two ways. Sometimes I would have 5,000 aspirins in my house, and I was never sure how I was going to explain it to The Man if he found out. And soon I had $20,000 in cash too, which was just blowing my mind. How easy, how wonderful...get the world high, and get paid for it too.

Before long the time came for me to meet Owsley. I was visiting Alpert's apartment in Berkeley, maybe six months after I'd met Alpert at Homer Lane, and Owsley came in and sat in the corner of the room, staring at me very suspiciously.

I didn't know at the time who he was and that he was interested in me. Highly sneaky, he usually knew just what he needed to do. A few days later I scored some more white babies from Richard, and he told me who the guy was, and that he would like to meet me. I was elated. I was in the major leagues, a Mr. Big in my own right, heading straight for the top. So, dressed in my farthest-out fashions, a real wheeler-dealer, I went to his house to meet him, to get initiated into untold fame and fortune.

Owsley lived in a small palace filled with amplifiers, instruments, owls, and dope. The strangest people I had never seen kept coming and going, getting high and talking to me like I was their brother. I felt so groovy and got so high being with him, that when Owsley asked me if I would like to work for him, I just sailed up to the ceiling.

In six short months I had more money than I knew what to do with and would be earning more. I soon saw why Owsley was interested in me. I looked very young and innocent, but had successfully taken on the "Mr. Cool-as-a-Tool" facade of the hip voyagers. Owsley could have an agent who would not arouse much suspicion by his looks and was cool.

And he needed someone like me. During this period only the farthest-out of outs dropped by his house: hair to the floor, dope dripping from their eyeballs, no one in any condition to somehow deal with the outside world and keep this part of Owsley's scene happening along with the part that was real, the laboratory. I was tasked with scoring certain supplies and transporting them, mainly various chemicals and apparatuses needed to make the lab happen. And it was happening full blast. I was excited and scared; it immediately took on the air of a James Bond movie, and it was fun.

I quickly got to know this mysterious acid kingpin and formed a bizarre, unique relationship with him.

Owsley was a short man with long hair that he was constantly washing and drying in front of the mirror. He had an excellent body, which he frequently showed to everyone in the palace. He liked to fuck a lot and with almost anyone. He strutted around, always attributing his good body and health to ballet as a youth and the meat-and-vitamin-only diet he was on, as well as his good dope. I was wondering at that time if he really was a chemist, for he was always talking of formulas and chemicals, books and whatnot, but he was never at the lab.

Owsley was a strange bird to deal with one-on-one. He had an attitude, a position on every issue, a certain self-centered confidence that quickly put people on edge, a self-oriented inner-drive often seen in powerful, shorter people. It was always "my way, or the highway." I had very few real conversations with this man. He preferred to do the talking: "Listen to me, remember it, and always agree." And he could go psycho-ballistic if someone he knew disagreed with an Owsley absolute proclamation. He had no close friends that I ever met other than a few trusted associates, and seemed to appreciate my candor and my ability to follow his detailed instructions. He was adverse to being photographed, and refused to let me take any pictures of him. He hid his face under the oversized floppy brim of a heavy dark leather hat that was way too big for his compact, lean body and height, and I felt this attracted attention wherever he went. Then there was always this one giant bear-claw, big as a clenched fist, pointing out at you, front and center on his chest, hanging from a thin strip of leather tied around his neck. He once told me about the special powers he received from his claw, powers that came to it from another plane of existence – crazy shit that I could still believe was possible.

I seemed to be the only person that he liked that was not a 'yes-man' to him. I had acquired a Chicago street cynicism in my youth that somehow gave him food for thought. Most of the frequenters were fellow workers and friends, but they never seemed to question his plans.

For my first task, Owsley and I rented a station wagon and we headed south on the I-5. There were a few things that still needed doing before we left for the new lab. The industrial cities of northern Orange County were home to many chemicals and lab gear distributors, the real goods that Bear, as Owsley liked to be called, needed to crank out a new batch of his infamous White Lightning acid. I rarely ventured off of the interstate when passing through the heart of John Birch territory, and for good reason: Orange County was infamously unfriendly to hippies in 1966. The cops were notoriously red-neck motherfuckers, known for random stops and illegal searches of suspected Pinko-faggot-longhair dopers, or someone looking just like I had only a few days before. But not on this trip, no way. I had shorter hair and no mod-style clothing for this mission, my first working road adventure with Owsley.

Owsley hadn't a clue how I'd react under stress, if I'd freak out and get us both busted. It was my trial by fire. He was checking to see if I had the balls for the job. So, while he was having another steak-only meal in a nearby Denny's, I headed over a few blocks to the warehouse to pick up the order, nothing I couldn't manage. If the order raised any eyebrows, I'd play dumb. Owsley assured me it was all legal and that these suppliers sold to all the legitimate pharmaceutical and chemical companies, and likely to other underground labs. The only problem would be if Bear showed up himself; he looked like a drugged-out, aging hippie nutcase. It made no sense to risk showing his face. I'm just the driver doing a dickhead job. Do I give a shit what I'm picking up?

Apparently, finding someone suitable to hang in with Owsley's clandestine, intensely narcissistic worldview was almost impossible. I mean, 24 hours a day with a stark-raving, paranoid genius was harder than it sounds, especially when you can't choose even the simple shit, like what to eat, unless it's red meat. It was not a cake-walk lifestyle, and very few could handle being with Bear for more than a very short time.

Plus he had an arrogant, somewhat tedious, and perhaps even dangerous, personality. He had an insecure desire to hang with and impress rock stars. He wasn't careful enough with the law in my book. But I held back and didn't spout off with any critical words, something I rarely held in check in those days.

For some unknown reason, I really liked this mad genius. He was so fucking brilliant and his super-large ego was pure entertainment for me. He'd intimidate or piss-off most everyone by just being himself. I watched Owsley treat even his closest associates, many as smart or smarter than him, like juveniles needing a stern lecture, inferiors who didn't know enough to step in from the rain. He was often wrong, but the facts didn't matter, as his friends understood his failings, but still appreciated his good work as creative art. Many wrongly mistook his innate paranoia for disdain; he'd mutter nasty criticisms when confronting or dealing with stupidity, and rarely thought of himself as ever being nasty. He was just being careful. His physical appearance was outrageous, but his conversations were never as flamboyant, always reserved or non-existent. And this man had every reason to be paranoid. He was Number One on The Man's most-wanted list of drug criminals. His strange personality didn't offend me, as Bear was only trying to avoid making bad decisions or stupid mistakes. He had little tolerance for stupidity and got agitated and somewhat abusive whenever he deemed it important or necessary for everyone's safety.

But, at the same time, he consumed ungodly amounts of his own products, enough to drive most people bonkers. Yet he never seemed zonked, or even slightly out of control. I carried the dilemma he presented with me and never figured out the answer. Why be so careful and careless at the same time? He was the first person I ever encountered to cover, maybe douse, his body with the unforgettable fragrance of patchouli oil. This bold statement of body scent, broadcast to the world, told everyone that Owsley was in the vicinity, making a public appearance, no doubt about it. Everything about his appearance, his dress, his erect military posture, the way he strode down the street, his thinning, styled Prince Valiant haircut (Owsley was the first man I knew to blow dry his hair), and eclectic taste in jewelry, made him stand out in public like a scarecrow. You couldn't miss him, especially if you were The Man and hoping to bring him down. I found myself trying to act like I didn't know him when we were out together in public. He attracted too much attention, which fueled my paranoia. But his public persona never caused him any trouble, and he appreciated the occasional compliments and recognition by his fans.

Everything about him tapped into something weird inside me and others he interacted with. He had just the right combination of brilliant intellect and weird hippie shit to activate most people's inner alarm systems: "Warning! Beware! Drug-crazed hippie in the vicinity!" But Bear paid little heed to his effect on others. He chose his own nickname, and seemed to be incapable of dressing himself any differently, even for his own safety. I believed he hired me, because, unlike him and his associates, I could dress for any role.

My first test was no problem. I played a great errand boy, bored stiff and caring less about my job while on the company's dime. So what if the company is phony and I'm delivering to a non-existent address? All this was happening, of course, in a time before Google Maps, where a quick search could easily have blown our cover.

In the relative safety of a Hollywood chain store parking lot as the sun was setting, we repackaged the lab supplies into the four sturdy metal foot-lockers I'd purchased earlier, then headed towards LAX. In those earlier, innocent days of airline travel, Owsley had discovered a major airline loophole which allowed one to ship baggage on a flight before purchasing a ticket for the flight. You'd get to the airport and give the skycap at the curb a worthy tip to handle your baggage. Then he'd tag each bag with the desired flight numbers and off he'd go, taking the bags inside the airport to be shipped. No ticket or proof of flight was necessary. An Owsley associate would be waiting to pick up the foot lockers at the destination and if there was something wrong he could simply walk away. Bear said we'd leave the following day and didn't want to be on the same flight as the lab gear, in case of problems.

Owsley gave the curb-side skycap a generous tip to cart the metal lockers inside while I waited in the car. He still hadn't told me where we were headed – where the lab was located. All I knew was it was too far to reach by car.

Bear changed his itinerary frequently; he never arrived anywhere on time, and no one ever knew for sure where he was at any given moment, unless you were there with him. To further distance both of us from the lab supplies just shipped, he'd decided that we'd return to Berkeley that night to tie up some loose ends before heading off to lockdown in the lab.

I asked again about where we were going, and Bear barked back, "Don't get so bent out of shape, dude. You'll know when it's time. Got it?"

I knew he was right, why did I need to know where the fucking lab was until I was already there? What you don't know can't hurt you.

Chapter 12
The Dead and Cassady

"Before we fly, I'm stopping by some chicks' in North Beach," Owsley told me. He used his fame and cult status to entice the exotic younger female trippers into bed whenever he got the chance. He seemed quite fond of one youngster in an apartment near Coit Tower filled with hippie chicks, and shortly after arriving, he left the room with his favorite. I was laughing to myself that this older, crusty, leather-clad, self-centered man could appeal to the seeming child, and vice-versa. Everything seemed unnaturally weird yet quite seriously humorous to me at the time. I was supposed to pick one to fuck myself, but had no desire for sex when I was busy talking with the paint on the walls, so I slipped out the front door to sit and wait in the truck filled with the lab glass.

Just after midnight, as soon as Owsley'd left his parting mark and returned to the truck, we continued on. With me skillfully manning the controls of the shape-changing, swirling red pickup, we left North Beach behind, giggling and wired out of our skulls – nonstop talk exploding with psychedelic insight. We were making an official Owsley exit from San Francisco, which had to include the Dead's[1] house on Ashbury. Owsley had to inform them all that the Bear was leaving on another sacred mission. It was both a ridiculous and a hilarious gesture, two sides of this complicated stoned genius I was now traveling with.

We pulled to the curb in front of the Dead's house as the

---

1   The Grateful Dead.

The Dead and Cassady

STP[2] seemed to reach a peak.

"Hey, Frank, wassup man?" I greeted the passing Freewheelin' Frank, who was mumbling gibberish, in a hurry while swishing a long sword back and forth. I recognized another familiar face standing under the green light of a mercury vapor lamp across the street.

"Bear, it's Cassady. Hey! Neal!" I greeted Neal as we crossed the street to climb the Dead's front stairway.

Neal was bobbing and weaving without moving his feet, backed up against a parked car, a small transistor radio held up to one ear, a sledge hammer bouncing in and out of his other hand. I'd been bumping into him frequently since I'd met Cassady at Kesey's in La Honda. He'd never once been without the heavy hammer, which he'd continually toss in the air and always catch on its return, never missing, never looking at its flight, and always doing something different with his other hand, all the while chattering away as only Neal could do. He'd talk to the air if no one else was listening to him. Neal was a holy man and a speed freak, maybe the fastest-reacting man alive.

"Yes, now Dean-47 Olds Cou-pay, what a beauty she is indeed, must check the front tires swing arm shocks you know. Well, as I was just saying you understand I am standing here on the chance that well, you see, with Mr. Owsley's latest I am no longer a free thinking being. STP stole my mind it did and has greatly affected..." bantered Neal, three nutcases heading up the front stairs to the Temple of the Whacked. Together we entered the Dead's house, Neal rapping at top speed about the world as he knew it, and, apparently unhappy about Bear's latest lab release, but still very fond and liking my 1947 Oldsmobile two-door coupe. He'd wanted to take the Olds' for a quick spin ever since he'd first seen me drive up in it at Kesey's. But mainly, Neal was telling us to stay away from Owsley's latest product that I'd recently ingested, talking about the damage it had done to his memory.

---

2   STP stands for 'Serenity, Tranquility, and Peace.' It was slang for a psychedelic drug that Owsley briefly produced and distributed in 1967.

"It destroyed the connections from historical reference...can't see beyond..." on and on, Neal wove his tale, working in theories about time, the Dead, places and people named and unnamed floating in the universe, the whole shebang explained almost in the same breath.

Cassady's rap ripped to my inner core. Was it just the effect of the STP? Whatever it was, this was the first time in the months since I first encountered Cassady that I could follow and understand his convoluted, free-form, non-stop monologue. The drug kept my mind and perceptions moving at a pace equal to Neal's and it was a revelation, privilege, and pleasure to be there in complete sync with Neal's huge mind. I understood every word, connection, and relation to my own inner life while his psychedelic vision unfolded.

Owsley seemed annoyed that he was relegated to playing second fiddle to Neal, upset by not being the center of attention he usually commanded in a friendly group. And he was pissed by Cassady's accusation about his latest batch of STP. Bear sat down with Neal and me at the kitchen table, barely pretending to be interested or even listening while Neal and I circled around and around, back and forth, discussing every known issue that flowed freely from our minds. Before I knew it, it was the next morning and Neal hadn't stopped once. In fact, it felt like he was just getting started. The secrets of his mind and his take on life made total sense to me. I was blown away, captured, and enthralled by the clearness and depth of his every spoken word. Owsley, after a few hours, interrupted the magical unfolding exploration of time and space that his own hands had made possible, looked at me, and abruptly interrupted our connected space with a direct order – boss to employee: "Let's go."

I immediately lost my grip on the unifying thread of Cassady's web of stories that my mind had actually tied together. Neal had woven a historical biography from a cosmic perspective combined with current events and related people into a complete statement about his life, God, and mankind. And it all made complete sense. His tale took at least six hours to wrap into a coherent personal, yet universal, account of this man's life. As I got up to follow Owsley out the front door, I knew two things. First, Owsley lived in a similar state of mind, understanding where Neal was going with his story. Second, what I'd just experienced was an extraordinary trip, a beautifully complete personal history of mankind related to me by a very wise, wild man. Until that evening I'd never taken Cassady seriously. I hadn't had the time or patience to listen to his stories from start to finish. But that night *I got it*. I only wish that I had a recording of Cassady's rap, as I can't remember even a word of what Neal revealed to me that night, sitting at a table in the Grateful Dead's kitchen.

Chapter 13
The Lab

Owsley and I drove to the airport, shipped the lab equipment trunks to Denver, and put ourselves on a plane to LAX, taking a roundabout route to Colorado, a diversion while trying to figure out if The Man was following us. The only problem was, by the time we reached L.A. later that morning, both of us were spaced-out, ragged-edged, and drugged-out weirdos, wild-eyed and paranoid, but thinking we were looking and acting real cool. What a joke. The Man could have spotted us a mile away.

By the time we hit the Continental departure lounge in the airport, having to wait a while for the next flight to Denver, we must have been quite a sight, completely whacked on a variety of psychedelic and stimulating substances. And I was still holding two sensimilla joints in a secret compartment I'd sewn into my overcoat, which would help us both avoid a ragged come-down later when the other drugs finally wore off.

Ticketed and having to wait four hours for the Denver flight, both of us were exhausted. Owsley decided to take a nap on the floor of the waiting area. I couldn't believe it, seeing him sprawled out on the rug, dressed all in black leather, face covered with his silly giant hat. Was he hoping to attract the attention of airport security? It might have been comical if the stakes weren't so high, him looking like a mafia hitman, or something worse. I didn't want to get busted as Bear's accomplice, and for sure he was holding who knew what sorts and amounts of illegal drugs in the

The Lab

multi-pocketed black leather vest he wore, or in the Renaissance-style, bright purple puffy shirt pockets underneath the vest. He looked like the King of the Hippies, or a deranged serial rapist, and I wasn't in the frame of mind to deal with the hassle that would be visiting us soon.

So I decided to act like I didn't know the man, tried to distance my own tired body from his, and sat down as far away from him as possible on the far side of the waiting room. I was in the very silly sort of situation I always tried so hard to avoid. Owsley stood out like a sore thumb, but he probably thought if he went to sleep, he'd just disappear and could rest out of everyone's sight. There was this strange sleeping creature, still wearing those too-hip, mirrored aviation sunglasses, the huge bear claw hung around his neck. You couldn't see this guy and not wonder, "What the fuck, is he gonna hijack the Denver flight?" And, of course, the 30 feet that separated us didn't fool anyone. My eyeballs must've looked like spinning bottle rockets while I was sitting down, staring at nothing but the wall. Actually, I was getting worried that the end might be near, as I was sure there wasn't a soul in the waiting area stupid enough to not notice that I was with that crazy man crashed out on the floor.

The flight was finally announced, and both of us bounced up to claim our first class position at the front of a long line. And as soon as we were checked in and headed to board the plane, two suited-up cops stepped out from somewhere flashing their badges and asked both Owsley and me to follow the leader into a side room for a conversation.

"Hey, man, we're going to miss the plane. What's going on? We got a concert to set up tonight in Denver," complained my now rock impresario partner. "Can't miss this flight, they're depending on us," Bear explained to the cops.

They searched us for weapons, and somehow missed the drugs that Owsley surely had stashed somewhere on his body, and the joints I'd hidden in my coat. But we were too different to just let go.

"Let's run a check through headquarters. Let me see your driver's licenses." I about shit my pants. I knew that

Owsley had a drug-related record in L.A. County, was a suspected illegal drug manufacturer throughout California, and that the next search would get us busted. My career as a rich, LSD flower hipster was close to its end. My name went in first. I was clean, so nothing came back about me.

"Final boarding call for Denver" over the PA system, and both of us pleaded with the cops. "Hey, officers, we can't miss this flight, both of our jobs depend on us being on it."

So while one cop spelled Owsley's name on the phone, the other cop relented and let us board the plane just before the gate was closed. This reassured Owsley that he was still invincible, and he decided to keep the acid and STP he had hidden in his vest, even though I was sure we'd get stopped again in the Denver airport, and just in case, we smoked up my joints in the plane toilet. But Denver was a breeze, no one met us as we deplaned and no one was following us when we left the airport, although we thought it wise if someone else came back to fetch our baggage later that evening. Owsley says, "Charisma."

A taxi took us into one of the straightest neighborhoods I'd seen since I left home, and we got out and walked a few blocks, always looking over our shoulders for The Man, to a very straight house. Brick with flowers, a mowed lawn, and a fenced-in backyard, inside was one of the straightest scenes ever, just like home. These guys knew what they were doing. There were six of us there now, and this was the lab. Where? In the basement, brother.

Down the stairs, through a door, and into another world, walls and floors filled with bubbling flasks and tubes, pots big enough to boil a human filled with coils and motors, another room with more walls of stuff, and another room filled with supplies and gas bottles, shelves and shelves of different containers. There was a complete bottle washing scene, and a room with a vented hood for the dangerous fumes produced.

I am in and on a spaceship, with no relation to my previous life, and headed for I know not where. And this is Owsley's paradise. He immediately sheds his giant ego and takes me around, showing me this and that. "Here is where we are making the DMT, look how this blue light shows where it is forming the cone. And over here we are extracting essence of hashish, one tiny drop will send you off for eight hours."

And, of course, there was the acid area and the STP experiments, where they were devising altogether new methods for creating this drug. Owsley completely blew my mind when I realized that he was indeed a chemical genius and so were some of his fellow workers. Their background amazed me, for I knew nothing of organic chemistry. They drew original conclusions about processes and then invented new apparatuses to actualize their concepts.

A blackboard was constantly in use, and I was quickly put to work watching and checking things, a 24-hour-a-day operation, pouring this and weighing that. But mainly my job consisted of three things: Go out and buy the dry ice needed to condense something into something else, buy the best steaks I can find, and poke fun at these madmen, provide some other kind of fuel for them to think about besides their work and the pressure of the business.

One fellow, a chemist, had been intensely involved with a radiation lab at the age of 16. He felt that his abilities were as good as Owsley's, and this thought was a constant source of friction between them. Another guy just kind of sat in the corner with giant eyeballs and I guess was constantly running errands. Owsley spent giant amounts of money keeping and feeding his scene, and I soon discovered that I was the smallest dealer doing business with him. Some dudes were selling as much LSD in a day or two as I could sell in a month.

It was a big operation and a lot of money moved in and out. Owsley was constantly doing things for people, buying this guy a car, renting that one a house. He had a scene, and was trying to carry it off righteously. And he had a beautiful old lady, who was more or less the initial brains behind the whole project. She originally got Owsley from electronics into chemistry, and was then a full partner in the business. He demanded a certain thing from her, and when he didn't get it, there was tension between them. Will she say yes or no to him this time? He was an egomaniac, but brilliant, and he kept me high.

After spending almost a month in the Denver lab house, I woke up feeling for sure I was very close to losing my mind, and decided it was time to split. I told the other crew on board Owsley's Spaceship that I had to take a break, that I was close to losing it and couldn't keep my shit together. We'd all discussed the potential risk, or side effect, of working in a lab and handling all the chemical agents of change. The compounds were constantly being absorbed into your bloodstream, through the skin, the lungs, the cuticles. I was staying loaded all the time, and was now too fucking high to function sanely doing my daily tasks out in the world.

The day before, while I was carrying a few hundred pounds of dry ice from the garage behind the house to the basement, I saw a neighborhood kid walking by in the alley behind the house. He saw me and stopped to ask me a question. He couldn't have been much older than 10, or 11, but he scared the living shit out of me when he said, "Hey, mister, are you guys making LSD in there, or what?" I responded somehow and he seemed satisfied and went on his way.

How could a young kid know enough to ask such a question? He had to have overheard some adults talking about all those funny people in the house on the corner. Later at dinner, everyone's sphincters either tightened up or spasmed when I mentioned the kid and his question to the group. Most of the substances were ready to sell, so the next morning no one objected when I decided to return to California.

Chapter 14
Yamananda, Bliss of Death

Over the next few days everyone I ran into, even the guy selling cigarettes, would straight up tell me that I was acting totally insane and completely out of control – not like the Dean they were used to. Well, after a few days of reports like this, it finally started to sink in and force me to question what might be happening. And WHAM! I woke up to the fact that I was in the grip of the drugs I'd been making in the lab, and that whatever it was that I was trying to express to all who crossed my path, it wasn't being heard, and my condition wasn't going to go away. The drugs were wearing off, and I was still as crazy as shit. How much fun is that?

After I'd been hiding out at my brother's place in the redwoods of Zayante in the Santa Cruz Mountains for a few days, Cleve, the Apache man with the piercing eyes, dropped by. What a strange-looking, almost threatening character this guy was. I'd met him earlier at the Hip Pocket Bookstore in Santa Cruz, one of the many different sorts who hung around in the store's back room or next door at Bubble's Bakery. One of the Pranksters, Hassler, who also co-owned the bookstore, told me this guy Cleve was a real in the flesh yogi who claimed to be an enlightened being. It was hard to believe he was hanging out with the Pranksters, but then again, where else would he choose to hang out?

Cleve, aka Yamananda, the one who'd stolen Hassler's ex-girlfriend, lived outside of Placerville in the Sierra foothills of California. Cleve had a small farm where he hosted and presided over a small group of spiritual searchers, mainly the wayward and the lost. The small farm was built around a historical stage coach stop, called Coles Station, and between five and 15 followers would be there, arriving or leaving frequently, at no preset times. Cleve was tough to take, and many newcomers would leave as quickly as possible, as soon as they found the nerve or courage to hit the road.

Cleve somehow came into my life during this time, just after the Cream concert. I had been way too high for over a week when I ended up in Zayante. Cleve knocked and I opened the door and invited him in. Then he stood directly in my path and looked long and hard at me, like this stranger was somehow looking deep into my soul. After a few minutes of just staring at one another, which I had been doing anyway for the past week with anyone and everyone I'd encountered, he asked me if I wanted relief from my pain. Feeling he was likely into something better than what I had going on, I said, "Yes, I do."

He was born a mixed-race Apache in the Southwest. He said he grew up near the Superstition Mountains in Arizona, where he left his tribe to pursue a life of crime in Texas and states east. He was forced to join the Army during the Korean War; that or go to jail. He told me he'd been raised as the scorned and hated mixed-race on a reservation and grew up knife-fighting Apaches who wanted to hurt him only because of his white blood. And so, being experienced with knives, he had no moral problems when he was trained in the art of silent jungle warfare and became a knife warfare specialist and Commie-killing machine for the U.S. of A. They sent him to fight in the jungles of the Philippines, where he and his finely-honed machete willingly participated in putting down the Huk Rebellion insurgency. Then the Army sent him on to the battlefields in Korea, where he was badly wounded. All of his jungle skills were no match for the ultimate power of real bullets. Hospitalized in Japan, Cleve met an Indian Hindu patient while recovering, and the Hindu talked to this wounded Apache warrior about God and enlightenment, asking Cleve whether he knew just how close to spiritual awakening he already was.

Yamananda, Bliss of Death

The man invited Cleve to visit an ashram in India upon his release from the hospital and Armed Services. Cleve accepted the invitation and spent the next nine years studying yoga until he found freedom living in India. He returned to the U.S. an enlightened being. He ended up living in California just as acid was hammering its way into the spiritual minds of the '60s youth, and instantly found he could gather followers who only stayed with him if they were hellbent on discovering 'The Truth.' He could muster an instant following whenever he turned on The Charm, but not many could stomach the reality of the truth about themselves that he sooner or later revealed to them. Cleve didn't lie. He took no pride in destroying someone's sacred ego, but didn't waste any of the precious time we are all allotted to live on Earth. He called himself Yamananda and literally considered himself to be Yama, the Hindu god of death. He talked about the Bliss of Death and spoke about survival in the jungles each of us faces every day. He took possession of whoever and whatever he wanted or needed to survive. I heard him claim many times to be the Savior we were all looking for.

The hardest part for me to understand about Cleve was his blatant engagement with his sexual desires while also claiming to be the road to spiritual freedom. Cleve was the ultimate ladies' man, exhibiting a profound love for sex and female flesh, always with answers for anyone who dared question his motives or sincerity. I, too, was often dealing with a personal confusion on this matter of choosing between desire and freedom from desire. One time, fucking one of his girlfriends on a twin motel bed while I was trying to sleep on a foam pad on the floor next to the bed, Cleve leaned over and, peering down at me, laughed at my predicament, asking me if I had been hoping it'd be me up there getting laid instead of listening to God doing it. And he was right. I was jealous, hopeful, and confused, all at the same time. He often said that he was the very last man alive in his line of Apaches, and his goal before dying was to populate the Earth with as many blood children as was possible; survival of the species.

Cleve had entered Hassler's life at a critical time, saving

him from the real monetary suffering of the failing bookstore Hassler had opened in Santa Cruz. He liked Hassler for all of his inner qualities, and for attracting all the local young beauties that hung around The Hip Pocket. Hassler liked anyone who spoke the truth and attracted women as well.

So I was the only person home at Lee's that day the yogi showed up. Cleve was an impressive piece of work standing there with an ear to ear grin when I opened the door. "What's this guy laughing at?" I wondered. "And why's he staring so deeply into my still-zonked-out, crazed, and now feeling a bit paranoid eyes?" His black eyes seemed to be looking way inside me, maybe to my very soul. They felt like the eyes of knowledge, of a spiritual being.

I looked back into those dark eyes. I felt overwhelmed with what I thought they were seeing. His eyes seemed unconnected, acting all on their own, separate from the person I was greeting, inviting inside. And just like that, in the blink of an eye, WHAM! BAM! SHAZAAM! Cleve stepped right into my life, looked through my eyes into my troubled, garbled mind and, instantly, just like that, I calmed down. All the wild thoughts and tedious mental gyrations were suddenly gone. They disappeared, vanished. I knew without a doubt that this tall, dark-skinned stranger standing in my brother's doorway and gazing into my eyes had just done some real magic on me. He somehow, miraculously, just ended my pain and confusion, returning me to my conscious self, which I recognized immediately as my sane mind.

Chapter 15
Hassler and Lee

The following is a letter Dean wrote to a Hollywood producer, Peggy, from Boron State Prison.

~ ~ ~

19 January 1984

Dear Peggy,

Hassler was the first of the Pranksters that I became really close with. He and I spent many months in 1967 and '68 traveling here and there, in the pursuit of God and pussy.

After Kesey had split for Mexico, and left many of the gang hanging out in L.A., after they all had been down to visit Kesey in Mexico and returned, I think the original in-group was getting their fill of thrills and chills of 'Total Rat Living.' So after many Acid Test happenings, they decided to have the one big final blowout, the 'Last Acid Test Graduation.'

Kesey snuck back into the States and was on hand for the gathering. There's a whole documented account of this time, but after the very last Acid Test, the Acid Graduation, many of the Pranksters started to head off on their own, whatever that meant. I hired Hassler to be my chauffeur, to take me places in my old truck, which he had ended up with.

Hassler had been jilted in a love affair when his girl

had decided to dump him for their mutual guru, Cleve the Apache man. So Hassler had his eyes on some young beauties in school at UC Santa Cruz. I had a house nearby, so he sort of moved in with me in Zayante, and even got me interested in these young pretties too, as my wife had run off with the Pranksters to Mexico, got pregnant along the way, acquired assorted venereal infections, and was no longer interested in me.

Zayante was a refuge for all kinds of outcasts, including hippies, and my brother, Lee, had discovered this place in the Santa Cruz Mountains after the courts ordered the house in La Honda shut down and The Spread in Soquel got too crowded. Kesey was doing time in an honor camp, and the Pranksters were on their own. So Lee and Space Daisy (Lee's second wife) decided to spend her dead husband's money on a new life in a postcard-pretty valley with a fast-flowing creek cutting through dense redwood forests to the north of Santa Cruz – Zayante. They bought a house, filled it with exotic monkeys, and acted like things were going to work out just fine. I followed Lee's good intentions and rented a cabin nearby.

Lee discovered that acid opened a personal communication channel to the mysterious outlaw of yore, Joaquin Murrieta, a Robin Hood character from early California modern history who supposedly hid out in the remote Zayante area a hundred years before. Joaquin appeared to Lee in his backyard, rising out of the rushing stream that bordered the back of his property. Joaquin became my brother's muse, apparently meeting him many times, and Lee started writing again, a good thing, while also staying true to his beatnik serious drinking habits.

The meaning of life was closer at hand in the mountains, and I could quickly get back from San Francisco to my mountain studies in my new Porsche, to count my new acid earnings. I had come into some seriously good money, using the new monetary system: I give you God in a pill, and you give me money. So Hassler saw a good thing, and moved himself right in with me. He had his toothbrush in his pocket, and his heart on his sleeve.

Hassler looked like Prince Valiant, with a wholesome smile running from ear to ear. He preached proper dental hygiene and a tuck-in at night. I fed him, and we rolled around for a few months, first capitalizing on his Kesey-earned fame to hustle UC co-eds, and then on to New Mexico, to take a closer look at the alternative communes sprouting up there, claiming to live in peace and love. Taos was becoming the new spiritual center of our generation.

-*Dean*

Chapter 16
The Outlaws

Who was behind this new earth-shaking rock 'n roll lifestyle?: the outlaw pirates. We had many faces; we were writers, poets, musicians, diggers, explorers, students, smugglers, chemists, risk-takers, dealers, the counterculture, the kids who suddenly woke up and knew they could make it happen and were learning how to enjoy the process of driving the rising waves higher and higher.

I was a founding participant in the first wave, and, unfortunately, the last group of a well-intended, honest, and trustworthy breed of pot smugglers. The Man called us criminals, but we were honored and respected as homegrown, in-the-flesh folk heroes by our own generation, the customers we serviced. Our group risked it all to stay living on the outside, a small bunch of rogues who took great pride in beating the law to earn a living. And man, what a great living it was.

The pirates I knew were rascals who trusted one another with their very lives. They made far-reaching decisions based on first impressions and overcame incredible obstacles to do whatever was needed to sustain the flow. They created new chemistry, new products, new drugs, new kinds of families, a new world, and made money – lots of money – doing it. And then they managed to give it away just as quickly as it had accumulated, without a moment's regret, and went back to make more money. The lifestyle and brotherhood of the honorable outlaw I'm talking about was almost a spiritual discipline, a calling. It was all good, and, in fact, as good as it ever gets, and we knew that what I'm saying here was all true in the moment it was happening.

I was working in this trade at a crossroads in modern drug history, before the time when a few small independent smugglers were forced to shut down their endeavors. They were replaced by a different breed: real criminals with larger corporate operations, who carried guns and used them to fight for total control of the business. No, I was just a small-time indie-type smuggler, a lifestyle outsider whose word was good, who didn't rat off a friend to save his own ass, and was skilled in what he could do...including knowing how to have fun. The competition was 'The Law,' not others in my business, and I enjoyed winning when pitted against The Man. I was in the first wave of California acid-heads that spread LSD and marijuana across the land, living day to day as if there were no tomorrow. I was a cunning pirate of the highest order, running fast and staying as low as possible. We sailed the open seas and braved the unforgiving deserts in the name of...? I never could decide what I was really looking for or where I was heading, other than looking for love, more fun, and more money. I lived in the existential 'here and now,' always chasing and then always finding the girls. It was mostly about getting laid, truth be told, when all was said and done. Like a man once said to me, "Dude, ya' know, I'd eat a mile a' yer shit jes' to get to the pussy..."

I'm still only setting up some of the history here, painting a verbal backdrop for a grand and dramatic live stage production. We had a blank canvas for a painting that many beginning outlaw artists were actively engaged in creating day by day, going for it with their newly acquired sense of adventure, enthusiasm, and excitement. Ah, it all was so much fun, even the dangers we faced, honing our skills at understanding the unknown and resolving the potential problems; those strange, unexpected twists that suddenly appeared during every outlaw adventure, the part of each outing that we all expected, even knew was coming. There was always a real challenge to overcome in the game we played. When the risks and unexpected results seemed to block the road forward, we knew we could work through it, no matter what, and even during the very worst moments, all of it could be dealt with, handled, and knowing this was a cause for more celebration.

Could you say that I was avoiding adjusting to adulthood, that I was holding on to rather immature beliefs, that I had a senseless trust in my own immortality? Of course! But don't we all take unnecessary risks when we're young and willing to risk everything for the freedom to keep searching? Of course, and before The Man got wise to our ways and our world, no outlaw I knew ever truly wanted to give up or turn their backs on such a grand source of entertaining adventure and real income because nothing else provided so many thrilling, up-close and personal encounters, with reality, with sex, with feeling really alive, living in the moment.

Experiencing actual, real camaraderie was the basic glue that allowed for such a thrilling life, although for many it became more like a serious addiction. Living the life rediscovered in the '60s, I felt that what we were doing and pursuing was a good thing, a beneficial addiction, it was really OK. Society labeled the lifestyle outlaw, criminal, but the smugglers and underground chemists were honored and respected, even praised by the subculture of seekers. They were the cultural heroes who mattered to their friends, many of them customers. The outlaws were just like the people they served, who were peers and equals, and their work was the impetus that drove the movement forward, the customer base that supported our illicit efforts. Most never knew our real names or faces, or how we worked or what we were capable of pulling off, but we had our generation's solid backing and approval. They loved our products, appreciated the skill and effort our work represented, and this was important for a long time in my trade. It was all us, the hippie counterculture, including politicos, meditators, hippies, musicians, students, diggers. Everyone, no matter why they were dancing in the '60s parade, knew the bottom line: It was all of us against The Man, for real, and it'd been this way for a long time. People were willing to take real risks on your behalf, to do whatever it took to maintain the supply of great products, and what a great kick it all was too. So many unsung heroes chose to keep everything about their lives and work quiet, for the sake of the lifestyle. Some chose to confront The Man face to face. Many of us hoped to out-smart The Man, and we were very good at doing so for a long time. The outlaw bottom line was simple: no weapons, stealing, or threat of bloodshed, you had to be honest. We really believed, beyond any doubt, that we were doing a good thing for a lot of people, most of the time.

Chapter 17
The World Smoke Ring Champion, '67

I am the first and the only 'World Smoke Ring Champion,' having competed in and won this title, the top honor, at the world's first and only World Championship Smoke Ring Competition event, organized and administered by the four official judges who formed the World Smoke Ring Commission. The Commission hosted the showdown event in an airtight sunroom in Julius Karpen's North Beach San Francisco apartment, where Nick Gravenites and I fiercely faced off in one final grab for victory, fame, and the worldwide bragging rights to be the one and only champion.

Nick and I were both highly skilled in the art of blowing smoke rings. We'd been unofficially competing with one another for months, meeting up frequently in San Francisco's North Beach bars, always maligning the other's splendid smoke ring work. Our ring-work reached such competitive heights that the two of us were invited by the founding president of the World Smoke Ring Commission to compete in an event that would decide, once and for all, which one of us could actually claim to be the world's best.

On the day of the competition, the judges, plus a group of wild enthusiasts, crowded into Julius' tiny apartment. Nick and I were sealed inside the apartment's separate sun porch, the only room with no air circulation to interfere with our smoke rings. We were separated by glass doors from the cheering friends, spectators, and judging officials, all gathered in Julius' living room, adjacent to the competition's air-tight sunroom.

Nick won the coin toss and chose to compete first. He was fully prepared for the match, grinning ear to ear while lighting up a non-filtered Camel. He led off with one of his favorites, a large and thick single ring, exhibiting a perfectly outrageous 'Taurus Approximation' endgame approach and with a near-perfect elasticity technique. His next series of smoke rings were truly incredible. Nick gave everyone a tremendous performance, and I knew his popularity as a Chicago blues singer with the crowd, along with his amazing ring-blowing skill and effort, would be tough to beat.

But I was born with a special gift, a unique ability: Whenever I find myself suddenly challenged or threatened in unexpected ways by some unfamiliar or extreme pressure, I can simply open myself up to the situation, without fear, become totally relaxed and focused, and then rise and respond to the occasion, whatever it might be. I enter a mental zone of calmness, a center of inner motivation, and acute personal awareness, a temporary state from which flows unlimited self-confidence to embrace, deal with, and usually resolve the looming crisis. And so, when everyone had settled down and all were eager to see me compete, I was 100% prepared to show off my stuff; the new champion had arrived. I stood up a transformed being. At that moment I had 'The Magic,' I was in 'The Zone' and all would be as it should be.

With a grand flourish I released the two brass clasps and opened the leather briefcase sitting at my side, reached inside, and produced a beautifully-engraved wooden box, only slightly larger than a pack of cigarettes. I carefully placed it on the table in front of me. The gathered crowd went wild, appreciating such a classy opening move. I opened and removed a pack of Kool Filter Kings from the box, my 'weapon of choice' for this first and only championship duel which would crown only one of us the victor.

With a grand display of confidence, I began my smoke ring routine, blowing a perfect machine-gun burst of tiny rings, aimed at and landing squarely in The Greek's now-stunned face. I asked Nick to extend his arm and point one finger at me, which he did. I immediately wrapped a giant, single, glass-smooth ring, blown from at least six feet away, around his extended middle, fuck you digit. Loud cheers and applause filled the apartment, rattling the porch's glass walls.

Next I blew a concentrated, highly-compacted single ring, a huge white donut that hovered three feet in front of my face, followed by a series of smaller, symmetric rings discharged at lightning speed, all passing cleanly through the donut hole of my larger, still-hovering beauty without the slightest contact with the large ring, and finally dissipating after hitting, and careening off of Nick's astonished face. The crowd went wild.

To finish off The Greek, once and for all, I improvised an unplanned assault on my powerful foe. Turning away from both Nick and the judges, I unbuckled my pants, letting them fall to the floor, forcing all present to look directly into my naked, bare ass. I swiveled my body around so all could see my face, wrapped my tongue around a burning, half-smoked Kool King, and tongue-flipped the burning Kool backwards into my mouth, which I then closed, the Kool King now completely out of sight. With a large flourishing twist I bent my head down from my waist, facing the crowd from between my knees, forcing the crowd to see my upside-down, smiling face below my shiny asshole, puckering open and closed, winking at the gathered judges and spectators. Then I blew one last perfect ring with smoke from the burning cigarette still hidden inside my mouth: my face, my bare ass, and my final smoke ring showcasing my world-class talent to Nick, the cheering crowd, and most importantly, to the judges. As my final gesture I flipped the lit cigarette out from hiding inside my mouth and continued smoking it, additional proof that everyone at the event had just witnessed an award-winning grand finale performance.

I was immediately crowned World Champion. My scores in all categories were rated above the upper-limits on the official scoring charts, including top honors for Taurus Approximation, longevity, accuracy, and 'Machine Gun,' as well as for exhibitionism. I'd earned the title, and was, for the moment, a hero to the crowd of beatniks and hippies gathered there in North Beach. Some in the audience later cried foul, as my brother was one of the four judges, along with Julius Karpen, George Gibson, and Al Taylor. But their decision was unanimous and final, and I still hold this championship title today, having won the first and only World Smoke Ring Championship title.

Chapter 18
The Second Hell's Angels Acid Test at Kesey's

The second Hell's Angels party at Kesey's was a defining moment for me. I finally reached a personal limit of laissez faire – a limit on accepting actions, but not responsibility for their outcomes. I got the shit scared out of me.

I wasn't able to make it to Kesey's second Angels party, but I gave directions to a new hippie friend from Berkeley who was really happy about going in my place. Leonard made it to Kesey's La Honda spread, drank some electric Kool-aid, and got way too high, higher than he'd imagined would ever happen. Consequently, Leonard went a little overboard, if not out of his mind that night, and for a long time afterwards.

He started introducing himself to every freak at the acid party in the woods. He'd say, "Hi, I'm Leonard and I'm cool, OK?" The Angels got tired of his repetitious rap and decided to tie him up with rope. Then one Angel somehow picked up that Leonard was a Jew, and even on acid, by god, they all still hated Jews, and that was the beginning of a very bad trip for Leonard. I later learned they'd hung him upside-down, the rope tied around his ankles, from the rafters in the center of Kesey's living room. They left him there for the rest of the party and no one present dared cut him down or even try to help this poor, lost fucker – another one who didn't pass the Acid Test.

Leonard was a very bright Berkeley student, just discovering his inner mind, or whatever, with acid. He had decided to really take enough to get off that night, and just as he started to peak, all this bad shit started happening to him. He was alone, had no friends, and wasn't prepared to deal with the Pranksters and their mantra, "Can you pass the Acid Test?" He got very weird well before the Angels got a hold of him. Someone told me later that he was acting quite obnoxious, but weird stuff happened all the time on acid. Usually someone in the know could step in and calm things down, but no one helped Leonard find a safe landing at that party while he was flying out on many micrograms of LSD.

There was no place or person for Leonard to engage with, and he lost it. That's when the Angels determined he needed to be strung from the rafters. And as he was swinging upside-down, the Angels all argued in front of him about which one of them was going to kill him, "the fucking Jew." It was the Angels' interpretation of putting on a big prank just like Kesey's band of fools always did, and even though they never touched Leonard, the poor kid was never the same after that evening. He dropped out of school, moved away from Berkeley within the week, and was never heard from again. I felt very bad about this, how Kesey could let things get so out of hand in his house – Kesey the Chief. Didn't he care at all? I still hold this against Kesey. I heard that Leonard was freaking out, screaming, crying, dying really, and no one would come to his aid. He didn't pass the Acid Test. And that was what it was all about.

Can You Pass The Acid Test? That was the new challenge, the big new question. Many of us could, and did all the time, but many others were thrown into an abysmal new reality with a shattered faith in themselves and their world. And I often wonder if I would have had the guts to stand up against 15 of the most-feared humans on Earth, to cut Leonard down. Was Kesey afraid of them too?

The Angels definitely had limits, rules, and I quickly discovered how far I could push an issue before they would turn on me. Kesey and Mountain Girl were pretty immune to their ways, but the rest of us were fodder for their fun. LSD didn't stop them from being mean and rude. Terry the

Tramp was a cut above. They said he had a degree from some Ivy League college, and he could carry on a conversation on a variety of topics. But most were truly bent on acting bad, and would only grunt at us hippies, a strange breed we were, without much in common to talk about. And as long as the party was staying fueled, they didn't fuck us up.

But after the Leonard experience, the thrill of these parties was gone for me, and I quit making special efforts to get to them. It seemed that Kesey was going to twist everyone out of shape. He was always pushing everything further, to the limit. No matter what it looked like out there at the edge, it didn't matter at all. It was the journey getting there that really counted.

Chapter 19
The King of Lompico

My career has been more interesting than most. Not only did I get to shake President Kennedy's hand while taking tickets at the main entrance to the 1962 Seattle World Fair, but 15 years later, in Chicago, I also shook Mr. Tony Accardo's hand, aka 'Joe Batters,' reputed crime boss of the Chicago Italian mob. I was visiting the Windy City to unload the 1,500 pounds of pot we'd just smuggled into the States from way down south of the Texas border.

In 1970 I was living as the 'King of Lompico.' What this self-bestowed title implied was that I, as the caretaker/controller of a 580-acre parcel of land and its redwood mansion, located in the Santa Cruz Mountains high above the city of Santa Cruz in dense redwood forests, which was also the actual headwaters of Lompico Creek near Felton, California, could do pretty much whatever the fuck I felt like doing on this property. For instance, while rowing a small boat around my private lake, wearing only a belted holster and semi-automatic .22 pistol, I could randomly shoot my gun at anything I wanted to shoot at; this was legal as I was the only legal resident living on the property and if a bullet ever hit another person, it would have been their fault, for my land was clearly posted for "No Trespassing." Standing naked in the wood boat, I would quick-draw and fire off 10 rounds in any and all directions, except, of course, in the direction of my house.

I lived in a hand-crafted three-story redwood log mansion, with a 25-foot ceiling built above a large, walk-in stone fireplace. There were hardwood floors, a forced-air furnace, and a three-car enclosed garage. I had an Olympic-scale outdoor swimming pool with an adjacent six-person sauna, curious waterwheels channeling fresh water into the pool, and a grape arbor and formal rose garden on a two-acre lake, held in place by a real cement dam. I controlled the level of the lake and how much water would flow out of my pristine wilderness, later to be captured again and consumed by the 1,200 residents living down canyon from my palace. I was in charge of the private dam that could block the stream's flow and any time I felt the need to assert my power, I could open it wide and empty my large lake and suddenly flood the valley, village, and people living below. Other than the loud and now infamous parties that happened on the land, much to the dismay of the locals who hated the hippie living at the end of the road, I was a benevolent ruler and dependable resource manager, never abusing my stranglehold on Lompico. No, I cared for the masses living downstream who depended on my largess for the water they needed to bathe and cook dinner.

Janis Joplin showed up at one party with her latest beau, another rocker, and today the Lompico lore is that she wrote many famous songs while partying on the land, inspired by Lompico to move forward to great fame through her music and voice. What she really did during her only visit to Lompico was drink and fuck, then fuck and drink again, over a one-weekend blowout acid-filled party in the redwoods.

Chapter 20
Funny Money

In 1968 I was flush with profits from my acid sales and looking to invest in some hip business that needed a cash infusion. I didn't know about 401(k)s or anything about investment advisors. Funny money always seems to disappear, whether invested in strange ways, or via dummy dust sent to one's brain through the nostrils. I was wary of money advice offered by various 'New Age' hippies in my circle of friends, remembering Kesey's advice: "Never trust a Prankster."

So when Lee introduced me to his SoCal friend, Joe, a recent devotee of LSD and successful rock 'n roll promoter in the Los Angeles music scene, I listened when he talked about his group of investors' plans for the Sierra Madre Theater. It was being converted into a performance hall and seemed like a great investment in people with a track record.

I visited Joe to check out the potential investment and future return via cash flow from the theater's profits. It looked good on paper.

Joe lived at the head of a beautiful narrow canyon in the Sierra Madre, part of the San Gabriel Mountains; a rural, open lifestyle setting that reminded me of Santa Cruz. He was cool, worked, and he knew lots of good people.

So, when Joe offered to just give me his family dog as my Route 66 travel buddy for another run I needed to make to Taos, I accepted his offer. This Jack Russell Terrier had attached himself to me during my visit and would be a welcome friend while I was wandering alone through the blossoming hippie world in the great Southwest.

A few months later, I returned to see the progress on my investment in the Sierra Madre Theater. Pulling up at Joe's cabin, I opened the VW bus door, and my little dog jumped out and ran into the open arms of a very happy little girl, a neighbor of Joe's.

"You've found my dog, thank you, thank you," the girl told me.

That was the end of two friendships: one with the dog and the other with Joe. I mean, who'd give away a little neighbor girl's pet dog? He was a stone cold dude, and in keeping with the rip-off frame of mind I now knew was the real Joe, the owners of the hip theater disappeared before any return on my investment ever saw the light of day. Funny money...

Chapter 21
The First Smuggling Adventure

My first actual smuggling adventure scared the shit out of me. My previous drug dealings had been easy in comparison: selling pot to hippie friends or delivering batches of LSD across the landscape to thankful searchers like a cool Johnny Appleseed. It didn't take a genius to conceal a gram glass vial filled with 100,000 concentrated, mind-blowing doses of liquid enlightenment and then fly it to New York. I delivered god-awakening hits of spiritual salvation to grateful, first-time seekers across the country, and in return, I was rewarded with deep respect and unexpected expressions of love for my efforts, along with lots of money. Everyone I was first involved with in the LSD scene, the lab alchemists, the wholesale or retail dealers, and the consumers, were mostly trustworthy fellow hippies who stood by their word and delivered on their promises. I skated through a few potentially close scraps. One time, after delivering 250 acid-coated aspirin in their original bottle to an apartment on Carl Street in the Haight, I happened to leave by the rear stairs, unaware the Feds were knocking on the front door. Nothing to do with me, though. I wasn't ignorant of the potential dangers, but at first, they came primarily from The Man. Duh, what's new?

But I had to change directions after The Man shut down my supply of good acid with Owsley's unfortunate bust in 1968. All the trust and spiritual fellowship which allowed for the '60s culture to expand so quickly were quickly replaced by the economic reality of needing to develop new avenues to create those wonderful piles of undeclared cash stacked on the table in front of you. The economic powers that have always run the world took notice of our Sixties generation's growing passion for mind-expanding, illegal drugs. Almost overnight the outlaw culture of openness and trust I'd lived and worked in disappeared, and it all happened before I was prepared to recognize some of the more obvious symptoms. I was a silly 'new age hippie,' whether I knew it or not.

Assholes and paranoids of all sorts appeared out of nowhere, a new culture of drug bosses. Suppliers and buyers moved into dealing higher quality pot and the more addictive, white crystal drugs. Within 10 years or less, the free-wheeling pirate channels where I'd learned the trade and sharpened my dealing skills came under the control of a less forgiving, never-taken-acid crowd of drug dealers. Smuggling's wild cast of characters and stories disappeared. Tales like I'm telling here were replaced by grim stories of greedy outlaws and dangerous criminals, most with just one idea in their minds: "Where's the money?" And with this greed came real consequences if somehow the cash was ever short, or misplaced along the route to the bosses.

My first, early-on experience in pot smuggling could have easily ended tragically and forced me to see how seriously stupid I'd been, thinking I knew enough to plan and pull off a smuggling operation. Fortunately, I was smart enough to recognize this hubris after the fact, and the insights gained from my trial by fire forced me to reassess my own dreams of grandeur. To survive in the new, real world after my acid supply was shut down, I had much to learn.

But in 1966, I believed I could just easily step into the role of pot smuggler. All I needed was a Spanish-speaking partner to get something started. What I didn't know was what it means to take on a partner. I mean, weren't the people I knew and already worked with all honest and trustworthy? Early on in my drug-selling career, a sharp snake oil salesman could have sold me worthless swampland in Florida, no problem. Hindsight is the real teacher. I foolishly asked a new Berkeley friend of another new friend to join

The First Smuggling Adventure

me in a smuggling caper. He was a hip pot dealer and lover of a girl who had also caught my eye. Randy claimed Spanish fluency and previous experience scoring pot in Mexico. He said he could get us the pot at the lowest possible price and I believed him. I had the name of a "solid" source for weed in Culiacán, Mexico, another silly assumption on my part. If 'Eliseo' had spoken English I wouldn't have needed a partner, but my Mexican supplier "no hable ingles" and I spoke even less Spanish. So my new friend became my partner, agreeing to handle buying and bringing a load of Mexican weed to the border. But he wasn't interested in smuggling it from Mexico into the States. I had the confidence of a fool to think this was the easy part. I'd get the pot across the border and back to Berkeley, where we had anxious buyers waiting. No sweat.

We pooled together enough cash to buy 100 kilos from Eliseo. Randy would drive his older Chevy round-trip to get the weed and we'd meet within 10 days in Mexicali to transfer the pre-packaged pot into my Chevy panel truck with secret compartments. We had it down, even to a day-by-day schedule for his drive to and from Culiacán, with three days to score and package the pot, and decided on three specific dates when I'd be in place, ready to meet him in Mexicali. Randy recommended a hotel in San Diego with cheap rooms, a good place for me to wait for his call. We were so together – two smart guys who could plan and agree to a schedule, real pros, and we'd soon be rich from our new career. If there were any delays, he'd let me know on the days I'd be waiting at the hotel.

The actual experience squashed my naive dreams of smuggling. Having to risk so much on off-the-wall people and unexpected twists to our plan wasn't worth the financial return or mental aggravation. Up until that point, my underground drug dealings were guided by my unfounded trust in the word of fellow acid-tripping outlaws, especially when they were from our San Francisco Area scene. Big bad wrong. I had to pay my dues and learn from experience how to smuggle and deal dope. The bottom line, the new basic reality of living 'The Outlaw Life,' was never trust anyone if your own freedom depends on people you barely know.

The plan was I'd look like a surfer, just another blue-eyed local returning home from some fun on the Baja beaches. I had built hidden panels into the truck's rear walls to hold 100 pounds of pressed pot. Randy would pre-package the kilo pot bricks into plastic-wrapped special-sized slabs that we'd transfer quickly into the secret compartments.

Randy decided at the last minute to take his new girlfriend, a wild and beautiful score herself, along for the ride. If he didn't, he knew I'd have been all over her. So Randy and the new lovely took all our combined money and headed south to make us rich. I spent the three weeks getting my truck in tip top shape, ready for the first big score of my life.

~ ~ ~

The hotel was a nightmare, a pre-WWII sailor's whorehouse located in the worst part of San Diego, with two floors of rooms just large enough for a twin bed, now converted to a stopover for the older poor and soon-to-be dying. There were no phones and it had a single-wall construction you could poke a finger through. The old guy at the front desk said that when I got a call, he'd come and knock on my door. He could have just yelled up the staircase.

For three days and nights I listened to hacking coughs, round the clock vomiting, and intimate conversations while trying to get some sleep. Sound bites detailing someone's last days on Earth filled my consciousness. What a fucked up place to pick to wait for a dope deal and get my nerves steeled-up for my smuggle. Man, Randy was going to hear about this shitty trip.

If I stood on my tub I could peer over the wall into the bathroom adjoining mine, where some shrinking geezer must have had TB. He wouldn't stop coughing. Funny thing was, I got the only room open, and I couldn't leave. This was where I had to be for the call. The first morning I decided to try the coffee shop just off the lobby. The clerk said he'd get me if the call came in. I didn't want to chance leaving the hotel because man, I had a lot riding on my performance.

The First Smuggling Adventure

So I was having breakfast, mostly old people, a few sailors, and me, the long-haired hippie sitting at the counter. The man on the swiveling stool next to me was eating some kind of oatmeal, and suddenly he just died. His face hit the cereal bowl on its trip to the floor, splashing me with some gooey porridge. This fit right in with the general ambiance of the place, nothing unusual to the rest of the breakfast eaters.

The vibe, man, I was getting a bad vibe. Randy, where the fuck are you? And so, after four days and no message from him, I said fuck it and headed back to Berkeley. No idea what had happened to Randy, and no way to check up on him.

Two weeks later I got the call, "Dean, come. I'll be in Mexicali tomorrow. I'll explain everything then." And off I went, non-stop to the border. I dropped a friend off at Louie's in Santa Barbara, where I was to regroup after bringing the pot into the States. I was upset that Randy turned out to be a flake and I was pissed at myself for agreeing to let him take the most beautiful girl in the world along to share in our impending new fortune. What was I thinking? She probably drove the Mexicans nuts. But as we'd all been dropping lots of acid before Randy left, and felt so cool and groovy, everything had seemed way cool. Sure.

Randy's only job, other than finding and buying good pot, was to package it in bundles small enough to be transferred quickly from his car to the tight compartments in the truck.

I met Randy where he said he'd be, but he was totally crazed and so was the girl. They'd been on a continual acid trip for the past month, and the whole operation had worn their minds quite thin. They'd been fucking non-stop and hadn't had time to repackage the pot. It was in gunny sacks, stashed under the hood, on top of the hot engine. Seems the Federales were on to them too. They had searched Randy's trunk once already just that morning. So we both drove south from Mexicali and looked for a spot to make the transfer. This is desert with some rolling hills, nothing more.

Randy finally pulled off the road into a sandy turnout,

saying he can't drive anymore. This would have to do. He was nuts, babbling, and the girl started wandering around the area, wearing only a see-through blouse, no pants and no panties...bonkers out of her mind. Cars, buses, and trucks were whizzing by as we were parked right on the side of the main highway. Everyone was honking and calling out, thrilled with our naked friend and her strange behavior, which turned out to be a good enough distraction for me to get to work.

Our original plan was to get the Mexicans to sell us special, saran-wrapped, smell-proof packages, half the size of the standard one kilo bricks, so the pot would easily slip in and out of the hidden compartments I'd added to the truck. Why on earth we thought this would be easy for the Mexicans to deliver, that's how stupid and working-blind we were. Did I think they had a factory with adjustable packaging machines to do this work? So the 'no-smelly-weed-to-avoid-a-bust' action in our plan didn't happen, which meant my careful welding of airtight spaces in the walls and fenders of my 1953 Chevy Panel Truck was a waste of time and money.

We dragged the burlap gunny sacks from his car to the back of my truck and I had to hand-stuff loose pot into the truck's secret panels. People were driving by, pointing, laughing at this naked girl running around in a field next to us, stoned out of her mind. It was really hot. I was stuffing and seemed to be getting nowhere, and I was starting to get scared. It felt like it could only be minutes before the cops showed up. Somehow I got the pot stuffed into the truck, reloaded the surfboard and camping gear, and then splashed a little gasoline over the whole mess to cover the smell. I mean the truck reeked of fresh, nearly broiled pot.

I hit the border ahead of Randy, just another surfer returning from Ensenada via the back roads. At the border, no one paid me any attention, all focus was on the car just behind me, on Randy and the girl, two crazy gringos.

I got waved right through the commotion as they prepared to hang my partner. But he was clean, and later they let him leave Mexico and enter the U.S.A. too. They strip-searched Randy's old Chevy, ripped off the door panels, slashed open the seats, slashed the spare tire, and tossed their clothing on top of the mess like salad dressing. But no pot was found in that car. Randy and I had quite a giggle after we got back to Berkeley. We sold the pot and made some good money, my first smuggling deal. It was my first, and last, venture with Randy, and I never heard what happened to that beautiful, crazy girl.

Working with a partner I had no experience with turned out to be a real drag. I toned down my grand plans to become, overnight, the smuggling kingpin of Berkeley.

Chapter 22
Chez Ray and Sleazy Dean

In keeping with the 1960s spirit of poking fun at contemporary cultural temples, I've always enjoyed riffin' with hipster friends who used spoken language for mutual play. Ray was a skilled Berkeley punster, and also a partner in the overnight Berkeley dining sensation, Chez Panisse. This game-changing, extremely hip restaurant was instantly recognized as a culinary phenomenon. Its founder, Alice Waters, established a new paradigm in truly fine, organic dining experiences, which became known as the 'Nouvelle-California' cuisine. Ray aptly bestowed upon me a nickname that served me well during the evolving 1970s wonder years. To fully explore the magical powers that this nickname brought to me, I only had to follow Ray's two-step process and then show up at Chez Panisse to reap the bounty of his gift.

Step One:

"Good Afternoon, Chez Panisse...How may I help you?" asked the person answering my phone call.

"Yes, hello, is Mr. Ray available?"

A well-known fact in Berkeley lore is that from its opening day, booking a same-day table in the front, downstairs dining room at Chez Panisse was next to impossible. I'm talking about up to a month's wait for a downstairs table at this popular, exciting gourmet eatery. But I possessed the power of Ray's two-step magical gift:

"May I tell Ray who's calling?" asked the receptionist.

Step Two:

Herein lay my secret sauce, two words that guaranteed me a prime dinner table at Chez Panisse, in the downstairs, front dining room that very evening.

"Yes, of course, please tell Mr. Ray that Sleazy Dean is calling." I was never once disappointed when Ray was working the day I called.

"Just a minute, Mr. Dean," the voice would reply and I was placed on hold until Ray picked up my call.

"Sleazy Dean, my most luminescent of luminaries! How ever may I assist you at this time?" Ray's greeting to me was always that of a perfect gentleman, host, and colleague.

"A romantic table for two, eight-ish, this evening, if possible," I'd reply.

"Of course! Can you please hold for just a moment while I check…?" as if he's consulting some reservation book close at hand, then always I'd receive the same reply.

"Sleazy Dean, you are confirmed for two. Eight-ish it is then, for this evening! Now, is there anything else I can do for you? And please, don't be shy, my most welcomed and promiscuous good sir."

"Well, perhaps, yes, there is just one, a simple request. We would be most honored if you might find a moment to join us, if only to share in my indeflatable joy with an aperitif or three just after this evening's gastronomic adventures." 'Aperitif' was our phone code indicating that I'd also bring a treat of my own, everyone's post-dining favorite, brain-stimulating Bolivian diet supplement, for the table's enjoyment. "Most assuredly," Ray replied. "Perhaps we might also find a moment to partake in a fine '68 Dom bubbly to honor the pleasure of a visit with my most favored of guests." And just like that, my evening's glorious, somewhat mischievous plans were a done deal.

I'd use my privilege only on special occasions, perhaps to impress the current object of my mind's romantic tendencies, knowing full well how positively the 'same-day reservation' ploy could impress the current focus of my affection's desires; it almost guaranteed the hoped-for result that would follow later, well after dinner. And Ray was always a man of his word: As soon as I was seated, a hand-painted bottle of Crystal, or a Dom Perignon, would appear at my table.

The fine bubbly was always Ray's treat, and it guaranteed our waiter an excellent tip from me for the uncorking service. What a wonderful time we all shared during those fine meals and all because Ray and I had become trusted friends while doing business with one another. I was a source for a variety of desired 'specialty' items, including worthy used cars, good weed, and the occasional pleasure of high-quality cocaine, my gift to our dinner conversation and enjoyment, no matter how one's appetite might suffer, and a pleasurable foreplay to the even grander thrills in store for later that evening.

~ ~ ~

Why did I sell used cars when I was already gainfully engaged in driving loads of weed up and down the eastern seaboard and making good money? Simply because I loved cars. I'd been seriously into cars long before I could even legally drive them. I especially liked the vintage 1940s and '50s regal road beauties that were still coming up for sale. In the Midwest, where I'd gotten into cars as a kid, most of the older Detroit creations had long since rusted away from the salted winter roads, beyond salvage. But in California's dry and warmer climate, they could still be seen on the roads everywhere, and usually in pristine condition. When sold, they went for almost no money at all. The owners were dying off and their inheritors were too modern to appreciate the flowing lines and design of these older 'ladies of the night.'

Before I fell into the car hustling business, I'd already been the proud owner of three 1949 Oldsmobile two-door coupes, a 1950 dark green Olds Fastback with a factory sun-visor, and a 1947 Olds two-door coupe, in which I delivered my first acid deals to Seattle and Vancouver, followed by a trunk load of weed to Chicago, before selling the car to Prankster Pat, who put another 50,000 miles on the gem before she died. Neal Cassady remembered me as "Dean with the '47 Olds coupe," which he'd always claimed was one of his favorite road trip cars.

These huge, heavy, and voluptuously-styled early American GM products were marvelous to sit and ride in, watching the scenery pass by, while looking over and beyond its long, full-bodied hood. It was like driving a well-endowed lover with generous soft cloth cushions to hold you firmly and guide you on the journey, such graceful, lovely sculpted lines extending forward to the large, full headlamps that would illuminate your night-time adventures. The enameled metal dashboards were pleasing to the eye, accentuated with chrome trim and numerous faux-ivory knobs to control the car's interior functions in elegant style. I also drove a '47 Cadillac crème-colored convertible with rolled red leather seats, which could comfortably seat eight people before the days of mandatory seat belts. I gave it to a musician friend from Chicago, Nick, who soon afterwards I'm told parked it in the north Sausalito mud-flats surrounding The Quicksilver Messenger Service's rehearsal studio. It's probably still there, buried under 10 feet of mud and ocean water.

I sometimes used my '59 lime-green Porsche 356 convertible, the first with roll-up side windows, to deliver my acid-soaked aspirin tablets around the Bay Area. Skyline Boulevard was my preferred route for driving fast in the world's second most beautiful open-air roadster. Before this, in 1963, I bought my first used VW cloth-top 23-window van in Chicago, and drove my first wife to San Francisco across the Northern U.S. It was one of many VW's I'd own over the coming 20 years, and the only vehicle that almost killed me. Having a wide selection of cars to choose from was an affordable hobby to pursue back in the day.

As I grew more passionate about the world of cars, and the art of buying and selling these 'Masters of The Universe,' the East Bay provided the best access to a wonderful supply of every sort of used vehicle one could imagine, from every country on Earth.

Mine was the first generation of Americans to take full advantage of the great new interstate highway system being carved into every part of America's landscape. At a time

The Substitute Asshole

when gas was 28 cents a gallon, older used cars were cheap and plentiful, and our country was a wide open canvas for the youth to explore. And explore we did. A three-day drive from San Francisco to Chicago might cost $50, and a pound of weed cost $100 and sold for up to four times as much, so 10 pounds meant a sizable profit for a few days of driving. Bart the Fart paid me $10 a pound to deliver loads from Miami to D.C., Atlanta, Chicago, or New York. A rented Chrysler trunk would hold 600 pounds, and I enjoyed making this drive many times a year, for many years. Great road cars were available in Miami in the spring each year, needing to be driven north for their elderly, cold-climate-avoiding owners, who'd driven them south to Miami for the winter months, but couldn't be bothered to make the return drive. I'd often drive a new Cadillac or Lincoln to New York or New Jersey for the owner from Miami, after filling the car's trunk with as many pounds of weed as it would hold.

Beginning in 1966, based out of Berkeley and Santa Cruz, I moved up the seniority ranks to become a major player in a small Berkeley group of hip used car traders, working the large market of student buyers always looking for affordable used cars. We facetiously called ourselves 'car hustlers.'

I'd put Chez Panisse's Ray in a fine used vehicle for a very low price, and he reciprocated with my special arrangement at his restaurant. It was a unique, short-lived period in the late '60s through mid '70s in California, when a gigantic loophole existed in California's DMV[1] rules, which was summarily exploited.

Our band of car hustlers were fierce competitors, each hoping to be the first to find and buy every suitable used car that appeared on the local market. We'd learned how to maximize any car's resale profit by abusing the lax enforcement of California's DMV regulations.

The law vaguely didn't not allow the first car buyer to pass on a car's title to a second buyer without first recording the sale with the DMV, thereby potentially bypassing the

---

1   Department of Motor Vehicles

cumbersome and costly DMV fees and paper trail bureaucracy. Our love of all things motorized and our free-wheeling lifestyles meant we were probably crooks in actual deed and the eyes of the law, but all of this was also unclear and our code was 'Ignore Alien Orders.' The services we provided earned us respect, even a certain heroic status, from our generation's buyers.

We scooped up the wide variety of used cars that local people needed to sell, couldn't afford to repair, or just wanted to get rid of. We then resold the same vehicles, many needing only minor repairs, to anyone looking for affordable new wheels. We took great pride in our skilled navigation of the DMV's poorly implemented code, which often proved quite beneficial to all involved in a car transaction. The sellers might be thrilled to finally be free of that hunk of junk, that unavoidable eyesore just sitting there in the driveway. The new buyers needed to find a good, affordable car to drive, no matter if it was still registered in the former owner's name. And we car hustlers desired to quickly pass along a working vehicle for a handsome profit with no paper trail leading back to us.

I took pride in developing finely-honed, sales-related negotiating skills that served me well in life. Usually I was buying from a student who was longing to be freed from the hated gift filled with so many years of unwanted childhood memories, the ten-year-old, family station wagon. Or, the car for sale was associated with hoping-to-be-forgotten events, or painful memories of a past situation that I'd look for, try to pry out, to sense or feel and as subtly as possible, dig into, work to bring out, probe at ever so gently, and use solely to get the seller to lower their asking price. And so, if 10 minutes of mind-gaming a seller could lead to the purchase of a used Ford station wagon with good tires, advertised for $400, for just $70, I won. Then, if I could sell this same Ford wagon for $700 within an hour to a buyer who would drive it hard for a few months, up until the current registration expired, this vehicle was solid gold. It was potentially worth thousands of dollars to the buyer, especially if the buyer was a frequent visitor to San Francisco, a city notorious for its expensive parking tickets.

The Ford's buyer could flagrantly park in red zones, bus zones, loading zones – anywhere parking was illegal throughout the Bay Area – because the new buyer simply hadn't bothered to register the car in his own name. Any new parking citations were charged to the registered owner of record, or the unknown seller. I was the middle man, separating the two, and the new buyer was really the law-breaker, and also very much appreciated the car hustler's services.

The DMV's loophole had been artfully exploited, with no real ethical considerations of potential outcomes ever mentioned by even one car hustler working in Berkeley and North Oakland. We were having too much fun, and making great money to boot. The comedic competition between us was hilarious. When a hustler was the first to spot a hand-written used-car-for-sale ad posted on one of Berkeley's three top community-accessed bulletin boards, he'd quickly remove and pocket the ad, for personal follow-up only. The extent to which one might go to beat out the other buyers for each used car that came up for sale, and for the lowest possible price, became wild, very enjoyable street theater for a few of us.

I was a silent partner in an auto repair garage in Berkeley, owned by two friends who both loved automobiles. Donnie Ducati (a motorcycle racer on weekends) was Chief Wrench, the ace mechanic of the business, and my go-to advisor. When a particular used car owner needed extra convincing that the vehicle up for sale was worth much less than the current asking price, I'd hire Donnie for an hour to accompany me to inspect the car, to act as my testing expert. His day job repairing older vehicles often left him covered in oily grease, so he usually looked like a mechanic. He had no problem crawling under the car I was wanting to buy, and grabbing hold of, say, a greasy tie rod arm, or shock absorber, anything he could get his hands around. He'd shake it side to side, up and down, supposedly checking out the car for any problems.

Needless to say, Donnie always found something wrong

with the car, often doing his thing in the dark, oily underside of the used car. He'd find some grease or congealed engine goo and smear the oily mess on his face and arms, all the while grunting and groaning during his inspection. Then, at the most appropriate moment, he'd emerge from under the beast, streaked head to toe with oil and dirt, popping out just at the moment I was telling the seller how much I really wanted to get this car. Donnie would jump to his feet, mumbling, "Piece of shit, man, needs a total suspension rebuild, new tie rod ends and ball joints at the minimum, and probably new brakes all around..." or something equally devastating. I'd be crestfallen, so deeply disappointed. We were performing a classic Mutt and Jeff routine for the owner. I'd argue on behalf of the car's good features while Donnie'd tell me I was out of my fucking mind. We'd go back and forth, maybe up to five minutes of good theater, intended only to get the owner to lower the asking price.

See, we knew that people usually only sold their cars when they were already convinced that the once-costly, valuable vehicle was now on its last legs and could blow up at any minute. They knew, deep down, that the car they were selling wasn't worth anywhere even near their original, hoped-for asking price. Often, even before Donnie and I had reached the moment to stop arguing back and forth, the seller would interrupt us, feeling like a piece of shit for trying to unload this worthless clunker onto some unsuspecting fool at any price. In their hearts, they were sure that this used car would soon cause the buyer a shitload of trouble, and were prematurely having seller's remorse. They'd just ask me what I'd pay for it. It worked!

And if this didn't happen, then, when it felt like the time was right, maybe after a good 10 minutes of our back-and-forth arguing about the car, I would stop, turn to the owner, and make a ridiculously low, cash offer for the car of my dreams. I might say, "Just in love with this model, I do want it, and hell, I'm willing to pay whatever it costs to get it back in shape again. Will you take (my very low offer) right now?" And then, not another word from either Donnie or me. And nine out of 10 times, the owner would accept my offer, and

The Substitute Asshole

we all could walk away feeling quite pleased within.

That's how the hustle went, and usually a newly purchased used car needed only minor repairs to raise its resale value up to 10 times more than the price I'd paid for it. Occasionally, there was nothing wrong at all, and the car could be flipped within the hour to the next buyer. I'd pay Donnie $100 for his help, and pay him again to fix whatever actually needed fixing. I could still make good money without charging the excessive prices that the greedy licensed used car dealers and repair shops gouged from their buying public.

Cal-Berkeley students became my prime source for used cars. They usually had school work on their minds when it came time to sell their clunker or buy one. When it was obvious that a student seller's next fantasy dream ride was a classy new Mustang or a stylish Camaro muscle car, my ruse as buyer became much easier: The more repair issues I could point out with the car they were selling, the easier it was for the naive student seller to justify taking next to nothing for the car, if only to be rid of the memories it brought back of those boring, middle-class, backseat outings into nature with mommy and dad. I once paid $70 for a like-new, pristine Buick Vista Cruiser. It would easily fetch $800 after I'd spent $40 on two new shocks, and steam-cleaned the engine to its original factory-clean appearance, an excellent profit for an excellent car. I mean, you could fold down the rear seat, drop some acid, lie back, and stretch out while watching the passing cloud movie above through the elegant, back-seat overhead skylight.

If a VW Bug needed major engine repairs, I'd pay up to $80 for one in otherwise great shape. Donnie could remove the VW's engine, rebuild the entire motor, and re-install the new motor in under four hours and $125 for the engine parts. With a new motor, the same VW would quickly sell for $1,200, meaning Donnie and I would split up to $1,000 for one day's investment. VW's were the car hustler's dream vehicle, easy to repair and easier to resell.

Hustling cars was great fun, but, as with most good things, there was a downside with consequences that we hadn't considered while in the thick of doing business. And when I finally realized the financial damage that our DMV shenanigans had caused a few of the sellers I'd bought cars from, I quit the business almost overnight. Almost a year after selling a fine station wagon to a close friend, Gerard called to tell me an interesting tale of what he'd just experienced regarding this vehicle.

While crossing the Bay Bridge from his waterbed store in San Francisco, Gerard had heard the unfortunate story of a used car seller being interviewed on a radio talk show, telling the listening audience about an incredible legal problem he faced regarding the sale of his family's station wagon. The owner had neglected to inform the DMV of the change of ownership when he'd sold a car, which he then described in detail; the make, model, year, color of the very car Gerard was driving at that very moment. This seller had never asked for and didn't know the name of the young man to whom he'd sold the car, which was me. As a result of this slight oversight in the official DMV protocol, the seller handing over the title to his wagon without notifying the DMV of the buyer's name, all legal responsibility for the car still remained with the seller, including the more than $30,000 racked up in unpaid parking tickets in San Francisco alone, with many thousands of dollars more in parking fines owed throughout the Bay Area. This man's problems led the state lawmakers to swiftly close this DMV loophole, basically ending our cozy little car hustling business.

After hearing the unfortunate story, including a detailed description of his car, Gerard took the first freeway exit on 80 East in Emeryville, parked the guilty vehicle on the first side street he came upon, and walked away, after clearing out anything he could find with his name on it, leaving the doors unlocked and the key in the ignition. He called me later, and we briefly enjoyed the ironic humor of the story about the car, and our good fortune at not being identified as the culprits.

"Sleazy Dean, please, the evening's on me tonight and my deepest thanks for another lovely evening," Ray said as we rose from the table and warmly embraced our goodbyes.

Chapter 23

Teenie Weenie Deenie

Franny opened the craft store front door, such a beautiful sight to behold indeed, dressed in a flimsy, yellow see-through gauze shirt and rolled-up worn jeans. She had a real nice 10-speed road bike hanging over her shoulder. Looking somewhat embarrassed she asked, "Do you know anything about fixing bicycles?"

Fucking-A, "I sure do, come in and let's take a look."

That was enough, she hooked me up and reeled me in. I was falling in love. She was a goddess with sparkling deep blue eyes that were happy and smiling. I mean, two minutes in and I'm thinking "I love you." I knew I wanted to spend time with her, and we did on and off over the years.

After spending a week together, she told me she'd pulled the bike chain off the gears on purpose and then so innocently asked me to help her, just to get to know me. Sure fooled me. Shit, she could tear down and reassemble anything like a bike blindfolded; she was talented. She spent the summer in Berkeley as a nanny, and we had a few great weeks getting close before she left in the fall for New York City to do her art. What a trip. She always kept it light and fun, enjoying our morning coffees at The Med on Telegraph; then she'd pedal off to this mansion in the hills and I'd be off to the craft store, all of it good. Her best friend from college was a rising power in 'Young Hollywood,' Peggy, and Franny thought I should meet her so I could tell her stories about the hippies. It could lead to something in a few years... "That's how it works in Hollyweird, Mr. Teenie

Weenie Deenie. I love you but I'm gone, moving to NYC. Anyway, you're already engaged, big guy." I was, in fact, engaged to Ellen,[1] whom I married in 1972. It all happened so easily, I just went with the flow and never considered what might happen next.

Franny had just graduated from a brand-name college in Pomona, California, and had friends from college living in Berkeley that summer, all smart and fun tasty treats "that you should probably enjoy after I'm back east."

And sure enough, after Franny had left, Ruth, Julie, and Sue, separately and together, all thoroughly shared their beds with me on a few of those cold, windy, and lonely nights that I had to face now and then. Franny and I stayed close friends for years, and I visited her in New York many times after that playful, happy summer in Berkeley. She'd single-handedly remodeled a second-floor Midtown sweatshop into her stained glass studio and designer-hip living space. It was also a great location to unload a shipment of weed. The area was always busy and I could quickly distribute to the few large NYC buyers. Franny let me work out of her place a few times when I needed to do so, and shared her bed with me in between her latest lovers. She was so striking to see walking down any NYC street, definitely a one-off original with incredible taste, known in the hipper artistic crowds for her fashion statements. She combined sophisticated second-hand designer labels, altered with her eye for new edgy urban design and style, distinctly one of a kind, and even dropped the simple name Franny, changing it to Nord, adding to her mystique. She died too young, another victim of NY lifestyle-living.

---

[1] Ellen was Dean's third wife after Ruby, his first wife, and a brief marriage with Terry, his second wife.

Chapter 24
Rockets and the Gopher

I always tried to hold a straight gig while pursuing my main job and passion: distributing the popular, but difficult to find, Colombian Gold weed whenever it became available. I'd sell some good shit here, and, for example, work on a government-funded drug awareness gig there.

In the mid-70s Dale hired me through a Nixon-funded program at the University of California, Santa Cruz to run week-long training conferences. I had the management skills, the East Coast 'hondeling' vibe, and public charm gained from managing the Ram Dass nationwide speaking events. I had the free time to work the occasional week when needed. If I could handle the logistics of a smooth-running pot enterprise or a week-long meditation retreat for Ram Dass, I could certainly help put on a live-in training conference.

My associate, Ron, and I put on some memorable, government-funded drug and alcohol abuse training conferences. Two post-60s characters and still-functioning former acidheads, we both saw the gig as a magnificent opportunity for mind-blowing grand theater for all who came for training. We came off to many at first meeting as two surviving weirdos from the 'Been There, Done That,' 'Summer of Love' generation, especially to the academic world of community development trainers we worked with. But we knew our logistics shit, and turned a rather boring, mundane role and job into a wild, outrageous learning experience for everyone involved. We became known as 'Rockets and The Gofer,' the two conference facilitators from Santa Cruz – two guys who put on and pulled off some memorable, game-changing training events. And it was great fun for us, too, interacting with all the diverse groups of trainees, however we decided to run the show. We especially enjoyed the one week of work at UCSC and the six weeks of leisure time before the next event. The gig suited both Rockets' and The Gofer's lifestyles just fine.

The training programs brought together parties with vested interests in one or more challenges of today's North American 'third world' social groups who were failing to achieve 'the American Dream' and instead were coping with their poverty and neglect by mainstream America through drug abuse. We trained groups how to work with their own unique community's big problem issues, putting on one to two weeks of intense workshops offering them leading-edge strategies to take back home. The work focused on all varieties of current social issues, and we took the participants out of their familiar home comfort zones and exposed them to different thinking about behavioral solutions and approaches to effect change in the communities where they lived and worked. I never mentioned a word to anyone involved about what I really did for a living.

By the 1970s, Native American alcoholism in North America ran high. The Gofer and I represented a radical alternative to the absolutes of current treatments for substance abuse: "Substances? No biggie, all you gotta learn is how to use 'em, not abuse 'em." We looked like two functioning, former drug-crazed hippies to the new trainees, but both of us were skilled at cracking through the stereotyped ideas these strangers had. Then we'd connect with each attendee as just another version of human being, reeling them into a social community based on mutual humor, laughter, and even trust during the week we had control of their after-work hours and social lives. The program brought community leaders and educators together for a learning experience, but Rockets and The Gofer ran the show and provided the week's real learning and even better, entertainment for all.

Chapter 25
Maybe You Use Your Mouth Too Much

1974

I'd been anticipating this sweat lodge for quite a while. Dale, my boss at UCSC, had asked me if I wanted to make the trip with him to visit Randall, an Arapahoe Medicine Man he knew who had a healing sweat lodge on some dirt-poor, downtrodden reservation in Wyoming.

I'd never met a medicine man with the powers that Dale described. But Cleve, the Apache yogi I'd traveled with, had shown me powers that blew me away, so I was ready and eager. Randall sounded kinder, gentler, easier to embrace than Cleve, who was all about the destruction of one's ego, plain and simple.

"Maybe he'll put the royal whammy on me, turn me into a swallow," I thought to myself. That was my typical cynical reaction to most '70s spiritual teachings, gurus, prophets, and their followers. Dale talked about the "Eagle Spirit" that manifests during Randall's sweat, the spirit who protects Randall's healings. "Sure, man, the mystical eagle," I told myself. Still, I didn't completely discount Dale's story or experience.

Dale, of Mexican-American blood, said that I'd be the first white man ever to sweat with Randall. Maybe it was too much hocus-pocus and too strange for most whites to deal with. But not for me, I was into it.

Over the next few months, I kept bugging Dale about

the sweat, and he kept saying it'd happen "soon enough, when it's supposed to happen." I was ready to make the trip every time I asked and didn't yet realize how seriously Dale took this ceremony. He wasn't making the trip until he felt there was a reason to go.

My fantasies about the sweat grew larger the longer we waited. At last, one day Dale said, "OK, let's go. It's time." We bought tickets and flew from San Francisco to Salt Lake City where we connected with Vernon Short, a tall, handsome, dark-skinned Cree from Canada I'd met at a conference.

Vernon was hosting our visit to Randall's sweat and we would enter it under the influence of Vernon's personal ceremonial pipe. Vernon carried a hand-carved, soapstone pipe, just like the 'peace pipes' Indians[1] smoked in old Western movies. New participants in Randall's sweat had to be brought to the lodge by someone already blessed by the sweat's purification. During every sweat I attended, Randall would pass his own pipe around the circle for each person to puff on during a short break in the sweat, and the tobacco smoke would be used to purify each person. Vernon was in his 20s, worked with his tribe's ongoing alcohol problems, and had initiated this particular trip to Wyoming. Harvey, a trainer for many of Dale's programs, made a last-minute decision to visit Randall's with us. We all rented a car in Salt Lake for the 350-mile drive to Lander, Wyoming, four very different people heading "off to see the wizard," each of us keeping his own unspoken, inner council.

Dale usually dominated the story telling, but kept quiet during the ride, as did both Harvey and Vernon, not one of them talking the usual alcohol program bullshit non-stop like they often did. And no matter how persistently I tried to stir up some conversation during the ride, I never got a worthy road trip rap started. By the time it was my turn to drive, my own, inner monkey-mind chatter had quieted down and turned inward. I started questioning my reasons for making

---

[1] Editor's note: Dean uses the term "Indian," which was the commonly used term at the time for Native Americans or American Indians, the more accepted terms today.

this trip. I don't often question an opportunity for the promise of a good rush, but everyone was acting so serious, probably hoping the sweat wouldn't be more than they could handle. The closer we got to Lander, the more pressing my questions and self-doubts became. Was it a big mistake to be on such serious business? Why was everything feeling so strange? This was turning into a very different sort of journey from a road adventure. I was already deeper inside myself than I'd ever imagined possible without first taking some acid, and we weren't even close to Randall's yet. This trip was starting to feel, no, actually be, way too real.

We hit Lander at sunset and quickly settled in at an older motel. Lander looked like a depressing 1940s, hand-colored monochrome postcard of a western cowboy prairie town that the new interstate highways had left forsaken; the sort of town where anyone out and about after dark was most likely drunk and where local high school kids cruised the one main street, flashing one another the hippie 'V' sign. The only cops we saw that evening were busy hauling a few drunks from a tavern. Lander was the local source for booze, and most stores stocked it – to the complete and total ruination of most Native Americans' lives. The town was full of flashing neon signs pushing the one commodity forbidden anywhere on the reservation. All of it was downright shoddy and hard to understand for a thinking human with even the slightest knowledge of U.S. history and the Indians.

That evening, after feeling judgmental about a conversation I'd just had with Vernon, I had a kind of epiphany. I could suddenly see beyond my own biases. I could step away from being the one who knows what's best for mankind. I had moments of living in a clear, self-aware space where everyone was really equal and each one was doing the very best they could. "What was that all about?" I wondered to myself. And then I had the answer: I was getting close to Randall's sweat. I'd been torn open and cleansed in preparation for the next day's sweat.

The next morning found all of us more relaxed, in great moods, and getting excited about the coming sweat. We lingered over breakfast, then hung around touring more of the town until early afternoon. We bought supermarket food for a grand feast at Randall's that evening. We'd bring the goodies and they'd provide all the fixings for the meal. The weather was clouding up and threatening snow. Even after my earlier insight about being judgmental, Lander was still a very strange town, full of cowboys and Indians, new Ford pickups and Marlboro-smoking 'real men.' And I was getting strange looks from the sober daytime locals, another one of those out-of-state, long-haired fairy pinkos invading their peaceful world. I was really feeling like a ghetto hipster in Straightsville by the time we finally left for Randall's place. These people were the real American rural working poor and my look must have upset the status quo.

The drive into the reservation didn't help any of us better understand the culture shock we had when we saw what was happening to our fellow American brothers. We saw new Ford pickups for cruising Main Street and ramshackle shacks covered in tar paper and cardboard to keep out the winter's wet cold. And it was really getting cold. After entering the reservation, the road quickly turned from blacktop to gravel, and then to deeply rutted dirt and mud. After a few miles of forlorn shacks dotting the landscape, and a few hard turns onto more dirt roads, Vernon pulled into a dirt driveway and headed towards a small house surrounded by two house trailers, numerous funky farming equipment shacks leaning sideways and twisted by age, a closed larger shed, and a nice pickup camper, suspended off the ground by four corner jacks. We'd arrived at Randall's place and here too was the ubiquitous shiny new Ford truck, the workhorse of today's cowboy or western rancher. I was thinking, "Oh boy, where's the Indian stuff? What are we getting into here?"

But I was the only one feeling any uneasiness. I followed my friends through a door and then a small, clean kitchen, into an equally small living room, dominated by a giant color TV blasting the details of some sporting event weirdness to this smiling, toothless man wearing a high-domed baseball cap, cowboy shirt, and levis. He was sitting on a worn-out sofa next to a large toothless woman, also now smiling at our group. Must be Randall and his wife, sitting together, obviously wanting to stay glued to their sporting event.

This was even more surreal than I could have ever imagined. Here was the original Mr. Funky and his heavy-set wife, Ambrosia, or Amby, and both greeted us with only a "Hey..." and turned right back to watching their daughter's high school basketball team. We all found enough chairs in the room to take a seat, but no one said another word. Then a lot of younger kids started clamoring through the living room, and I stood up and shook hands with each one, all quite formal and a bit tense, and not anything like what I'd imagined the Shoshone "Don Juan" to be like. I really wasn't quite sure what I'd expected, but it certainly wasn't this. And all the children – there were so many in such a small house. All the walls were covered with high-school graduation-type photos of the kids with large pictures of Jesus Christ interspersed here and there. My immediate first hit was that this man's life, his house and family, had been co-opted and influenced by the marketing forces of the white enemy, conquering him again. But this feeling didn't last for long.

Never had I seen a man so gentle and patient with his happy children, yet so firm at the same time. He had such a warm smile for everyone. In fact, he was always smiling, and when not smiling, laughing out loud. And so was his wife. I quickly understood that these were two of the warmest people I'd ever met. She had 14 children, and 11 grandchildren. Many were adopted, and came from different American Indian nations. Randall later told me that they'd adopted children from different Indian tribes just to prove that, when raised together from infancy, all children could be raised as one family. They could grow into adulthood without any cultural, bred-in hatred for other tribes and nations. Randall said they were proving that with enough love, all children could grow up without anger and fear of anyone. He was trying to put a stop to an Indian-held belief that one nation or tribe just naturally hated Indians from a different tribe.

His kids quickly welcomed me into their world, dragging us all outside to play basketball in the snow, which was a kick. I was feeling an unfamiliar sense of peace from just being around these happy, open people. I'd met four of Randall's daughters, very plain, obviously from different tribal ancestries, brown-skinned younger women, each starting to show extra weight. They were full of teenage giggles and whispers, and very shy. But not too shy to compete with their brothers. They soon went outside to play some serious basketball, and we were really moving that ball around.

Randall wandered across the dirt yard to a pile of cut-up logs, grabbed a long-handled ax, and started splitting the logs. I left the basketball game and grabbed my camera from our car. I had to take some pictures of what was happening. Randall tossed the split wood into a large fire pit hollowed out in the dirt, next to what appeared to be a mound of discarded tarps or blankets. Then I understood that this must be Randall's sweat lodge. Randall was adding the new wood to a smoldering fire, and a large bonfire jumped to life. I could see the fire was mainly on top of black rocks lining the fire pit. This was a good Kodak moment, and I headed closer to the fire to take pictures. Randall looked up at me and laughed, waving a finger back and forth, and said, "Please, no photos of the sweat. It's not allowed." Another hit of some mystical presence. I backed off, understanding his unvoiced message: "This is a holy thing we're doing and trying to capture it on film won't do it justice, so Don't Do It!" The thought loomed large in my mind that Randall was now telling me, without any words, what was happening. OK, I got it. I'm cool.

The sweat lodge, about 12 feet in diameter, maybe three feet high, was covered with old tarps and tent material. It looked very funky from the outside, almost intentionally built not to draw attention to itself. It fit in with the look of the rest of the farm.

Randall continued chopping wood and had a big fire going at one end of the lodge. I started taking pictures of everything but the lodge itself. He couldn't believe that someone would want to take his photo. Pretty soon he piled large pieces of volcanic rock on the fire, more wood on top of them, and soon everyone came and stood around the fire trying to keep warm.

Looking around the wide-open horizon, there was beautiful, open land for as far as you could see, with horses turned against the cold wind, and snow covering the low hills off in the distance. I started to remember, to realize, that this was the traditional homeland for these people, and had been for many centuries. It was their land. I was a visitor from some other United States. They were real goddamned Indians, and they weren't drunk like most of the ones I'd had contact with. They were genuinely friendly, not trying to hustle me for a quarter for more wine, and they were having me as a guest at their very important ritual, the sweat. Far out.

The sweat: It is the purifier, the medium which brings the four natural elements of the universe, earth, air, fire, and water, together so that man can pray for help from their forces, their spiritual essences, and also pay his respects to all four at the same time. I was really beginning to feel a subtle attitude adjustment; something very deep yet exciting was happening to me here.

Soon, a few teenage boys came running through the snow in swimming suits, and stood by the fire to keep warm. It was almost time for the sweat to begin. Just before heading off to change into our sweating gear, Randall asked each of us visitors from the West Coast to individually spend a moment with him to tell him why we had come to the sweat, what we each hoped to receive from the spirits of the sweat. I told him that I wanted my heart to be opened, for a better understanding of my heart and its power struggle with my mind. In the light of the blazing fire, he no longer looked like the toothless rheumy old man of my initial impression. When I spoke to him I was speaking to a much different being, now feeling his wisdom and ageless spirit. His eyes were focused on mine, and felt like they were penetrating deeply inside my being, a serious moment for both of us. When that finished, we visitors hurried to a small cabin to undress and then, in only shorts, ran through the icy wind and snowflakes back to the fire. And there we waited for quite some time, a bunch of almost naked men and boys huddled around the fire, laughing and joking. I really felt good, refreshed. Dale, Harvey, and I started to feel much closer, to share longer moments of eye contact, and a knowing smile that all was so nice.

Soon Randall came, and we followed him into the lodge. I had to squat down to walk around in near-darkness to the spot Randall pointed out to me, around and on the edge of a deep hole or dark pit in the center, I guessed for the hot rocks. As my eyes adjusted to the low light, the inside of this place blew my mind. It was beautiful. Long thin willow branches were woven into a frame that covered all of us, beautiful material covering the wooden web, with various little leather sacks and pieces of leather hanging from the wood frame. Soon the men and boys were in, and it was only half filled. The young kids were laughing at us, telling us how hot it was going to get. "You gentlemen must be crazy to come to such a hot place," Randall piped in and started chuckling. Soon all the women, some with babies, filed in, taking places across from where I sat, completely filling in the circle of humans sitting around the fire pit except for Randall's spot closest to the entrance.

I was sitting across from those daughters, and now, seeing them in the sweat, they looked completely different to me. I'd stopped being so fucking critical and was now accepting them along with however they manifested in their bodies. I was seeing way beyond their physical bodies, open to the real person inside each body. They were very real, sparkling, and energetic young ladies, and it felt good to have them sitting there. Randall's wife spoke about the sweat: what to do if it got too hot, and how to use the stalks of prairie sage each of us had picked up on the way inside. The glowing-red hot rocks were brought in and carefully stacked in the open pit in the middle of the lodge. I was ready. It was impossible to imagine the level of 'hot' that Amby was preparing us for. Hell, I knew 'hot,' I'd been in very hot saunas before, but I covered my bare shoulders with the towel I'd brought with me as instructed by Amby, just in case, to keep the steam from burning my bare skin.

The flaps closed creating total darkness just as she was telling us that if it gets too hot to bear, start praying to the Great Spirit. Pray for yourself and for everyone in the lodge. How do I do that, I wondered? We were packed together like sardines in a can, the sloping walls of the lodge would touch my back if I leaned back, and the fire pit was only a foot in front of me. Nowhere to go to find relief, and suddenly, it got very quiet. I could hear the water being splashed on the glowing hot rocks, "Hiisssssss..." and soon wet heat filled the space. The steam rose from the rocks, flowed across the roof and then down onto the participants. It was hot, but it felt good. A high-pitched screech penetrated the darkness, and I heard a man singing, chanting, "Hey Hey Yeh Yeh Hey..." and soon we all joined in. Without a thought about what I was doing, I started singing a Hindu mantra, a prayer I used for meditation. The hotter it got, the louder the singing. It took my mind off the heat. More water, more steam, getting harder to breathe; louder singing, such sweet sounds. Such harmonies I'd never heard before. And more water – it sounded like a whole bucket was tossed on the rocks, and for a moment the heat was too hot to bear. But just at that moment Randall called out in an Indian language, and the flaps were thrown open at both ends, and cool outside air rushed through the lodge. I was sweating profusely. Vernon, to my left, wasn't sweating, just smiling, and I realized that I was too, grinning ear to ear. Everyone was smiling, and there hadn't been one sound of displeasure from any of the infants wrapped up in the arms of the women. I felt incredible. The sweats were supposed to last for four minutes, with a four-minute break, for four periods of sweating. But time had stopped. Time was not important. I was happy when the flaps were closed and everything was dark and silent again.

More water, more heat, and such beautiful singing. I was praying for Randall, his wife, their beautiful children, and my friends. The shrill whistle that penetrated the air didn't seem a bit unusual with all the singing. This time the final bucket of water was so hot that I fell forward to find cooler air to breathe, and just as I was falling the flaps were again thrown open. Such relief, such perfect timing. This time as I gazed, smiling, across the pit in front of me, I saw such beauty in womanhood as I'd never seen before. The sitting women now appeared each to be the image of everyone's ideal of the perfect woman, full of such deep beauty and grace, peace and countenance, warm dark eyes full of the earth and it almost seemed that these ladies were rooted and growing right out of the dirt beneath us. I was completely overcome with a powerful love for these people, filled with their spirit. Randall prepared a large pipe with tobacco, smoked some, and then passed it around to each participant. I watched as Vernon puffed and then used both hands to bring the smoke down to wash over his body. Purification. A small ritual, but the act strengthened the bond between all of us. We were all sharing the same pipe, the same space. Then more darkness, the flaps were closed again.

The third sweat was totally timeless. It could have lasted for hours, I was so high and praying like I had never prayed before. I was laughing and singing, yelling, trying to harmonize with the Indian songs, never quite making it, but it didn't matter. Even the heat was singing, and the lodge was filled with the sound of people slapping themselves. Randall's wife had said earlier that if it got too hot, just slap where it was hot. I tried it, and the heat seemed to get worse. Must be something the Indians know how to do that I don't. I was spinning, ecstatic when the flaps were opened for the third time. The men and women gathered in this tiny space all came from the universe, and the children, their children were the most beautiful I'd ever seen, so light, so joyful. Randall turned to us and said that the spirit had spoken to him, and had told him that all of our prayers would definitely be answered, if only we would be good. We were all certainly feeling good, the spirit had come, everyone was happy. It was only much later that someone told me the spirit had entered during the second sweat, and that he had blown his own loud whistle upon entering. The whistle – no one in the lodge had a whistle, so who could have blown it?

OK, it was the spirit.

Darkness again as the lodge went dark for the fourth and last sweat. Again, I started to sing and chant a mantra I'd been given by the Maharishi, one that I'd repeated quietly to myself daily for over six years. I was going into deep meditation, transcending the heat and the darkness. There was a strange noise to my left, the sound of a bird flapping its wings, and just then I felt the wing of a large bird flapping, rubbing against my mouth and around my face. "Far out," I said. "I just got whammy'd by a bird." And then it moved on to my right. More chanting of my mantra, more heat, more incredible singing by everyone, such a sound, I could hardly believe it was really human.

Then I thought to myself, wait a minute, what's a bird doing in this place? How did it get in? It wasn't possible for a human to be moving or crawling around in here, there just wasn't enough room. Before I knew it, the flaps were opened for the final time. Everyone was so high. It had been some time since I'd experienced that level of communal spirit with so many people at the same time, not since the early days of LSD. Randall stood and backed out the opening behind him, then slowly we all filed out of the lodge, keeping to the left of a dirt mound just outside adorned on top with an animal skull. Everyone was laughing, oblivious to the falling snow.

The four of us visitors slowly walked to the changing cabin away from the main house, the snow melting as it hit our skin. As we dressed I asked Dale if he felt a bird flying around in the lodge, and he laughed at me. "Man, that was an eagle." I told him how the bird had flapped a wing against my mouth, and rubbed feathers over my forehead and hair.

Dale, with a broad grin, looked me in the eye and said, "Maybe it was telling you something, old buddy," then giggling and laughter from the others...and no one clued me in to what was so funny. Later I had a moment alone with Randall and mentioned the flapping wing on my face and mouth, and he looked me in the eye and said, without a drop of sarcasm, "Maybe you use your mouth too much." I knew he spoke the truth.

Dale said that the eagle stopped in front of him and blew cool air into his face, which kept him from freaking from too much heat.

By the time we were dressed it was time for dinner. A blissful calm had settled over the four of us, a state of mind so desired yet seldom experienced, and we agreed that something important had happened for each of us in the sweat, marveling at how high and open we all felt, a grand state of grace perhaps, and how beautiful everything now appeared to each of us on this strange Indian reservation land.

Inside Randall's house a banquet was about to be served. The women had prepared the fried chicken, roast beef, and other goodies we'd brought for the post-sweat feast. What a great meal it was too, sitting with the whole family at the table. Clyde, the ten-year-old, finished first, sprang up to a chalkboard behind the table, and wrote "Love is Happiness. Some bring it by coming and some bring it by leaving." And then he laughed, having put in his two-cents worth. We literally floated through dinner, and then we had to make the drive to Salt Lake City that night. After a warm goodbye of repeated hugs and hand-shaking with this group of Indians, all strangers just a few hours earlier, we set off late that night in a driving snowstorm.

Vernon drove us on and over a snow-covered road and often there was no road to see. We were traveling in a state of grace. The falling snow flakes looked like tiny strobe lights hitting the windshield. We passed over an 8,000-foot pass, slick and dangerous, without a hitch…we knew that nothing could go wrong. We had the power, whatever it was.

After a few hours of sleep in Salt Lake City, we caught a flight to San Francisco. Man, I had connected with the spirit, we'd all sat with the Eagle Spirit, and I'm still wondering 40 years later what it all means. I made many trips back to sweat with Randall, and each time was as miraculous as my first visit. Whenever I'd call Randall to tell them I was coming, Randall would always answer the phone with, "Hey, Dean! How's it going?" He knew it was me every time I called, no caller ID then.

Before one sweat I'd asked Randall if he'd give me my own "Indian medicine," which many Native Americans carry in a leather pouch around their necks. I wasn't sure why I'd asked for this gift from the Great Spirit, but I was pretty sure it wouldn't be a bad thing to have. Randall bent over in laughter, asking, "Medicine, you want medicine?" I felt pretty foolish after entering the lodge and taking my spot in the circle, the only Anglo in a large crowd. Randall's wife again mentioned the house rules before the sweat started and finished by telling the circle that this would be a healing sweat for a particular person. I followed her eyes and saw a woman lying prone just past the end of the glowing hot rock pit, wrapped neck to foot in white cloth, almost like a mummy. The woman was close to death, and it would be good if we'd offer up healing prayers for her to the Great Spirit during the sweat.

During the fourth and last period of this sweat, the chanting and songs hit a fevered pitch, everyone focused on doing their best to bring healing powers to the sweat on behalf of the woman. I know my own words and singing were asking for the spirit of the sweat to help her. In a blinding flash, a bright light shot out my palms and the fingers of both of my hands. What is this? Wow, I can shine this light around and see everyone in here. What's happening? Man, this is too weird. Wait, I know what it is. I'm supposed to shine this light on the sick woman, and that's what I did. I bathed her in the white light being channeled from the Great Spirit. I'm supposed to use this light to heal this woman, and I'm doing it. I kept the light focused on the lady until it stopped and went out just as suddenly as it'd appeared. OK, that was interesting. In the next breath I glanced down at the ground in front of me, and something glowing with a white light was lying on the dirt, a small pile of, I didn't know what. I knew immediately, this pile in front of me was my medicine.

For some unknown reason, the fact that I had produced magic white light from my hands and magic medicine magically appeared to me didn't faze or amaze me at the time. Not in any way. It just was another moment in Randall's sweat, and the Great Spirit used my body for a higher purpose. And that was that. So when the flaps were opened for the last time, I picked up the no longer brightly shining little pile of whatever, now my medicine, and filed out of the sweat. Randall and I never spoke about this particular sweat again. Forty years later, I still have no idea why the medicine came to me and what I'm supposed to do with it.

Chapter 26
Seventeen Strangers, 1972

It was one of those kinds of trips that sort of surpass description. Right from the start we all knew it was as close to heaven on earth as we had ever been before. And that includes three good years of total LSD weirdness a while back, as close to some total understanding as I'd ever come before.

Some of us met early in the morning at the Charter Airways counter in the Las Vegas airport. Chelsea and her friends were vacationing airline stewardesses from Chicago, my hometown, and we all had that special common background that brings strangers together. The short flight over the Grand Canyon and surrounding desert was good preparation for the week to come. In a flash it took us from the safety of familiar surroundings to somewhere totally new and strange to all of us. We had all innocently signed up for a long raft trip on the Colorado River running through the Grand Canyon. Seventeen strangers were gathered for the trip, all ready for a good time.

As soon as the plane touched the ground a large truck rolled out to meet us. The driver looked like Prince Valiant, a deeply tanned, blonde, blue-eyed giant, dressed in torn levi cutoffs and armed with a big knife on his belt and a pair of pliers. "Pile in. I'm Mike, your head boatman," he said with a big, ear-to-ear grin.

The boats look like giant plastic baggies; World War II portable bridge pontoons, large inflated innertubes, laced together with rope, and a metal frame secured in the middle to store the supplies. They are designed to give with the force of the river through the rapids, something that the earliest river-runners found to be the most important secret: Use a boat that has some give to it. The old wooden boats broke up on the rocks as fast as they were built, and it wasn't really until these flexible rafts came along that more than just a few people had run the whole river. Now there are 22 different companies sending hundreds of people annually down this wild river.

Our boat is on the water, and the beach is filled with boxes and backpacks, big rubber bottles, and more fellow passengers. What an interesting bunch of people. Some look prepared for a year-long safari into the depths of the Sahara, others are madly snapping pictures of everything in sight.

I am what you could call a 'California Longhair,' and the idea of being thrown together with seventeen unknowns was quite interesting to me, the kind of situation that I had always avoided with every brain cell I possessed. The notion of the Grand Canyon and its solitude had given me support for the trip. If I didn't like the other passengers, I could withdraw into my idea of a calm center, and just groove on the scenery. But man, there they were, a beach filled with weirdos and crazies like myself, along with many 'straights,' and even they looked like cartoon characters, dressed in cutoff khaki pants and white sneakers, jungle hats, and suntan lotion, all ready to plunge into that unknown abyss ahead of us.

Vincent comes running and twisting and jumping down the beach, out of nowhere. He is our assistant boatman, and he has come to make a money collection for beer. "Oh, it is so hot down there my friends, and you will be so thirsty. Kick in now while you have the chance." We get enough money for 24 cases of aluminum canned beer... "got to crush 'em up and pack 'em out, you know."

We set off from Lee's Ferry, life jackets cinched up as tight as we can get them, all of us sitting on the front of the boat, holding tightly to the webbing of ropes for safety. The boatmen have told us that for our good health we must sit down there and hold on. No one is wondering yet just why they are sitting up high on top of the load of supplies, smiling down on us. I can hear them mumbling and giggling to each other. Soon we hit our first rapid.

From the approach it seems quite harmless, a little rough water, but going through it is like falling off water skis behind a speeding boat. Suddenly there is a solid wall of water in front of you and then rolling over you. It's totally exciting, unexpected, so cold, yet so refreshing from the day's heat. The rapids are what this trip is all about on one level, that part of the trip that drove the first discoverer of this place to the brink of his mind and to kill some of his crew. I had read some of John Wesley Powell's writing about this river, and now I was beginning to understand. It was both frightening and exhilarating, one of those natural kinds of things that get you immediately high. It was the first experience that the whole group shared in common, and it got us all high and laughing. Instantly we were seventeen fellow voyagers, not strangers, and it felt good. Sitting high and dry on top of the load were the boatmen and their friend, Lou, laughing at us. They had skillfully taken us through some very dangerous water, but they had been spared the fury of the water suffered by those of us in the front.

We flow deeper and deeper into the canyon; at the beginning the cliffs are about 500 feet straight up, and very quickly they rise twice that high. Mike claims to be an educated geologist, and he tells us as we go along about the different rock formations we see, 50 million years old at this point. The colors are unbelievable – dark reds and browns. It doesn't take long for that old 'I am such a small part of the universe' feeling to fill my body and mind. I love it.

The first lunch break is fantastic. We jump off the boat on a beautiful sand beach, so much to see and explore, and the boatmen seem to be doing all the work for us, setting up and getting things ready. Hey, there go the three girls from Chicago down the beach. I'll just follow and see what is happening, and I find them sitting behind a rock smoking a joint. That sounds good. Here comes the head boatman.

Want a toke? "Sure, not too much though, got to try and keep my act together." We get so high, laughing and having our secret from the rest.

Before we know it, the sun is setting, the moon is rising, and it is time to stop for the night. The river has deposited soft sandy beaches, some with streams that flow from side canyons into the main river, many with groves of cottonwood trees and green bushes, quite different from what I had expected. My image had been of a hot and dry trip with only rocky ledges to sleep on, surrounded by scorpions and rattlesnakes. We pick a nice beach, terraced away from the river with big rocks and flat sandy nooks between them. You can spread out your bag and be in complete privacy, hidden by the rocks from your neighbors. I go off to find a nice spot to set up camp and to spend my evening half-hour meditating. It is particularly nice that night, I'm so high, my mind and body feeling so together.

I am a good watcher of interpersonal getting-it-on, and it is lots of fun just to watch the different people together. Our group is made up of lawyers, young veterans out for a good time, a housewife on vacation, a welfare worker from the West Coast, the stewardesses, and many travelers like myself. We are all meeting each other, creating some sort of social cohesion, all except, it seems, for Tom. He is an uptight lawyer from San Francisco, my idea of an anal reject from the Boy Scouts, possessive of his space and time. Tom has all the necessary equipment, but watch out, he doesn't want to be bothered. I found this out when I tried to snap his picture. He is here to have a nice easy-going, relaxing trip even if it kills him.

But who cares about Tom? We are too high and, after dinner, getting too drunk, all of us that want to, which it turns out is the hardcore group of longhairs and dope smokers. Mike breaks out some wine and I can see that his goal is to seduce all the pretty women on his boat. It is not a game I normally like, but this time I do seem to enjoy being the voyeur. One by one we break off for bed and it looks like no one has scored with the women by the time I leave. Too bad.

Lo and behold, what is this? Curled up in her sleeping bag right next to mine is that beautiful blonde from Chicago, the one with the good grass. Hello, I undress and slip into my bag, and we smoke another joint, and do I want a hit of some blow? Sure. We both agree that it is one of the nicest evenings we've ever spent. And it gets so much better as the night brings us toward dawn.

Soon we are naked to the moon, deep kisses and sweet tender bodies bound together under the stars and in the most spectacular, beautiful landscape ever imagined... so perfectly romantic, like in a fairy tale. We are fucking, making sweet love, moving into strange territory for me, something new, something I know will be unforgettable, right from the first passionate kiss through a multitude of orgasms, out-of-body love-making that I've always known was out there somewhere, just waiting for my discovery. We are soaring, stuck together with the juices of our love.

Chelsea and I are still awake for the new light, hovering about 10 feet off the ground. We share the love energy, the coke energy, the friendship energy and we seem to know each other so quickly, so thoroughly. Almost too much to believe, we both agree. Up until this trip I have been following a sort of drug-free living model, not wanting to interfere with the effects of my daily meditation, but now it seems so right. That moral voice from my dehumanizing Catholic upbringing seems to be quiet, or maybe just blown out by the good vibes. Chelsea and I agree to play it cool concerning our night of fucking, why, I am not quite sure, but it seems to be as good a drama to act out as any. Breakfast sees us as good friends having done nothing unusual the night before, except everyone seems to know what happened.

The second day really breaks down everyone's resistance to their new environment. The river cuts deeper into the canyon, the walls rise 2,000 to 3,000 feet from the water. Mike says the rock at water level is close to 200 million years old. We beach for a short hike to a ledge above the water, and walk among the ruins of an Indian village more than 10,000 years old, built by the ancient Pueblo people as a summer camp, a refuge from the waterless desert higher up on the rim.

The real hustle for the women by the crew and other trip members is fully on. Chelsea and I laugh. Our previous evening is still our secret. Tom, the lawyer, gets wet like the rest of us, and we sneak lots of joints in along the way. The straights are definitely getting a contact high, and Vincent is unusually giggly and funny this day. Every time we go into a scary rapid he screams like a stuck pig, at the top of his lungs, "Aaaaaiiiiyyyyeeee! Oh Lordy God in Heaven Save Meeee...!" which sends us all into hysterics, and we join in the screaming through the rapids. What fun!

I discover Vincent's secret that evening. He's been chewing peyote all day, and by night is a raving madman, jumping and yelling, running up and down the beach, falling down to rest almost in the campfire, and totally enjoyable to watch. I can imagine what the straights think, but no one seems to be upset, everyone is getting so loose, and it's getting harder to tell who is straight and who isn't. Jerry looks like the squarest kid you have ever met, with his close-cropped hair, maybe a high school athlete, big-time beer guzzler. Well, he is the one providing Vincent with peyote. The discovery that Jerry is a head blows me away, and, of course, everyone he offers the mind-bending cactus to accepts. I take four fresh buttons and start to munch. It tastes horrible, but it's such an incredible high.

Some others have also paired up and a general good energy seems to fill our camp. I even put out some food for the red ants so they too will be happy this evening. Weird. To be in the heart of Mother Earth and to feel so good, so real. And before we know it the sun is up again, breakfast is over, and we are on our way. The lack of sleep is no bother, the whole day before filling us with such peace.

For the next six days we chew peyote every morning and smoke as much dope as we can keep dry. Three or four of us seem to have weed stashes. We go deeper into the Grand Canyon and the walls rise almost a mile straight up at some points. The rapids must be like those huge waves the surfers brave in Hawaii. We are wet and cold, dry and hot, stoned and sober, and getting higher all the time. Tom has taken off his two layers of hiking clothes, and sits at the bow of the raft, riding it like a bronco, bearing the worst force of the rapids, loosening up. He is turning out to be OK.

One day we stop and hike up a stream to a beautiful waterfall, which comes straight out of the rocks at chest level. We strip off our cutoffs and flip out in the freeness of nudity and the warm water. I decide to walk back to the boat completely naked, and on the way pass Jo and Judy, two very straight ladies, who pay me no mind. It doesn't bother them. Our group is becoming a very close-knit unit, many of us sharing an awareness of ourselves and our common experiences which surpass any normal, verbal level of consciousness. There isn't a person aboard that I don't like, can't talk to.

There are about 10 of us who are getting stoned and running off together whenever we stop, and we vanish for about 10 minutes as soon as the boat hits the shore. We all wonder what the others think about this, but they don't ask and we don't tell – a pot bust means five years in the slammer.

I can feel the tremendous age of everything in my bones, with my eyes. I sometimes feel like an eagle, soaring through the canyon, riding the updrafts of heat coming from the sheer walls on either side of me. The peyote intensifies the already psychedelic colors of the rock and occasional grove of vegetation. The sun and rock are the paper that the river writes its never-ending poem on. The cocaine seems to be pure energy. I have never used so much before and it is such a sweet power to feel. Over and over Chelsea and I say, "Can this be for real?"

About the third night out Chelsea asks me if I have ever fucked with poppers, and I respond that I haven't, because I don't even know what poppers are. "Amyl Nitrite," she says. Now I'd inhaled amyls a long time ago. When partying, a small group would sit in a circle, break the glass capsule open, and pass the ampoule around real fast, so everyone could get off before it was gone. It caused convulsive laughter, but before long I'd decided it was a bit stressful on the old heart.

Well, it seems that if you are lying down and in the midst of serious love-making, it gives you such a mind-bending rush as you never imagined. And to pop one just at the moment of orgasm is one of the finest trips I've ever taken. The officials who made it illegal call it an orgasm extender, and that it is, oh yes. We shared such sweet, deep, and dramatic love-making that night. I knew this was as high as I could get. I'd always felt that the highest thing to do on this physical plane of the Earth was to fuck, and now it became even more real to me...oh god, for that first fuck with amyls. That first night was at Dubendorf Rapids, and we repeated this high every night from then on. I can remember it so well.

Mike and Vincent have been preparing us for Lava Falls rapid from the very first day of the trip, building in us such a terror and fear of this terrible man-eating stretch of the river that comes just before the end of the Taft ride. John Wesley Powell's description was enough to scare even the reader, and soon we had to face it.

We pull in at the head of Lava to prepare. It is incredible; a stretch of foaming, swirling water about a quarter of a mile long, giant spurts of water flying straight up where the rocks interfere with the flow of the river. Across the river there is a group carrying a smaller boat through the loose lava rocky ground around the rapid, on their shoulders, not risking the water. Lots of dope gets consumed, and Chelsea and I snort up a good hit of coke to clear out our heads. It is too much fun. Through the rapids we go. We get drenched, making it through like a hot knife in butter, and it's over a few seconds after it starts. Quickly we pull in the swirling eddy at the bottom of the falls and break open the celebration beers, standing in a circle and passing many bottles around until they are empty. Later I notice that Tom, the once-uptight lawyer, is playing tic-tac-toe with another lawyer on the sandy beach we're camped on. How childlike he seems with a big grin. There is a good feeling coming from him now.

At Separation Rapid a large jet boat waits to carry us back on the last leg of the journey to Lake Mead. No one wants to leave and no one can believe the trip is over, but we're so spaced out and high that no one resists. Before we know it we are in a van and on our way to the Las Vegas Airport, where we will be whisked back to our homes and familiar friends.

Chelsea and I lie in the very back of the van on a pile of sleeping bags and backpacks, sharing deep kisses and a good-bye bottle of red wine. No one can believe it's over when we pull into the airport. Where have we just been, what have we just done? It's over?

Chapter 27
Easy Money

I always knew which career best held my attention, was the most interesting of the lot, indeed I did. By the time I first met Curtis I was ready to take my outlawing expertise to the next level, maximize my earning potential in the shortest, most enjoyable time possible, and retire at an early age.

1976

I heard a knock on the front door, and opened it to a smiling man about my own age, "Hi, I'm Curtis, your wife's ex."

"Cool, nice to meet you, man...I'm Dean, welcome," as we shook hands and I ushered him inside. He was my height, with maybe 50 pounds on me.

Curt[1] said he was on a quick visit to Northern California, had stopped by to say hello to his ex-wife, whom I'd recently married. A while back I'd nick-named my wife's powerful Hitachi vibrator after her ex in jest, referring to it as "Big Curt." I sensed that Curtis had been hoping that I'd be away on a business trip, anywhere but standing there talking to him; hoping he could sneak in another sweet session of the erotic bliss he'd once shared with his ex, knowing as well as I did her keen interest and passion for all things sexual. The tension I'd first sensed quickly dissipated after I mentioned that I had no plans and hoped Curt could stay for dinner.

Within minutes of our meeting, Curt and I discovered that we had much more in common than my wife to talk

---

1   Short for 'Curtis.'

about. Wasting no time with small talk, in a brash expression of unfounded trust, we acknowledged to one another that we knew a bit about the other's outlaw history, relayed to us by our lovely, talkative wife. We discovered that our drug dealing experiences and skill sets seemed to complement one another perfectly. I liked this guy.

We laughed out loud, retelling a few favorite war stories, those unreal moments of dealing we'd survived that could only be truly appreciated by one who'd had similar experiences. Neither of us felt any need to embellish by adding macho exaggerations to our stories. It felt good to just speak the truth.

I soon realized the truth about what Curt was able to accomplish or make happen. He was a natural-born, gifted salesman who had powerful tools he used to quickly build trust and gain the confidence of absolute strangers. I mentioned that I had an unusual ability to see and handle the numerous, often unnoticed, logistical details that were key to a successful weed operation. Curt admitted that he easily lost interest in worrying about the minutiae needed to keep a smuggling business safely afloat, and always hoped that someone else would handle the "day-to-day grind." I mentioned my obsession around using only dependable, cared-for vehicles, and getting drivers who didn't get too fucked up while out on the road, all the little shit that could make or break each weed deal.

Curt was quick with numbers, had a financial savvy that I completely lacked, and a talent for steering the conversation in a direction of his own choosing. He came with established contacts on both the distribution and supply sides for obtaining good weed. He had the one key element that every smuggler needed: a trusted, established Mexican weed supplier. He had all the shit I didn't have and needed to learn about.

Curt was in California looking for volume buyers for Mexican weed, new markets other than those already in the Midwest. I'd developed contacts and buyers in Colorado, California, and the East Coast who were always looking for good pot to sell.

From the get-go it felt like I'd known Curt for a long time. Immediately we were trash-talking like Chicagoans often did, laughing hard with the city's skewered, cynical sense of humor. And we learned we had a shared obsession with the opposite sex, fueled by our mutual desire to have more of it.

Our first conversation then turned more philosophical. Some people, we both agreed, seemed to be born with innate criminal tendencies, some were born with a passion to experience excitement and grand thrills, and we each knew both types. But only a few of these outlaws' lives and actions seemed tempered by ethical sensibilities. Curt and I both agreed that the current working smugglers could no longer be depended upon to honor the unwritten codes of basic criminal ethics that had guided the pursuit of illegal activities since we'd both started dealing. I still believed in honoring social agreements such as shaking hands to agree on something, or 'word is bond' and 'never rat-out a friend or associate.' But these guiding principles of our trade had mostly disappeared by 1976. I felt I was born to be doing what I did; I was an outlaw but not a 'criminal,' not someone who would purposely hurt or cause needless suffering to another.

Neither of us mentioned it, but it became clear that we were actually exploring the terms of forming a future smuggling team from the first minute we'd met. We'd each made an existential leap of faith, trusting one another with private, personal knowledge and it was good knowing deep down that we could be working together fairly soon, putting together and pulling down some fucking-righteous outlaw capers.

I've often wondered since if I had been too crazy that day, being so open with someone I barely knew. I'd rarely before ever discussed any part of my personal life and work with people I'd known forever, let alone telling it to a complete stranger. Magic was in the air, and both of us talking so openly without masking the conversation with half-truths and lies felt right. Wasn't this what the '60s had revealed to us with all those deep insights into behavior and personalities? Both Curt and I agreed that life was too short to waste time dealing with lies.

Curt quickly convinced me that he was one of the few good guys left in 'the biz'[2] and that he totally understood what I'd been saying about trust. I was ready to sign up, and needless to say, eager to join in a smuggling adventure with this man before the possibility had ever been mentioned. Curt seemed to be that special, savvy kind of person I'd been wanting to work with, and was, obviously to me, a good enough salesman to sell refrigerators to Eskimos.

Curt went on about how he'd grown up with a streetwise take on the life around him and had understood how things got done in the real world, on the streets of Chicago, from very early on. He'd recently survived a small airplane crash in Northern Mexico that easily could have killed him, and had a few deep scars to show from the crash. I'd also had a similar, near-fatal accident experience. It wasn't often that I encountered another who could appreciate my two favorite sayings, 'Ignore Alien Orders' and 'Here today, gone tomorrow,' as much as Curt did.

Smuggling, selling, and using weed were considered serious crimes by the U.S. government, and could bring a world of hurt to anyone involved with weed who didn't understand the rules of this game in America. Get caught and suffer serious consequences. And, if ever caught, never rat out your associates or friends: Don't do the crime if you can't do the time. If you could live honorably with yourself, accept the outcomes of your own personal choices and actions, and abide by an honorable code while living life, then whatever it was you did, it was OK.

Curt told me about his unusual childhood in Oak Park, an all-white suburb just west of Chicago. He spent his teen years hanging out with the sons of the head of the Chicago mob, Mr. A, aka Joe Batters, aka Big Tuna. Mr. A, a family man through and through, filled his house with the best kid toys that money could buy. There were only two rules to obey without question when visiting the A's home: "Nev-

---

2 A term Dean used for the business of drug dealing/smuggling.

er block the circular driveway" and "never go into daddy's locked room in the basement."

These were simple, clear rules, not difficult or too intimidating, considering the man who'd created them. It didn't take a genius to see the need for both rules: Vehicles used the circular driveway day and night to deliver packages to Mr. A. The boys knew the delivered packages were stored in the locked room.

Of course, what kid wouldn't be curious enough to want to break the second rule, just to see what was really hidden behind the locked door? Curt said he snuck into the secret room just once. What he saw inside changed his life forever; the room was filled, floor to ceiling, with shoeboxes, and the one box he dared to peek inside of was tightly packed with $100 bills. Easy enough math for even a child to do, easy enough to understand that lots of money was stored in that room. Curt said from that moment on, he'd dreamed of having a room exactly like Mr. A's all of his own.

It didn't matter to the neighbors that Mr. A, formerly Al Capone's personal bodyguard and enforcer, was said to have whacked over 400 people by himself using a baseball bat, hence his nickname, 'Joe Batters.' Curt only knew the man as a good father to his kids, always generous and friendly to his children's friends. The bad rumors or stories only added to Mr. A's mystique. Mr. A took Curt on family vacations to Florida, which included many fishing adventures on his deep-sea yacht.

Mr. A's passion for fishing earned him his second underworld nickname, 'Big Tuna.' Curt had a snapshot of Big Tuna aboard his boat, curled up and napping below deck like a new-born baby. I mean nobody ever got this close to the boss of the Chicago mob while asleep and lived to talk about it...no one, and Curt cherished this childhood photo.

Now, later in my life, I can only get pissed off at myself. I should have foreseen what happened between Curt and me right from the start, considering he had told me about his money dream the day I met him.

Curt and I talked about the latest pop star in the drug world, and the most lucrative of all smuggling opportunities, importing and dealing cocaine. The elusive dream and addictive appeal of coke's easy money were rapidly making inroads with the pot smugglers and street dealers. Curt and I both agreed not to get involved with the white powders (cocaine and heroin); they were simply too dangerous in every regard. First and foremost, they received more than a fair share of law enforcement attention. We'd both seen what happened when drug smugglers started using too much blow. Many seasoned risk-takers suddenly became paranoid, unreliable, and made bad decisions during even the simplest activities, when everyone's tension levels were already high and on edge.

Drivers snorting blow to keep themselves awake were a big problem. One fellow driver I talked to said he abandoned a truck loaded with pot in his motel parking lot after noticing an army of miniature DEA agents crawling into his room through the air-conditioner, coming to bust him. He escaped by jumping from the bathroom window, running like hell into the night. I asked him why the Feds hadn't used the front door to get him, and, shaking his head, he said he'd asked the same question. Time after time you'd hear about a load being abandoned for no understandable reason, and it usually boiled down to the combination of cocaine and alcohol use behind the bad decision.

The bottom line: Curt needed help to meet and offload a planeload of pot, someone who could also safely drive the weed from the plane to Chicago. Within a week of meeting he offered me a job offloading a shipment of Mexican weed, time and place to be determined. His offer stroked my ego in exactly the right way, the pay mentioned was a real step up for me, and Curt seemed to have his shit together, so I accepted. The opportunity was exactly what I'd been looking for, and the outing appealed to my sense of edge. Stepping into the unknown definitely made my juices flow.

I'd worked too many loads in the past when I had to depend on too many unknowns, including smugglers who didn't plan beforehand for my safety. I'd driven loads in unsafe Winnebagos and worn-out pickups with funky camper shells, a wide variety of untested vehicles the smugglers expected the driver to handle without complaint.

I never understood how all the up-front cash investment and time it took a smuggler to plan and pull off a major smuggling gig would ultimately end up as a load in the trunk of a neglected vehicle, the kind that was frequently waiting for me to haul their product from Miami to New York, to Atlanta, or other cities along Interstate Highway 95. It always felt like a roll of the dice, hopping into a weed delivery camper truck that I quickly discovered had worn-out shocks, a bald tire, or bad transmission. There were so many potentials for trouble on the road and I was expected to just immediately drive away. 'Out of sight, out of mind' seemed to be the guiding principle. I understood how a smuggler might feel so tremendously relieved after successfully bringing a ton of pot safely into the States that they couldn't imagine the difficulties a driver often faced delivering their load. The delivery part should be really easy compared to what this team had just survived getting it safely into the country. But driving off in an unknown vehicle, with no time to check the car out first, was a bad way to begin the long drive through enemy lines. I'd reached a point where I had to stop risking my freedom by working with stupid people.

If I really wanted to feel safe doing my outlaw work, I was the only person who could make it happen. I needed more control over my situation, including time to check and see if the vehicle was safe before driving off with a million dollars of merchandise. Curt's offer was too attractive to refuse. And just to prove the point to me, that he was a man of his word, the first thing we did in preparation before the load's delivery from Mexico, was to buy a brand-new, top-of-the-line Ford ¾-ton pickup, with a cab-high, air-tight new camper shell sealed over the long bed. Perfect. I couldn't have known how soon this new vehicle would prove itself completely worthless, but that's part of the thrills and chills of the outlaw life.

My first outing with Curt pushed me to the limit, tested the strength of my resolve, skills, and self-confidence, and I proved myself to be unshakeable, able to function under extreme duress in a dangerous situation. And later, when I realized what I'd helped Curt and the pilot pull off, the after-glow buzz I felt was psychedelic. To be up-close and personal in a well-planned, dangerous, and lucrative pirate outing was a total gas, and I was up to the challenge.

My stepping up instead of freaking out when everything promised to become a total disaster, my contribution that night, was immediately and generously rewarded. Curt offered me an equal partnership in his smuggling operation. We worked a ton of Mexico-grown, imported chills and thrills each month for many months, and I collected some large 'green,' or cash money, in return for my effort, and did this while having the time of my life.

Chapter 28

Word Is Bond

I couldn't remember the moment they'd changed the rules. See, I was believing we were partners, you know, for the profit or the loss. Our word was bond.

And the cold was really getting to me, my knees were shaking waiting out there in the garage. Especially knowing my partners were inside talking, all toasty warm...at least I wasn't standing outside dealing with the howling Chinook blowing down off the Flatirons. That wind was fierce, moving everything it touched. Hey, my job was done. I did real good and we'd all agreed to sit down soon to divvy the cash piled up inside. But I couldn't get in there, the door was locked.

James[1] stuck his head out of the door to the garage, caught my eye, and nodded for me to follow him outside. We both left the garage. The wind didn't help a bit. I was feeling pretty agitated at being left outside, and now we were headed over to my parked rental car.

"Chill out, brother, this frickin' wind isn't helpin' anyone," James told me. He then stepped real close and whispered in my ear, "I just convinced Roberto not to kill you."

Bam! Talk about a rush, whoa! What, it was already a done deal? Not a partner, or maybe soon to become a silent one. Change of plans!

"He asked if...shit, if we wanted to "disappear" you, you know, back in Colombia...crazy talk. The Brothers and me, we said no way to that BS," my former good friend said qui-

---

1 A smuggling partner to be introduced in chapter 34.

etly into my ear.

Fucking-A...this is nuts! They're actually talking about killing me? The fuck's that all about? Get me out of here, like right now. "What's goin' on, James?" I said just loud enough to be heard over the wind. While my brain was yelling, my mind was jumping everywhere, loaded and locked on rapid fire. The Chinook's famous for driving people out of their minds.

I'm a key player in the whole show, from all the planning, through the waiting bullshit. The endless rolls of quarters dropped into payphones. I was in from the get-go, and still feeling the high, the huge rush that comes with pulling off another load, that beautiful big plane full of Colombian Gold, way the fuck out there in the Louisiana swamps, man, and sending off a small fleet of trucks loaded with the goods, delivering to our buyers. We'd pulled it all off. I should be a fucking hero, for Christ's sake.

You know what it is, dumbshit...come on, you know that's what it is...it's the money. Some greedy assholes you've been in bed with, dude! You dumb shit, didn't see it coming...how they screw the nice guys first. The motherfuckers! But you know it's your own fault, you weren't looking for it, and you never thought they'd turn on you.

"Thanks for the heads up, James! I'll be leaving like right now," I replied without showing him the malice I felt inside.

I hopped in and fired up the car, immediately shutting out those crazy wind noises, and a lot more to follow upon leaving Denver on the next flight out. Word is bond? Word is shit.

~ ~ ~

Curtis is screaming over the blowing storm into a handheld microphone, tethered to the suitcase-sized, two-way airplane band radio. During the non-stop lightning blasts of bright light, I see that he's hunched over, trying to cover it from the rain, but standing in a river of water flowing over the highway. The rain could be nails hitting the pickup roof. Curtis is straining against the sideways angled slashing wind and rain, trying to talk to our pilot, he needs to reach our pilot, who's somewhere close by, flying in the darkness overhead.

Jesus, now Curtis is holding the chrome antenna up over his head, like that might help. He needs to get through to Sky King right now. All I can think is that Curt is a perfect lightning rod if I ever saw one. Cuuurtiiis!" I shout out the open truck window. "Hey…CUUURTIIIS!" but he can't hear me, the weather's too insane.

"DO–YOU–READ–ME? Sky King, do you read me? ABORT! Abort, do you copy?" Curt is totally focused on his radio, shouting out our new reality, repeating it over and over into a flashing white, then nothing, black sky.

Thunder shakes the pickup, BAAMM! A bolt of lightning strikes way too close to both of us. "Curt! CURTIS! Get the fuck inside," I scream at my partner, now invisible in total darkness. "You're gonna get fried!"

But Curt stays put. We're in the biggest storm we've ever known, somewhere, nowhere, in the middle of butt-fuck Oklahoma. Just a few minutes before, a motherfuckin' tornado tracked our asses, running alongside us on the interstate, just off to the right. What a sight! It could have crossed our path easily. Our plane's due, it's flooding on the highway, the landing strip's under a foot of water, and we're about to be electrocuted, fried while waiting on our bird and the load of pot.

It's all bad what's happening out here, but then again, I gotta say, man oh man, it's sure damn exciting. I'm thinking to myself, "Man, is this crazy, it's so fucking real, and I'm loving it, and am scared to death at the same time."

Suddenly the radio is chattering, clicking, making sounds; we both hear it coming in over the flashing racket of the storm. The pilot's here. He's getting back to us: Sky King's close-by and he's OK. Then a crisp, clear voice says, "Copy, oh mighty ground control, I'll be headin' off now to the alternate…please do copy, over…"

"Copy! We copy, Sky King! That's a mighty ten-four, over and out!" Curt's laughing voice says over the airwaves. The change of plans is confirmed…we're off to the alternate landing strip.

Curt is drenched, but out of the rain now, riding shotgun. We're headed back the way we came. He is grinning ear to ear, and we share the sort of look that says it all, what a trip we're having out here, that's for sure...!

"Yooooooo Cuurtiiisss!" I'm shouting, pounding both hands on the steering wheel. "It's gonna happen, we're still cool." The bird's headed a hundred miles west, to the alternate landing strip, far from the raging storm; the load's gonna happen!

The 'Special Moment' is what can happen from what we're doing, being night-fighting pot smugglers, risking it all for something...and the closeness we sometimes share in the heat of doing this work. I'm sitting next to a drenched, laughing madman, the same as me, and it's all about what's behind that look we've shared, the essence of what's beyond the money, why we're out here doing what we do.

"It's time, Curt," I tell my partner. "Do it, OK?" Curt is nodding in agreement as he pops the tape into the player and cranks up the Eagles to blast-off volume. "Take it, to the limit, one more time..." The Special Moment tune of the week.

I drive west into Texas, and just before Amarillo turn right and then take a dirt road that runs into the local airport. The Piper Aztec is bathed in light from a green vapor light, one engine's cowling is sitting out on the wing, and a large man seems to be working on an engine. Good old Sky King, just doing his thing.

I flash the truck's headlights and drive into the airport. It's 2 a.m., hot and very sticky out here while the rest of the world's asleep. Sky King looks around and then points toward the far end of the runway. We find the 1,200 pounds of Mexican weed piled under a plastic tarp, just waiting for us to load it into the truck. We heave the fifty-pound gunny sacks into the camper in less than four minutes, then drive back and refuel the Aztec, and the rest is history, another load on the ground, and headed for Chicago.

What can I say? Holy shit, making that trip time and again, it's really something, nothing else I've ever done is quite like it, such a mind-boggling rush! Such a sense of accomplishment. All the logistics, the planning, the little pieces that have been so finely tuned and come together in one big show.

How many times can we keep doing it, and still come out on top? Each time we safely unload our good smoke, we both wonder if the odds are stacking up against us for the future. Bullshit, no way. Each trip starts out with a clean slate; luck is only one working part of the game. We learn from each venture, each time refining, tuning the logistics, and the constant effort seems to be working in our favor. No surprises, no fear, everything depends only on what we alone put into it to make it work.

We were still living off the good will and brotherly love generated by LSD and the new 'Hip Generation' that had swept across America during the '60s.

I introduced Curt to three friends currently living between Boulder, Colorado and Miami, three ocean-sailing hash smugglers that I knew from work we did in Europe. The two Italian brothers behind the hash operation we called 'the Pizza's,' and the meeting I stewarded went very well. There was electric energy when we decided to work together, and we formed a new working partnership to set up our first big pot adventure. They asked both of us to partner with them in a much larger smuggling operation they were planning. We brought access to a lucrative, steady market for good pot in Chicago and many other regions outside of their experience.

So whatever it was that happened later, whatever caused Curt to decide to dissolve our relationship, I've never had a clue. It was so damn good and so much fun for a long time. I tell myself, "It's about the money, stupid," and this must be right, but what about the rest of it? What about the special moments when we knew we were both really alive, and what about all we accomplished together, what about trust and life and death, what do they mean? Nothing could have happened without both of us and the pilot. Curt broke it up and I have never figured it out.

Curt owed me three grand, peanuts in those days, and

I owed the Brothers three grand, and as Curt was flying out to meet the Brothers the next day, he agreed to hand them my cash to settle my debt, all would be cool. I didn't give it a second thought. It was a done deal. Wrong.

My partner didn't give my money to the Brothers, he kept it, and I didn't tell the Brothers that Curt was supposed to settle my debt with them. I was relaxed about such a small amount of money, and I trusted Curt with my life, so I never mentioned it or thought about it again. Duh, it became a big problem later, but by the time I found out, Curt had moved on, having dissolved our partnership without a word to me, and that was that.

Curt got seriously involved with a Chicago beauty while all of the Colombian plans were being set in place. Our vision for the future of our pot smuggling operation changed shape and grew. Small plane loads morphed into an idea of doing fewer loads in much larger cargo planes, like maybe doing one great big finale in a four-engine DC-6, 20 tons in one fell swoop. And why not? We were good at the logistics. Everything was cool at Curt's wedding and elegant evening party, and then he flew off to Hawaii to chill.

The Brothers thought I was withholding my debt to them, when I believed all was straight between us. No matter it was only three grand, they immediately started cutting me off, moving me from a trusted partner to the outer edges of the partnership, someone not to be trusted. This happened almost overnight and without my knowledge. I only found out I wasn't a partner when I was told that my life on Earth was currently under consideration. Wow! Hurt like that goes deep.

Chapter 29
Waiting for the Load

1978

Stillness, absolute silence. Humid-sticky night air, the two of us standing outside the pickup in total darkness, waiting in waist-high weeds and grasses that grow profusely off the south end of the cement runway.

The only thing I can make out from a 360 horizon scan on this moonless Oklahoma night is the feeble green glow from a mercury vapor lamp mounted high up on what appears to be a barn, about a mile west. There's no breeze; the only sound comes from swarms of buzzing insects. The bugs are nasty little fuckers, buzzing everywhere and biting through the polyester plaid, itchy-as-hell cowboy shirt that I am wearing to blend in with the locals. Mind you, we're both totally lit-up, on full-tilt-boogie alert, every sense geared up and working overtime.

"What's...that?" There's suddenly a substantial grinding, chomping, rumbling noise, close to the ground, punching through the summer weeds, heading towards us, getting louder and closer until we're sure it'll smash into us. Suddenly, without prompting, we simultaneously jump back inside the truck, pulling both doors closed as quietly as possible. I risk shining a flashlight into the dark weeds and out pop the snarling, snapping jaws of a pissed-off badger charging straight at us. Just before headbutting the front tire, it veers hard right and starts running in tight circles next to the truck, snapping and barking. Next thing I know we're both bent over, cracking up at the weirdness of it all.

There's always some unexpected strangeness. It happens every time we meet a load. It must come with the territory. I mean, a charging badger's hard to beat. The interlude offers a moment of relief from the mounting tension already ripe in the air. It's always high stress, you can bank on it in the hours before the next load is safely on the ground, delivered air express straight from the jolly green growers way down in Mexico.

The next sound we hear, though, is unmistakable, a beautiful, familiar, double-clicking electronic chattering coming out of our suitcase-sized, portable air-to-ground radio; the pilot's transmitting the pre-arranged code alerting us that he's close by. He'll come in real low, at the same ground-hugging altitude he flies at when crossing in and out of Mexico, low enough to fly beneath U.S. Customs border-guarding radar. He brags that he flies so close to the ground, he clips the tops off the desert cactus he's passing over... "Ah, where've I been? Oh, ya' know, been out prunin' me some cactus..." he says. He's a for-real, Texas-born country boy, who's also an ace pilot and fearless smuggler.

Some background: Our pilot's journey begins from one of many southwestern U.S. airports, where he files a bogus flight plan with the F.A.A. for a trip to some city off to the east. Then, after taking off from, say, Phoenix, he turns off the plane's flight-tracking transponder just before diving down, losing altitude to fly "close to the deck," then heads due-south, under the range of the radar while crossing into Mexico. Once past the reach of the U.S. Air Force's radar scrutiny, he regains altitude and continues due south. Bryan pilots our Piper Aztec through Mexico's rugged Sierra Madre Mountains to Mazatlán, and lands on a flat stretch of the four-lane highway connecting Mexico to California. This busy international road has been temporarily closed to traffic just outside of Mazatlán by our supplier's associates and guardians, the Mexican Federales, for the 20 minutes it takes to land, load the bales of weed, and refuel our plane. This gives Bryan just enough time to get out and stretch, relieve himself next to the plane on the asphalt, and stuff his belly with El Jefe's catered lunch before returning to the States. Bryan goes on about the fantastic Mexican food that always awaits him after he lands on the highway, a bright spot he looks forward to during the long and dangerous flight.

It's just easier and safer to land unnoticed on the paved highway than on the nearby international airport or on a local bulldozed dirt strip. We've been told that the air controllers are on the payroll and will warn the highway ground crew of any local problems that might interfere with our plane's return flight north...they've got their shit together down there in Mexico.

~ ~ ~

Bryan was paid for each pound of weed he delivered to the U.S.A., and he always flew back with as many pounds of weed as the Mexicans could cram into the plane. Bryan would crawl on hands and knees across tightly-packed gunny sacks of weed to reach his left-side pilot's chair. Once he's securely belted into his seat, the outside crew would put more sacks of pot into any remaining cockpit space, completely blocking Bryan's right-side view and the plane's only exit. Escape in an emergency situation would be next to impossible. It was only about making more money. Our pilot never questioned his own flying skills or worried about the plane's ability to perform. It took this foolish level of self-confidence for Bryan to fly week after week, knowing so many things could go wrong. In response to my asking, "How's it going, Bryan?" he'd just shrug his shoulders with a smile that said, "No worries here, all's good."

A year earlier, in 1976, a similar flight south almost ended in total tragedy. Curt and his former pilot-partner had just flown over the U.S. border into Mexico from Arizona in a Beech King Air during a late summer afternoon's cloudy, often windy monsoon weather, flying just above the desert floor and over the mountainous terrain. The pilot suddenly tried to gain altitude a moment too late to avoid touching the plane's under-belly on the rocky mountain terrain that rose abruptly in his path. Had he pulled up a second or two earlier, the bird would have cleared the mountain slope. Instead, the plane scraped the ground, was no longer airborne, and continued skidding and bouncing uphill along the mountain's rugged, rocky terrain. An endless shower of lethal sparks lit-up the crash site as the plane skidded over the ground until it crashed nose first into a house-sized boulder blocking its path.

The abrupt impact sent the heavy 50 gallon fuel drum, the fuel needed for the return flight to the States, stored in the plane's forward luggage compartment crashing backwards into the cockpit, pinning both men in their seats. Injured and bleeding, both smugglers agreed that an immediate change of luck for the better was not only called for, but necessary for their survival. Things were not looking too good for the two at that moment, but both were seasoned smugglers, prepared to do whatever was needed to resolve their dilemma. Amazingly, the plane hadn't already burst into flames from the impact, considering the sparks and the likely chance of the plane's fuel leaking from a ruptured fuel tank or from the drum, spewing a liquid horrible death over the crash site.

Curt found the plane's functioning, two-way radio microphone and broadcast out an emergency S.O.S. call for help, and was able to activate the plane's radar transponder, necessary to guide any rescuers to the remote site. This was in the days before anything like GPS existed.

Only a few miles into Mexico from the border, Curt's distress transmission was received at a nearby U.S. Army base, and the Army dispatched a rescue helicopter to investigate his call for help.

Curt held his cash-filled briefcase tightly to his chest, dragging his nearly-severed leg out of the plane. The bottom line for a smuggler is, "Save the cash, fuck the rest!" There was nothing incriminating yet on board the plane, and, if the rescuers suspected the two crash survivors of engaging in any illegal activity, there was no proof to support such a theory. The pilot's official story, that he'd simply veered a bit off course, was believable, as he'd earlier filed the required

Waiting for the Load

flight plan for a flight to El Paso with the F.A.A. Their story was just believable enough to satisfy the U.S. Army.

Of course, problems arose before Curt and the pilot could be flown away for any needed medical attention. As the Army had also illegally crossed into Mexican airspace on this rescue mission, the Army officer in charge decided the injured men couldn't re-enter the U.S. carrying anything "other than the clothes on their backs." They would have to abandon everything, including all luggage. They could only leave Mexico with the clothes they wore if both men wanted to be taken directly to an American hospital. Otherwise, they would be dropped off at the nearest Mexican medical clinic and forced to fend for themselves.

"No problem, officer, yessir, please, your generous American hospital option works just fine for us! We'll leave the luggage."

But Curt wasn't about to fly away without his cash. He considered burying it in the Mexican desert, then getting someone to come pick it up in a couple of weeks. Yeah, right. The locals would pick the crash site clean before the next day passed. So, with no possibility of saving his briefcase, Curt did what any right-minded smuggler would do. He stuffed the bundles of $100 bills into his righteous Tony Lama cowboy boots and his bloodied jeans, making both legs appear hideously swollen, and doing it before any Army rescuer could object. The stuffed money fell within the Army officer's guidelines. Curt would re-enter the U.S.A. with only the clothes he was wearing and personal paperwork. The pilot did the same, rolling down his shirt sleeves, hiding the expensive Rolex watches up and down both arms that he was taking to the Mexicans.

This is the stuff of great smuggler tales. Curt loves to tell his story, and the punch line is too real and too good to miss.

The injured men were hustled into the emergency room in the closest U.S. hospital. Curtis' pant legs were swollen tight inside his pants, from the blood and crushed wads of sticky cash, so that the emergency room attendants were forced to cut off his levi's to determine the extent of his injuries. As the scissors sliced through the stretched denim cloth, the compressed wads of wet money exploded out into the small emergency room in all directions, plastering everything, floor to ceiling, including the medical staff, with bloodied, sticky $100 bills. Curt says it looked like a ripped-open red and green down feather pillow was being tossed around the room. But it's still legal to carry cash in America, and he got to keep his money.

~ ~ ~

Back into the sticky, humid Oklahoma night:

WHOOOMP!!! The sudden rise in air pressure pops in my ears, a startling, loud crack breaking the eerie, silent anticipation that's been building while we wait for what seems like forever in the pickup as our twin Aztec swoops by overhead, barely a couple of feet above the roof. Next, I see a bright flash of white light in the total darkness when the plane's landing lights are switched on, illuminating the narrow ribbon of runway cement for the plane's landing, so bright it looks like it's daytime. I watch for the blast of smoke that shoots out when the plane's rubber tires first touch down on the hot cement, meaning Bryan's on the ground, followed by the penetrating, air-splitting roar when Bryan reverses the propellers, helping to slow the speeding outlaw ship down to a crawl, then absolute silence again after both engines shut down. The bird's quietly coasting now down the runway, heading to the optimal spot to unload. Another delivery has made a perfect landing.

As the airstrip action unfolds, the truck bursts out from the weeds and accelerates hard down the landing strip, no driving lights while catching up to the rolling plane. I've already flipped the special switch that kills the truck's brake lights, rendering us nearly invisible if any curious locals should be out and about after hearing all the landing commotion so late at night. We follow in the darkness, behind the plane until it finally rolls to a complete stop.

We pull in just behind the right wing, barely able to see the plane in the complete darkness. We're out of the truck

Waiting for the Load

and...wham! My world, my life switches into high gear and everything's moving in non-stop motion: It's 'showtime,' 'partytime,' the 'moment of truth' that separates the men from the boys, the 'serious business time' when it all shifts from planning into action at our end. It's about living for real in the present moment.

I've heard stories about former ground crew/offloader first-timers who've freaked out at this critical point in the caper; it's too real, too much pressure. One newbie-helper went catatonic, simply froze up, and wouldn't budge from the truck when Curt pulled in behind the loaded plane. Then moments later, a helper took off running across the runway and into the night. The loaded truck, on the road to Chicago, picked him up on the highway a few miles from the airport, walking alone on the white center line.

But not this crew, not tonight, no way! We're fully into it, all synced and psyched up, following a 'Just Do It Now!' game-plan for offloading a planeload of pot. We're using the unwritten, time-tested, unofficial smuggler's guide for bringing tons of pot into America, day or night.

Curt is up on the wing, pulling open the cockpit's only exit, and is knocked backwards as the hinged door flies out from the plane. Gunny sacks follow, flying out helter-skelter, propelled by some serious force from inside the plane onto the wing. I can barely make out the flashing blur of Bryan's hand-crafted Tony Lama rattlesnake and iguana-skin cowboy boots as he kicks the bales from inside the cockpit. When the plane's empty, Bryan emerges onto the wing, all smiles, dressed in a two-piece, polyester leisure suit, laughing as he quietly yells, "Outta my way boys, gotta piss like a racehorse..." and his fly's unzipped before his boots touch the cement.

I'm grabbing, yanking the heavy gunny sacks off the wing, hurriedly dragging two at a time to the rear of the truck, and stacking each 40-kg burlap bag full of reeking Mexican weed inside the camper shell as fast as I can move. There's no time to wipe the sweat pouring into my eyes, just keep on humping the shit into the truck. Curtis has already pulled the long hose from our camper shell and is pumping the 50 gallons of aviation fuel we've brought with us into the Aztec, enough gas to fly the plane on to Albuquerque or Oklahoma City.

In less than 15 minutes it's over. We've unloaded and refueled the Piper twin, stashed almost a ton of valuable contraband inside the smell-proofed camper shell, and my two partners are accelerating down the runway for takeoff. "Damn! Like clockwork." And not a single real problem so far this night. But I know my real job's only just beginning: driving the load 1,500 miles northeast to Chicago.

I'm the only vehicle on the two-lane rural road late at night. It's after 1 a.m., and I can just make out the faint buzzing sound of the plane's engines, revved-up and gaining altitude, off to the west. Then I notice a blinking red strobe light. That's got to be our bird, now flashing high above the western horizon and this steamy Oklahoma farmland. Alright! I'm chuckling with relief, remembering the frickin' badger that tried to eat us. Man, was that creature for real? Don't matter now, good buddy.

At last I'm in the groove, doing what I do best, driving a load through the unfamiliar wrinkles and edges of alien Midwest cultures, with their unfamiliar state laws that I must navigate to safely pass through. It's like being super-alive, totally aware and conscious in the Now, existing in an enhanced physical and mental state of centered, acute awareness, and it's happening to me out here in the middle of nowhere. I'm on a mission...yeah, everything's cool. I'm back on the road and heading to my childhood hometown, Chicago. The Eagles song is swirling through my mind, "take it to the limit, one more time..." God I feel good, this is so much fun.

Dean in the early 1960s.

Dean sporting the look that he referred to as a "California Longhair." 1960s.

An undated photo that appears to show one of Dean's six marriages (he married six times, and divorced five times), or, Dean poking fun at the irony of the words contrasted on the sign.

Dean always had a thing for classic cars.

Ken Kesey in Springfield, Oregon, after an afternoon brawl with locals, according to Dean. Credit: Dean Quarnstrom

Grateful Dead lead singer Jerry Garcia dropping acid at a festival in San Francisco. Credit: Dean Quarnstrom

Former Harvard professor Richard Alpert turned LSD spiritual leader, 'Ram Dass.' Credit: Dean Quarnstrom

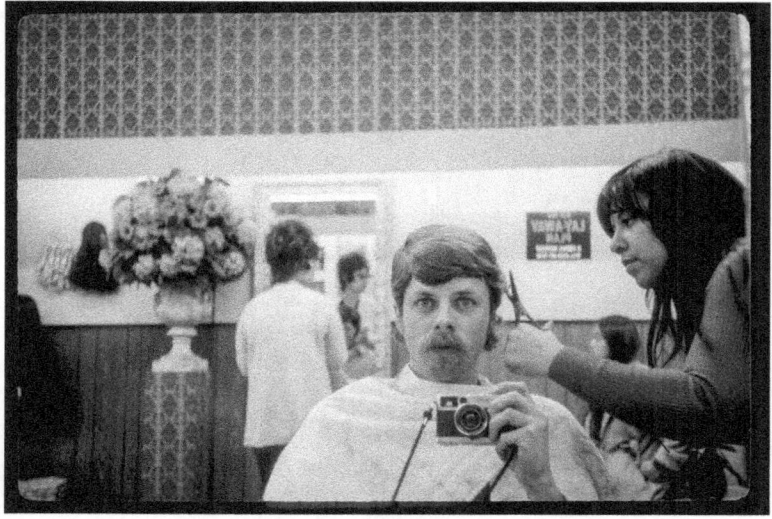

Dean getting one of his business wigs fitted and trimmed.
Mid 1970s. Credit: Dean Quarnstrom

Above: Dean and friends, including Dale (right, with back to camera), play basketball in frigid winter temperatures before a 'sweat' on the Wind River Reservation in Wyoming in 1974. Below: Randall, the Arapahoe Medicine Man who invited the guests and led the sweat.
Credit: Dean Quarnstrom

Dean (right) and business associates on Clark St. in Chicago. Mid 1970s.

Dean on one of his many trips to the Grand Canyon, one of his favorite places in the world. He's also wearing one of the pink bandanas he loved to wear while hiking or working in the yard.

Dean and his three children in the mid 1990s, from left to right: Evan, Nik, and Anne.

Chapter 30
The Stash Houses

1977

Curt and I needed a safe place to unload and work each load close to the Chicago buyers. We started out using an industrial warehouse owned by Curt's relative in an upscale, suburban Chicago business park. As soon as the last employee had left for the day, Curt would back the pickup truck into one of the indoor loading bays, out of sight from passing traffic, and we'd remove and weigh each bag before a buyer took delivery. His cousin was OK with our arrangement. The rental fees he earned for ignoring our after-hours activities were substantial.

One, or both of us, met each buyer separately in different nearby fast-food or roadhouse restaurants. While the buyer ate an evening meal, we'd take their vehicle to the warehouse, pack the pot in the trunk, and return the load to the buyer before he'd finished dinner. The exchange was based on mutual trust; each of the buyers negotiated a separate deal with Curt, and when each buyer had paid-up in full, Curt and I would sit in the cousin's office and each count the cash. Often it was dirty, crumpled-up, small denomination bills, straight from Chicago streets. We'd count and rubberband it into bundles of $10K each, then hide cash-filled paper grocery bags overhead, behind the acoustic-tiled office ceiling. It wasn't unusual to put four hundred thousand dollars, in stacks of tens and twenties, directly above the guy's desk. There wasn't a safer place to hide or

The Stash Houses

keep the bulky green paper. The only problem was getting to it, which could happen only after working hours.

It could take four nights of in and out vehicle activity to sell each load. Often there'd be three buyers waiting in three different eateries, each choking down their burgers and fries while Curt and I made the pot available to them. From the get-go, the after-hours, back-and-forth activity might seem fairly obvious to any passing cop or security guard paying attention. For the first three loads, our luck held and nothing bad happened. As a mutual trust and friendship developed between us, we decided this warehouse was too unpredictable, too open to random trouble for our otherwise well-run operation. We needed a safer stash house to unload, store, and distribute our product.

We'd compiled a list of the essential requirements for the perfect smuggler's stash house. It should be an easy drive for the local buyers, where bursts of in and out traffic wouldn't seem out of place. The storage had to be close to an interstate, able to service two or more vehicles hidden from public view, and have the indoor room to park our truck for unloading and handling the weed.

It also needed to be possible for the wholesale weed buyers to examine the tightly-compressed, 50-kg burlap sacks of weed before leaving their cash. One knife slit in the middle of the bag told its story, revealing any hidden pockets of added, unsaleable junk weight mixed in with the weed. Mexican suppliers were notorious for adding extra pounds of pot seeds and shovel-fulls of dirt and rocks to the bags, which really pissed off a buyer if discovered later, after he'd already paid for the whole sack.

But what was beautiful about working with most of the Mexicans early on was that they never argued because they knew that they short-changed the gringos, or that somebody helping on their side stole some. We had been working with these guys for many years, and it was all pretty much on the up and up. If we told them that a bag was short a certain number of pounds, they said "OK, cool." And that was that.

After a while, our Mexican suppliers never wasted anyone's time by adding useless weight to our weed, which helped distinguish our product. Still, we couldn't argue with a buyer who'd been burned this way before and demanded to check each bag before driving off with their pot.

On the other hand, it was a given that all Colombian weed suppliers added junk weight to every bag in a load, and they were reluctant to own up to this fact. If a lazy smuggler in the States didn't pay close attention to each pound he'd received from the Colombians 'on the arm' (fronted to the smugglers with or without a down-payment), this person or group might wind up owing more to the Colombians than the total profit he'd earned from its sales. Most burlap bags of weed from Colombia were numbered and weighed by the suppliers, for accounting purposes. The Colombians were clever and completely crooked. Each sack had to be reweighed after reaching the States, with someone recording the actual weight and the bag's identity number. Then, each bag had to be slit open and the added stones and pockets of seeds removed, and then the bag and pot weighed again. The bag's lower weight was recorded with its original weight, and the unsaleable junk had to be stored to prove the discrepancy to the suppliers later, or you'd owe for product you'd never received. When it was time to settle up with the Colombians, disagreements over the amounts owed were inevitable. Unless the smuggler was prepared with accurate records and physical proof of the shortages claimed, the smuggler owed for the extra junk weight. And when working with Colombians, unresolved disagreements over actual weight could prove fatal.

The biz was complicated, left room for the cheaters and crooks to try and fool everyone, and when the South American stonier weed drove down the demand for Mexican pot, a complicated business turned even harder.

This new stash house for our loads had to be hidden from any neighbor's view, as rural and suburban folk tend to be nosey. They like to wave "Hello" when they see you. The more curious neighbor will even drop by unannounced, just because that's what friendly neighbors often do. We needed to do our thing out of sight, and the typical Midwestern rental, a two-story brick house with an attached, two-car garage, didn't work for us, making most rentals close to Chicago unsuited to our needs.

In the 1970s, Greater Chicago (including its suburbs) was small compared to its size today. Chicago was flanked on three sides by fertile farmland, numerous small lakes, and summertime vacation homes for urban dwellers. Most were an easy drive to and from Chicago. Today, 45 years later, most of this open farmland is covered with mini-ranchettes and cookie-cutter housing tracts, suitable only for indoor pot farmers. But back in the day, the rural farms surrounding Chicago were the best place available to set-up our warehouse hideout.

We also rented a small apartment in the heart of Chicago's Fun Zone, near Rush Street, a necessity for one's sanity while waiting for updates on our next load's arrival, and for any bad weather to pass during the smuggling season. Smugglers always faced a variety of hurry-up-and-wait drug situations; unpredictable delays were expected with each new deal. If I wasn't at home in California, ready to jump on a flight out the minute the next opportunity popped up, I would stay with Curt in the Chicago apartment, where the waiting and planning were more interesting because there were so many tempting, entertaining venues always close at hand, all within walking distance of the apartment.

The first weed warehouse we rented seemed, upon first inspection, to be perfect. It was a decrepit, two-story farmhouse that was so unappealing you wanted to look away and avoid having to consider the unfortunates who were actually living there. The only neighbor was an open-pit gravel quarry, which it turned out, operated 24 hours a day. The sounds of gravel mining were unearthly, a continuous ground-rattling cacophony from the digging and loading machinery, frequent and disturbing dynamite explosions, and huge diesel trucks hauling rocks at all hours. We discovered this only after signing a year lease. It turned out that this constant bone-jarring, teeth-rattling racket, the miserable state of the place inside, plus having no TV or cable reception, made it impossible for us to kick back and relax between loads.

But the upsides to the property were too good to overlook. It was 10 minutes from the Northern Illinois interstate and three miles southwest of a small town interstate exit. The farmhouse, on the edge of a steep 1-acre yard, appeared slightly lopsided as if it had sprouted like a mushroom in a heavy wind. Looming above, on the crest of the hill, was a mammoth, faded red, wooden barn, the biggest barn I'd ever seen up-close, with enough space inside to park a fleet of pickups and an aircraft carrier. And, on the positive side, our rural patch of offloading torture was only 40 minutes southwest of Chicago. We put the big barn to use for many loads, locking up what wasn't yet sold inside and hurrying back to the Windy City for our rest and recreation instead of trying to tough out the waiting there.

Eventually we got a second farm, which came along at exactly the right moment, just when we had decided to abandon the gravel pit once and for all. The replacement proved to be beyond perfect. We couldn't have found a better scene or rural location to run a smuggling gig: a 150-acre 'gentleman's farm' only a few miles from Chicago's premier, year-round recreational playland, Lake Geneva, Wisconsin. The large brick farmhouse, with numerous barns and sheds, sat on rolling grasslands, divided into sections similar to a golf course by rows of mature evergreen and deciduous trees. No neighbors were visible in any direction, even from the large second-floor dormitory, with its six or seven twin beds spread randomly around the room. Our new base of operations came with everything needed to keep a person entertained day and night while working or waiting between loads, with a variety of man toys and creature comforts, like a tennis court, pool table, and skeet-shooting range. For kicks in the snow, the farm came with an open, four-wheel-drive Jeep with a snowplow, and a huge fireplace for added inspiration on those romantic, cold winter evenings.

This farm was 15 miles west of the interstate connecting Milwaukee to Chicago and only a few minutes from the Lake Geneva Playboy Club, a safe haven to flash some cash on a lonely, country night. Much about being in the drug biz has to do with the creative use of too much free time with lots of cash, as frequently the days turned into weeks of waiting between each load's actual arrival. It was tricky to beat the boredom of anxiety-filled days of waiting, and more waiting, without going overboard to avoid its tenacious grip on a lively mind. The pursuit of new sexual encounters was always an interesting, boredom-reducing pastime. Lake Geneva offered a range of opportunities and green pastures for fresh adult entertainment.

Most of the new arrivals to this Wisconsin playland were weekend partiers or vacationers from Chicago, and the traffic in and out of our farm never drew any attention from the few locals who hadn't yet sold their farms to the weekenders and land developers. We never saw or had an encounter with a curious local while we were using the land. While getting our new business off the ground, we hosted some wonderfully wild gatherings of close friends, associates, and a few new investors, as well as the occasional one-night lover. We were just another bunch of crazy Chicago commodity brokers up for a few days of insane fun if anyone ever asked.

Our main distributor of the Mexican weed in Chicago, Mel, was our first weed buyer to transition into dealing coke as well as pot, but he kept his good humor and trustworthy demeanor while groovin' down with the powder, and before long, many others we sold to followed suit. Cocaine has a profoundly seductive allure; as a social stimulant it makes everyone quite chatty and everything one says seems quite brilliant. As an effective sobering solution to drinking too much booze it works wonders, and as a subtle, driving aphrodisiac when buffered with a pure grain alcohol, it's marvelous, magic. Coke brings on an insidiously grand and bright state of mind, an exciting high that stands in the lexicon of highs all by itself and is hard to beat, that is, until it wears off only a few minutes later, and there's nothing that comes close to its addictive hold on the mind, the desire to just do a little more.

After unloading a trunk-load of our Mexican weed in Mel's garage, Curt and I sat down at the kitchen table to count the piles of loose, unsorted cash still in the paper bags it'd been delivered in, a dirty job for the counters, but made more bearable after a few lines of Mel's blow. Counting bills of different denomination paper money isn't ever fun to do. But we were into it, trusted friends taking care of some drug business. Mel's long-time, live-in girlfriend bounced through the kitchen on her way to the basement, poking fun as she passed by about the "poor ol' big-shots having to touch all that dirty paper." We were separating the crumpled-up cash into separate stacks, laughing at our manic, coke-infused jibber-jabber. She was headed downstairs carrying a load of dirty laundry, one of her boring household chores. A few minutes later, as we got close to completing our money work, Mel suddenly froze, looked around wide-eyed and screamed, "Shit!" then jumped from his chair, tripping and stumbling badly down the basement stairs. He yelled, "Honey, HONEY! Tell me you're NOT DOING THE WASH! OH FUCK! NO! NO! FUCK!" But of course, that's exactly what she was doing.

He'd hidden two, $25,000 kilos of cocaine in the washing machine, not a bad hiding place, and he was way too late to stop the rinse cycle and keep his cocaine from being flushed away into Chicago's sewer system. In a rather typical cocaine-snorting relationship, with a typical male fear of his female partner's lust for more coke, Mel hadn't told her where he'd hidden the stash.

By the late '70s, The Man was getting much better at his game, and started intimidating the weaker-willed druggies they busted, threatening them with long prison terms, squeezing them until they'd rat out their doper friends and drug sources, in return for some promised hope of getting a reduced criminal charge. They were as efficient and brutal as modern cops could be, and as ruthless and dangerous as the worst of the dopers. It didn't take them long to let their hair grow long and easily infiltrate the street scene, then on up the drug chain, learn the hip lingo and behave like the hippies they were trying to catch. And in this arena, the mob people were light years ahead of us newbie, free-spirited smugglers. The 'families' already had 'the fix' in place, buying off The Man well before anything bad ever came down on them. The bottom line was: Never snitch and never trust anyone you don't know like family.

Chapter 31
El Jefe

1977

On each flight to Mazatlán Bryan carried a bag, the cash payment due for the previous load, to hand directly to El Jefe. The Chief always met the arriving plane, often casually stretched out on a folding lawn chair strategically positioned in the middle of the empty highway that Bryan had landed on, most likely put there just because he could do it without regard.

After one successful mission, I agreed to deliver the cash payment to the Chief in Mazatlán, traveling there via commercial airline, in the time before U.S.A. airport security seriously searched anyone's carry-on baggage. My only instructions from the Mexicans were to make sure I was the first passenger exiting the plane in Mazatlán, and to carry the cash in a Halliburton, shiny-aluminum briefcase, quite a popular accessory with Mexican smugglers at the time. I made sure this happened. I apologized to the passenger ahead of me at the door and elbowed past him, so I was indeed the first to walk down the rolled-up stairway, shiny briefcase in hand.

Stepping off the stairway, I was immediately greeted by my new "best friend," a man I'd never set eyes on before. The stranger welcomed me with a full-on body hug like we'd known each other from birth. I returned his embrace in kind, two old friends happily reunited, both all smiles while the man efficiently ushered me without hesitation through the Mexican customs inspection line, through the airport's lobby, and out the airport's front door. "Mi Amigo, mi amigo," the only words spoken by this middle-aged, heavy-set, ebullient man, dressed to the nines in an expensive, finely-tailored dark-blue suit. He opened the passenger door for me on the black Ford Crown Vic waiting in the 'No Parking' zone at the curb. I hopped in and was driven directly to a large bank in downtown Mazatlán.

My host ushered me through the bustling bank lobby to a large office at the rear. Gold lettering on the thick wood door read "El Presidente," and I sat down behind the only desk in the large office. Still smiling, he held out both arms, indicating it was time to hand over the shiny aluminum briefcase. Keeping to our all-smiles, no-talking conversation, I reached across the yacht-sized expanse of the mirror-polished mahogany desk to put the case into his arms. My banker opened the briefcase and, with experienced, incredibly nimble fingers, fanned through the rubber-banded stacks of $100 bills, counting the money by hand as quickly as any machine could do it. Dude knew his shit, no doubt about it.

Nodding with apparent satisfaction, my man stood up and, in a somewhat awkward effort, reached across the vast slab of wood, offered me his plump, fleshy hand to shake, then pointed at the bottled soft drinks buried in an ice bucket off to the side, still not a real word uttered by either of us. As I swallowed my first sip of the sugary Mexican Fanta, a second, dark-suited, grinning man appeared in the office and said, "Aeropuerto, señor!" adding two more words, making for a grand total of four spoken to me since my arrival in Mexico. Off we drove back to the airport, in the same Crown Vic I'd just arrived in. I made it just in time to catch the last flight that day to San Francisco, which happened to be on the same plane and with the same crew that had delivered me to Mazatlán only a few hours earlier.

Was the banker I'd encountered the real 'El Jefe?' I didn't ask and I never found out. This was well before the brutal cartels took control of Mexico's smuggling activities. Still, I can only imagine what might have happened if my cash delivery had been short: It could easily have turned into "Adios Meester Deen." During most of the '70s, a pot entrepreneur's word was still considered bond.

Chapter 32
Butter and Woodstock Gail

1978

On a hot, humid East Coast summer night, I sat down on the only available stool in Albert Grossman's bar, The Bear, in Woodstock, N.Y. I was celebrating, albeit alone, having successfully pulled off another action-packed episode in my own magical mystery tour. I was feeling like, and also had stashed in a rental car parked outside, a million bucks. Earlier in the day I'd filled a Chrysler's extra-large trunk with burlap bags of Colombian weed that I'd driven from Atlanta to Manhattan, stashing it in a friend's second floor warehouse on Sixth Avenue near 31st, in the heart of the busy Garment District. Workers passed by pushing long racks of clothing all day long, and paid no attention to me or my U-Haul double-parked on Sixth as I schlepped gunny sacks of pot from the rented truck across the wide sidewalk and upstairs into the apartment. I can't remember how many up and down trips I made from the truck to the stash, a herculean feat in the stifling summer heat, without a hint of a problem.

You can carry or push just about anything on Manhattan's streets, day or night, and never be noticed by another living soul. Every person walking on the streets carries at least a paper bag, a backpack, box, or maybe piles of stuff hoisted up on a shoulder. Everyone. You could probably carry a body over your shoulder and never be noticed unless by a person thinking about taking it from you. A New

Yorker never asks, "Hey, pal, what's that you got there?" It's none of their business. The rules are easy: Never make eye contact with a stranger, mind your own business, always keep moving, and act like you know where you're headed, and you'll never have a problem. The hardest part of working in Manhattan was climbing stairs in the July heat and humidity, the dealing pot part was simple.

I'd arranged to sell the last of this load of top-grade Gold to a buyer who refused to drive into Manhattan. I agreed to deliver the weed to his motorhome, camped in the dense forests a few miles south of Woodstock. No problem, this sale would conclude my business in the Big Apple and leave me time to visit friends in Woodstock. I rented a full-sized Chrysler (with the living-room sized trunk), parked in front of our Sixth Avenue warehouse and quickly packed my clothes and piles of counted cash in a large duffle bag. I carried the bag and the remaining bales of pot downstairs to load in the car trunk, waved goodbye to Franny watching and smiling from her loft window, and headed out of New York for the north woods. After meeting my buyer near Woodstock, I had no immediate plans other than delivering the cash to Boston in a week. Driving loads, delivering drugs, and keeping track of piles of money, all of the pressure combined could cause some serious stress. I was looking forward to a few days of fun and relaxation before driving on to Boston.

Delivering the load to Woodstock proved to be way too weird, meaning too scary for my tastes. The buyer had rented the largest motorhome made in America, probably big enough to sleep a football team, to store and transport the weed that fit in a car trunk. It was so long that he couldn't find a safe, out-of-sight place to park to make the transfer – typical hippie too-stoned, hang loose planning. I wasn't shocked, but unplanned stupidity really pissed me off. We drove for miles through the woods on narrow, rural two-lane back roads until we finally came upon a large enough turn-out to park both vehicles off the roadway. It screamed 'way too visible' for my liking, but it'd have to do. The harried transfer seemed right out of an old Laurel and Hardy movie, one guy turning his fat body in circles while pulling at his long hair with both hands, and the other nervously running in place, all of this in broad daylight, as he scampered back and forth into the motorhome with the bags of pot. We had to look suspicious to anyone passing by with our out-of-state license plates and the manic scrambling to move the large sacks, a tempting sight to even the sleepiest sheriff's deputy patrolling his county highways. It was scary and frantic, and not what I'd planned on dealing with. I had to sit in my car where anyone passing could see me counting the cash, the final step of a deal before either of us could leave, but the money was right, and at last, off we went in opposite directions. It was getting late as I headed into Woodstock, looking for a place to crash and somewhere fun to eat. I stopped at the infamous The Bear Pub, one of Woodstock's better-known fun zones.

"Hey, 'Butter,' howya' doing, man?" I said. Another Chicago pal, Paul Butterfield, sat slumped over the bar on a stool to my left, and, to my right, sat a beautiful, wild-eyed, smiling woman I'd never seen before.

Paul had crashed at my crib when he first came to San Francisco, early 1964, checking out the West Coast scene for gigs for his band, The Butterfield Blues Band. Our mutual Chicago friend, Nick 'the Greek' Gravenites, brought Paul by my apartment. I had no problem giving a Chicago brother a place to sleep. Butter was a rising star in the '60s post-beatnik blues scene back in the Windy City. I would spend many future nights in Chicago at Big John's dancing to the Band's music.

So Butterfield and I had shared history and it'd been a few years since I'd last talked with him. I didn't expect any extra-friendly response from him, especially since hearing he'd become a full-blown junkie. But his response was downright and unexpectedly nasty...he cranked his head around, just enough to see who it was sitting next to him, and mumbled in a 'what-the-fuck-do-you-want, asshole' tone: "Do I know you?"

"Butter, it's Dean, you crashed at my crib in Frisco, Nick the Greek..."

"Fuck off," Butter mumbled, interrupting me. "I'm tryin' ta forget those days." He then swiveled his head and drink back into some other world of interest there, off to his left, more appealing to him than the one I offered...oh well.

But swiveling on my barstool to my right, there sat an even more interesting surprise, the beamingly beautiful Gail, and she was really smiling now, seemingly quite impressed that the handsome stranger, just arrived in town and now sitting so very close to her, knew the infamous Paul Butterfield. She was even more impressed when I mentioned my much better friend from high school, Mike Bloomfield, the best blues guitar-playing white boy who ever lived, former lead guitarist in Dylan's first rock/blues band. Mike and I stayed in touch and good friends since high school, right up until Mike died a few short years later.

Man, the love gods were working on me that night. I knew it was going to be something special right from the start as a power passed over and through both of us, a deep, pure sexual charge that each of us recognized. Without hesitation or thought, we were holding hands, then arms, then I touched her face, knowing anything was possible, right there, right then. I was holding, kissing an incredibly beautiful woman. It was perfect. My heart was soaring and something beyond words was happening. We both knew it was for real, an unspoken, deep connection without seductive foreplay, lies, or bullshit. Sex was already a foregone conclusion; this was so much more and turning swiftly into a full-blown, real love affair, a wonderful, unpredictable, coincidental coalescence of energies that was becoming a way of life for me.

The fact that I knew my life could end any moment seems to be the key to my openness. I was open to love, and always looking for it. So when an unexpected gift fell into my lap, I was ready to go with it, if it were real and leading to the ultimate connection, showering both of us in intimacy and pleasure without limits. That is, until it happened all over again. I mean, how many times can a man fall so deeply in love without facing an overwhelming guilt or the wrath of a scorned woman?

My first deep love was Jeanie, who was too young to believe in it, then Ruby in Winnetka, Marilyn in North Beach, who opened my mind to the possibilities, and when Jeanie reappeared and offered her soul, I was too focused on bodies. April in Seattle offered body and soul, but quickly set limits while I was prepared for outer space. And I fell head over heels for Terry two days later, and my heart was torn to shreds when she left without a goodbye; everything being only what it was. I learned there was no such thing as rejection or love lost. Every experience had been good, and opened the door to greater knowing, and sex was the key to the gates of heaven. There was a second luscious April in Berkeley, and after two days and nights of lust-filled bliss, when I dropped her off on a street corner in Berkeley, she whispered her goodbye, "Don't worry my love, this will soon pass." Her words opened another door…she'd been a hitchhiker dressed in a worn, plain dress, and a few months later I saw her once again. I'd noticed an elegantly-dressed beauty step from the chauffeured Bentley parked in front of the crafts store I temporarily managed in Berkeley. The woman slowly gathered a few items and wanted to pay when I finally figured out how I knew her. I smiled and said "April, please, take them, a small gift to you from me." We stood for more than a moment lost again in the other's eyes, then she said, "Thank you, Dean." We kissed briefly, lightly on the lips, and she left. As she closed the front door, we both smiled softly in acknowledgement of what we knew and what we'd shared, then was gone forever.

Ellen filled my heart one night, then invited me to marry her. I said yes to everything. She was all I ever needed, except what I wanted. Chelsea tore open what I'd been wanting, and handed me the secret to life on the sandy floor of the Grand Canyon. Then there were Lana and Nancy, the list is much longer, and maybe even Stella, in 1982 in Soquel. And Nord, Lisa, and Rainy in Arlington, and Kay on the plane, and Ricky and Karen in Miami, and Kay in Vail, and this very special Gail in Woodstock, and all of them leading me onward to, after all has been said, done and digested, the best ever, Jeanie, who I first fell in love with over

The Substitute Asshole

50 years before. And so many others that could have been real, felt so close at first bite, but quickly vaporized into a passing dream in the night...still wonderful and full of life juice. I lived for this level of love and searched for love. I was hurt by love, but have never stopped believing in love.

As our bodies intertwined, our two bar stools merged into one. In complete submission to the love flowing through our bodies, I lit a cigarette and blew a marvelous giant and perfectly-round smoke ring that hovered above our heads. I asked if she'd like to hear a story from my past, about the world's first and only smoke ring competition, and her reply was perfect. She said, "I'd love to know everything about you, but only if you'll tell me later this evening, or in the morning." I about fell off of my stool with her invite to spend the night. She was for real.

Everything I was feeling about this woman, the physical, mental, spiritual, was coming together. Our two souls were moving, without effort, swiftly into one joy, so tactile, eyes locked on one another's, melting into an unexplored, yet familiar space, carrying each of us deeper and deeper. We were both consciously inching closer and closer to one another in every possible way, with each new breath, sitting there on two stools in this rural upstate country bar. The attraction and profound feelings moved us into deep, tender kissing, and after each break for air, each kiss lasted longer and went deeper than the last.

I drove the two of us slowly over a rough dirt road that cut through a dark forest to Gail's remote cabin next to a running stream that carved its way through the woods and hills to the west of Woodstock. Once inside, our bodies moving as one, she gently pushed the front door closed behind us. No hurry now, all the time in the world was ours as we slowly undressed one another, exploring and touching everywhere, kissing, licking, tasting. Time ceased, disappeared. It could have been hours or days, gently moving through fields of arousal and awakening and more exploration to such deep fulfillment of a love that was ours for the rest of eternity.

Re-entering our bodies, still entwined into one connected being, all we agreed on was that the hot sun was high in the sky. We had unconsciously moved outside of the cabin and were both lying naked in the stream, cool water flowing over our bodies. It was so good, both of us hungry for more and fully satisfied, in a cosmic state, and everything was perfect in every way, except for one thing: I'm a married guy living thousands of miles from Woodstock, the only part of my story that I'd left out of our conversations. Later in the day, while smoking a very pleasurable cigarette, I blew two perfect smoke rings. Each one approached, hovered, and then wrapped itself around each of her perfect, erect nipples. Gail was amazed at the skill I'd demonstrated for her, so we agreed to take a brief break from our passion so I could tell her the story of how I'd become, and still held the title of, World Smoke Ring Champion.

Chapter 33
Colombian Gold

1978

A smuggler Curt had known from before we met had an emergency and needed a big favor: a safe place to unload and sort through a 40-foot trailer filled with Colombian Gold. His tractor hauling the container was on the road and heading north from Miami. We traded him the use of our barn to offload his weed for a worthy piece of his load. It meant exposure to outsiders, but Curt had history with the man and felt his word was good.

His 40-foot tractor/trailer powered up the steep dirt driveway and was easily concealed inside the barn, with plenty of room to unload and examine the hundreds of gunny sacks of glorious, aromatic, valuable Colombian Gold. If things went as he'd planned, it would be this smuggler's final load. This one truckload should soon make him a retired multi-millionaire. Every smuggler's dream included this exact exit plan, parked right there in our barn. Seeing actual proof that a small group of pirates could pull this off was encouraging, and this friend of Curt's planted the seeds of change in our brains.

The end of that year's Mexican weed supply, facing a few months of no business, was a good time to take a break and relax, and begin looking for a source of Colombia's finest. During past breaks in business, Chelsea and I learned to dive in Maui, rafted down the Colorado through the Grand Canyon again, visited friends in Spain and Bangkok, and trekked in the Himalayas.

Mexico's weed supply followed the spring and summer growing seasons, and we stopped working when the growers' annual harvest was finished. But Colombian weed flowed north year-round, meaning, with a Colombian source, we could continue working our distributors year-round. Curt and I decided to search for a trustworthy South American connection. We'd just witnessed what was very possible, and felt certain we could pull together a major weed operation from Colombia to the States.

Right then, the beginning of a major change, a paradigm shift to our business world, became Curt's and my dream: our hope for a successful exit from an increasingly dangerous lifestyle. Just like flipping on a light switch, our focus switched from the Mexican suppliers (they had no access to Acapulco Gold) to the more lucrative growing fields to the south, in Panama and Colombia. Curt and I started searching for a source that we could trust to supply quality South American weed, with the potential for greater profits than the Mexican. We could make it happen without significantly adding more risk than we already understood and could deal with.

Chapter 34
Pulling Off the Big One

I reached out to James, a friend I'd known since my Berkeley days who was now involved with other acquaintances in moving pot and hashish between Miami and Boulder. He'd been smuggling Moroccan kief into Spain, which I also hoped he'd turn me on to when I visited to help him reconstruct an ancient stone house on his property near Valencia.

It was 1971 when James and I drove his modified VW Camper to Tetuan, one of Morocco's little-known growing centers at the foot of the Rif Mountains. He'd built airtight secret compartments inside the VW to hide forty kilos of pressed hash bricks, and we filled the hidden spaces after another strange adventure. We were trying to find a good supplier for kief, and this turned out to be through a kid, maybe 15 years old, who approached us with an offer of something to smoke. Most of the people in Northern Morocco spoke Spanish, and we drilled down through many bullshit layers of lies before actually finding a large supplier. This kid would have tried to sell us pressed anything instead of actual kief, and he kept returning to our bus with different samples of worthless shit, but we were determined to score something to smuggle back into Europe, and kept insisting on talking to someone a bit older and not so obviously trying to rip us off.

We'd given the kid 24 hours to produce a decent product before we had to leave, and at the last minute, he finally introduced us to an older man, sitting nearby with a group of the town's elders, all of them wearing white robes and cloth turbans, indicating they'd visited Mecca and were now saved from a bad afterlife. This one guy had been sitting in the same place for hours, like he was praying, and paying us no heed. Now he rose, walked to our van, and accepted our offer to come inside for a cup of tea. We sat down and immediately negotiated a deal for 30 bricks of drugs. As soon as we agreed upon the price, the kid knocked on the door, and produced a gunny sack filled with bricks of solid pressed yellow flowers of whatever plant they'd harvest for kief, and this shit did its job quite well. This was all happening where we'd first parked the day before, in the center of town where the locals all passed by day and night, each peering at the camper and scrutinizing the two white foreigners who'd parked there. They took their time watching us before opening the door to their hash supply, and, as can happen in any drug deal, they waited until they knew we were packing up and about to leave before making the first real offer to deal with us two strangers. They were solid horse traders for sure, and after all was said and done, and we'd safely returned to Spain, we finally realized what those country folk had done, and they surely had the last laugh.

It turned out the bricks had just been pressed, probably while we waited for someone to make us a decent offer, and they'd used some kind of animal or human urine to bind the flowers when they were pressed into bricks. A few days later, when we unsealed the compartments on arrival at James' place back in Spain, the van reeked of piss and ammonia, and no amount of air-drying could reduce the awful odor of the drugs we planned on selling.

There are more than likely two or three lessons to be learned here for smugglers planning to work out of Morocco. James returned to Tetuan after I'd left in the VW, while I took my half of the stinky shit north to Amsterdam, where the smell didn't matter. I was welcomed and treated like a returning war hero, having taken huge risks driving the kief through Germany and into Holland without being caught.

Entering Germany I was ordered to pull over by an American soldier, who held an automatic rifle and a leashed

German Shepherd dog. Oh shit! Now I'm really fucked! How many years will I spend in a German jail? Things looked pretty bleak. What the fuck. Why is an American guarding Germany's border? "Sir, I'd like your permission to have my dog search your American-licensed vehicle. Do you agree to this search?" I only nodded to the U.S. Army man's question. I was feeling quite ill like I was sinking into mud that would soon cover my head. I was in a bad movie with no good outcome. I had no other option but to agree to the dog's search, knowing it would happen whether I agreed to it or not. Dumb leading on to dumber, to put it in a nutshell. But I left that border unscathed and in the end, I appreciated the Dutch treatment I received. I made many new friends in Amsterdam and a little money to boot for all of my stupid maneuverings through unfamiliar territories.

James returned to Morocco enough times to find a quality, volume supplier and sailed many loads across the Atlantic to Florida. He, like me, was quite taken with the biz and the smuggler's life. His partners had long-established family roots in Miami's Italian community and sold their annual trans-Atlantic loads of hash locally, as well as in Boulder, Colorado. During the '60s and '70s, it was inevitable that the Italians living in Miami would develop friendships leading to drug contacts with the influx of South American visitors. Miami had become the smuggling capital of the U.S. trade in Colombian weed, as well as quaaludes and cocaine.

When Curtis' and my attention turned to finding a South American weed connection, my Berkeley friend and his Boulder/Miami partners were looking for outlets for Colombian Gold. Their source was interested in shipping his weed on airplanes, and my friends, with no airplane experience, were searching for exactly what we could bring to the table, and vice-versa. We were into aviation, Curt had access to larger four-engine cargo planes, and knew skilled pilots that could fly the weed to the States. We also had buyers in the Midwest and California, while the Miami group had access to high-grade Colombian weed and buyers set up throughout the western states. It felt to both groups like a righteous joining of talents and trusted experience, and we became a partnership of seven: two hippies and five non-hippies, the latter unfamiliar with the psychedelic practice of hanging loose. And, of course, there came another one of those 'I told you so' or 'you should've known better' life-learning events.

And this all came together because Curt and I had trusted a fellow smuggler who'd unloaded his semi truck in our barn. The experience had seeded a major shift of plans and focus in our business, and we quickly transitioned into smuggling pot from Colombia. With its arrival, everything changed. Mexican weed was suddenly too pedestrian, impossible to unload in America and make any decent profit. Switching to the better, more-profitable product posed different, but manageable problems, all within reason. We increased the scope of our business from the smaller twin-engine variety, capable of hauling 1,500 pounds, to a larger cargo plane that could fly a heavier load for a longer distance. Back in the day, with the advent of jet-powered flight, many older, gas-powered, four-engine cargo planes were easy to locate and then rent or buy. Ex-military pilots, trained to fly these older birds as cargo support for the war in Vietnam, were either already in the biz, or real easy to find.

The logistics and planning to move up to a DC-5 operation were more sophisticated and complex than we'd faced before, but a challenge we were confident we could handle, and the danger was really not much greater than our recent Mexican ventures.

The bottom line when planning a new venture starts with one important guideline: Use other people's money to fund a startup operation, and it's the responsibility of the investor to perform due diligence. Chicago was filled with new and old wealth, and Curt had lived and grown up around friends and families with 'buu-cuu bucks.' The truly greedy and overly ambitious in his inner circle of "most trusted" were excited at the opportunity to invest in a high-risk, but glamorous operation that could double their cash and their cachet amongst their Rush Street social crowd. Chicago could be the heart and soul of America's most addicted gamblers. All you need to understand to know this is true, is that the Windy City is the home of the Commodities Exchange, 'nuff said. The math was easy for an investor to appreciate, promising unheard of profits over all other commodities; Curtis' reputation, street creds, and established, on-going success rate, made for good gambler stats, meaning a good bet to a savvy investor, and investors were coming out of the woodwork for a piece of the action.

Transporting hothouse-grown flowers was the name of the game at the time. South America was just beginning to fill the U.S. market's demand for the disposable beauty of cut flowers. Curt and one hip, willing investor set up a legal business as a cover for our Colombian weed endeavor, enabling our new flower importing company access to the larger, busier airports that could accommodate landing a loaded DC-5 transport plane and offer our company the ability to fork-lift our goods from our plane directly into our own semi, all in plain sight at some remote unloading/staging area at the airport. On paper, it sounded like an OK plan, but, in reality, it was something quite different.

I got so caught up in our group fantasy of pulling off 'the big one,' of amassing enough cash to retire from the smuggling game, that I dropped my role of playing the devil's advocate. I stopped voicing my logistical smarts or concerns. The bigger egos took control of planning, and anyone who raised an objection was trying to interrupt the energy flow with negativity, and discouraged from pointing out any obvious or potential difficulties with the planning for our grand Colombian opportunity. With some calmer, more critical thinking, it was easy to spot many potential flaws, and with some refined thinking, we probably wouldn't have jumped into action so quickly. Hey, everyone involved got on board the ego train, eager to make this major score possible. Why not take the A-ticket ride, seize the day by the balls, and maybe even realize my dreams?

Chapter 35

Bart the Fart

Bart and I were working out of Franny's second-floor loft on Sixth Avenue, in New York's Garment District. I pulled up to the curb and Bart appeared to help me unload the burlap-bagged 'goods.' Bart had already been in Manhattan for a few days, enough time to assume his special N.Y. personality, while I was fresh off the turnpike and spaced from the long drive from Miami.

Returning to the loft after parking the car nearby, I found Bart in quite a frenzy, running around the long, narrow loft, yelling that he couldn't find his money, very close to being out of control. I mean, he was heading into a solid freak-out.

I was standing and watching his antics from the door when he rushed past me, down the stairs, and through the door to the sidewalk, shouting, "Where's my money, where's my money!?" I followed him until he left the curb and entered the northbound, always-insane Sixth Avenue traffic, ranting about his lost money at anyone and everyone passing by. This was a bout of insanity.

With my own paranoia unfolding considering the fresh-off-the-boat Colombian Gold that we'd just stashed in the shower stall upstairs and its powerful odor, I locked myself inside the loft and started searching for the missing money. And sure enough, there it was, a pile of green $100 bills sitting on a table in plain sight, right where Bart had set it down.

I could have done what most people do in a similar situation and just pocketed the cash, but no, I was for real, the one and only Sleazy Dean, and, for the practical purpose of warding off any unknown, future karmic retribution, a man who never stole anything from anyone.

But I was hopelessly convinced The Man would arrive any second to grab that madman out in the traffic and get us both in some very serious trouble. I pried open the 8-foot, floor-to-ceiling glass window facing the street and the scene below, and somehow got Bart's attention and got him back inside.

I had forgotten the great N.Y. lesson that Bart the Fart had taught me earlier: People often 'act out' in public all over N.Y.C., day or night. Bart was behaving no differently than people did all the time on those streets, and it was not a problem. No one stopped to help and no one cared about the screaming.

Chapter 36
Abandon Ship or Save the Load

The Miami I discovered through Bart, and came to know through the colorful smugglers I met over the following year, was wide-open if you desired; a wild and magical experience. The sensual, tropical ambiance permeated everything. Each day had an exotic, hypnotic rhythm, an alluring, background body-high hinting at pleasures to come, touching every sense, an arousal of unfamiliar desires awakened by Miami's fragrant, warm ocean air, wild dreams with the promise of fulfillment. This purely-Miami experience unfolded out of sight of the beach-worshiping tourists and vacationing masses. It flowed slowly through the sultry evening breezes while I was cruising on Biscayne Bay, or gazing at the dramatic, towering afternoon clouds always rolling by overhead. The Miami sky was a horizon-to-horizon movie screen with mind-blowing sound and light shows hitting every nerve with sharp cracks of thunder, shocking flashes of lightning, and sheets of blinding rain, inspiring a vivid imagination with one story after another. It inspired dreams physical and close, deeply romantic whenever I relaxed and opened up to this pulsing Miami mood. And there were so many exquisite, insignificant culture hits, like biting into the now-famous Pollo Cubano from Café Versailles in Little Havana along the river, and the 'Media Noche,' a grilled ham and cheese sandwich on a soft roll, a Miami-Cuban late-night snack – so many pleasures that pushed my 'I want more' sensual buttons.

I was living in Bart the Fart's old place on Fairview in

Oakland. He called, saying he had work for me in Miami. Would I like to drive a big load to New York for him, 1,000 pounds, $10 a pound? Sure, why not, if you cover expenses, which he agreed to do.

I had shoulder-length hair at this time, so I ran out to the nearest straight person's beauty salon to get fitted for a wig. I wasn't about to cut my hair, but I was smart enough to know that having long hair was like waving a Yankee flag down south in those days. I went to a ladies' wig parlor and bought a wig with the same coloring as my own hair. The stylist showed me how to bobby pin my real hair to fit under the wig, and then she gave my wig a haircut, no extra cost. I took pictures of the process in the barber shop mirror, great stuff. I made it to a red-eye flight to Miami that night – off to the races.

We stopped briefly in an iffy Miami neighborhood, white-washed decaying storefronts on the edge of Miami's black neighborhood and Bart ran inside a busy shop, returning shortly with two, to-go Cuban coffees: small paper cups filled with a powerful jolt of sweetened thick caffeine that snapped my eyes wide open. Thirty minutes later I dropped Bart off at the Ft. Lauderdale Airport before hitting the I-95 North.

The Miami-to-Georgia's state line stretch of I-95 was always dangerous for smugglers. Tons of South American weed moved north on it and tons of outlaw cash payments flowed south on it. A major hurdle for smugglers working the Florida interstate could be either of two known evils: a crooked cop who would steal your load, or worse, a law enforcer offended when offered a bribe. Either cop could cause a dope driver some serious trouble.

The thieving Man, always hard at work making personal income insead of drug busts, was a line item expense if you were working in Florida. Now I'm not saying all I-95 cops were crooked, but for sure a few understood the lucrative potential for personal gain or fame that was theirs for the taking. "Hey, why shouldn't I stop that guy, looks like a smuggler to me?"

Every smuggling operation knew about the two Highway Patrol super cops working I-95; both were successful at ferreting out many loads leaving Florida, and neither could be convinced to look the other way. These cops had a sixth sense for spotting the most sophisticated smuggling ruses. False compartments carefully hand-built into rental trucks were too easy for these two wizards. They used tape measures to compare the outside against the inside dimensions, as a 19-inch false wall added inside a 20-inch van could fool anyone unless it was measured, and it could hide a fortune in weed. For years, hand-crafted secret compartments in vehicles had been the top-notch solution for moving weed before these two super cops showed up.

If a car visibly drooped in the rear, then the trunk must be filled with pot. In Florida, anything that popped into a cop's mind to stop and search a vehicle would hold up in court as probable cause. These two lawmen were responsible for way too many illegal, random freeway drug busts that were always allowed in Florida courts.

There was another well-known, dope-adept cop on the interstate near Ogallala, Nebraska. He had the same uncanny ability to pick the one pot-hauling 'needle' out of the passing 'haystack' of highway traffic. He busted many loads heading in and out of the Denver/Aspen area in the mid-1970s. This Nebraska officer parked in plain sight just off the interstate shoulder, stood outside his cruiser, looking relaxed while leaning back against the hood, just watching the passing traffic. He'd only chase and stop the one vehicle out of the thousands that carried drugs. The smugglers, of course, tried diversions to fool him, like using a stoned druggie to drive a suspicious car, but with no drugs onboard, and four women dressed as nuns a few cars in front of it, who were driving the load. The cop would stop the nuns every time. Rumor had it that a sizable bounty had been placed on the man's life. This cop was that good. I never heard how this story turned out, except that someone had tried a drive-by but missed the officer.

On a trip from West Palm Beach, Bart bought a new Datsun pickup with a camper shell in Miami to carry 600 pounds of Colombia Gold, which I drove non-stop to Washington D.C. and parked underneath an upscale townhouse overlooking the Key Bridge and Potomac River. While waiting for Bart to pick me up, I felt a thrilling rush of Kundalini energy shooting up my spine. Some call it 'the whips and jingles,' followed by a mild epiphany. I felt an overwhelming sense of accomplishment to be standing where I was, gazing down the river. In the distance I could make out the Pentagon building, which I'd driven past only minutes before, thinking about all that this building represented about my country, it being the cause of so many useless wars, including the DEA's effort to eliminate the flow of pot into the U.S. The moment's awareness left me filled with a sense of pride for pulling off another little success in plain sight of them.

I delivered tons of pot from South Florida to garages, parking lots, motels, hotels, and shopping malls, to rural farms and high-rise office towers all along the Eastern Seaboard, from Athens, Georgia, Columbia, South Carolina, north to Boston, Northampton, Woodstock. I also survived a few unexpected, incredibly tense vehicle breakdowns on the roads. One stands out as the freakiest I've ever experienced, and was due totally to good old Bart. Cruising along in a half-ton pickup with a cab-over camper on I-95 North, just below Macon, Georgia, in the broiling summer, Sunday afternoon heat, I felt and heard simultaneously a sharp explosion, a tire blowout for sure. BOOM! And I was wide awake, either that or die, as I struggled to keep the swerving, top-heavy truck on the road, thinking, "Fucker's trying to kill me...break loose and roll over, holy shit!"

After an intense few moments of hard steering using both hands, my bad-weather winter driving lessons kicked in. I regained control as the truck slowed and tracked straight on the pavement again, enough so I could pull to a stop on the narrow shoulder, scared and exhausted after the adrenalin rush wore off. Couldn't do a thing about the rear bumper jutting out a bit into the traffic lane.

I was telling myself before stepping out of the truck, "Hell, Dean, jack it up, swap the flat for the spare, be outta here in a flash...hell, we're not on black ice in a fricking snowstorm, no biggie here. Wow, sure is some mind-staggering heat in this fucked-up state of Georgia. No problem, get this done fast, be rolling in 10 minutes...it's why I make the big bucks."

Fat chance, good buddy!

Bart had met my flight earlier that morning, driven us quickly through Miami, then over a toll bridge, and a short while later, made a sudden left onto a dirt driveway cut through a dense pine forest; a swath of open space and blue sky had been opened in the trees for just one small summer house up from a sandy beach, with a million-dollar, blue water ocean view.

"Wow, a little rest and a swim, what a place! And the white sandy beach could be real nice," I was thinking to myself, gazing at the beautiful blue-green water paradise, not far off the one road that runs through Key Biscayne. President Nixon, I'd read, spent endless vacations with his buddy Bebe Rebozo on Key Biscayne, and I could see why he did so. It was spectacular. A few years later, driving to meet a business connection further out on Key Biscayne, I noticed while passing by Bart's forest that the spot had turned into the Sonesta Beach Resort Hotel, what a pity.

I should have been ready for what happened next. Before I was awake enough to really consider an ocean swim, still reeling from the grueling, no-sleep redeye from San Francisco, I wasn't able to recognize the typical Bart the Fart working scenario. Before I could think to pull back, Bart guided me to a pickup truck with a cab-over camper partially hidden in the thick growth of fir trees, pulled open the driver's door, and ushered me inside behind the steering wheel.

"OK, you're good to go, time to hit the road," marching orders delivered with a big Bart the Fart smile. "Toll money's on the seat next to you." And he slammed the door shut. I started the engine and as I drove the large camper slowly towards the highway, saw the still-smiling Bart waving goodbye in the rearview mirror. I honked twice.

I learned later that Bart's smugglers had offloaded their speedboat on the secluded beach the night before. Bart had clearly wanted me on the road as soon as I arrived, and I'd left without looking over the truck. My bad.

"So big D," I'm telling myself after the blowout. "It's my fault, isn't it? Well, NO it surely the fuck isn't! This pile of shit had bad tires to begin with, so it's Bart the goddamned Fart's fuckup!" But I knew not to mention it before I'd been paid for the run.

I'd moved on to thinking about the flat as I hopped from the truck, telling myself, "OK, get the jack and change the tire, I can do this." But I quickly discovered I'd been sent on this dangerous journey without a jack, without a spare tire, without anything that could help me solve the problem. What the fuck!

"What a fucking drag! Fucking asshole Bart!" A silly jingle kept repeating itself over and over, looping through my brain, "and you're up Shit's Creek without a paddle…and you're…"

Shortly after leaving Key Biscayne, I'd pulled over and carefully arranged the wig to cover my real hair, and kept wearing it for the drive through Georgia. So standing outside the truck, with no spare and no jack, my body already baked evenly top to bottom, feeling very claustrophobic in the sizzling hot, muggy weather, I caught my own reflection in a window: Oily strands of long, brown hair had escaped from their confinement up under the wig.

"Oh Shit!" I screamed out loud, "I'm so fucked!" No way, it was too sticky in that humidity to get them all tucked safely back up and under the wig.

If a cop stopped now, if only to help, I was busted. The afternoon sun had been cooking the concealed pot, and its smell was oozing out from the camper like sweat from a ripe armpit. I took a few deep breaths, trying to contain my anger at the lack of preparation, the lack of respect The Fart had given to protecting me and this load. I had only two options to consider: Abandon ship and walk away from the danger right now, or try to save the load.

This wasn't paranoia, not a simple mind game that I was imagining. I could feel the handcuffs being cinched down tight, digging into my wrists. Then, "in for a dime, in for a dollar..." another insightful saying popped into my thoughts.

"Wow, really out there, isn't it? Hey, far enough out on the edge for you this time, Big D?" Today I have only good memories of these unexpected smuggling moments that pushed my mind and body to their limits, cool that I could hang with them each time they happened.

My mind was very alive, hadn't yet quit working from the fear I felt. I was worried for sure, but knew myself well enough to realize that I liked balancing on these crazy high wires now and then. I knew I could pull this off, thinking, "Yeah! Let's go, let's get this show back on the road."

I started walking on the dirt shoulder towards the next exit. No other action plan came to mind, and I had no idea what might happen or was waiting up ahead, but at least I was moving, even though the whole episode was scaring the shit out of me.

"Your cool free time on Earth could be over any minute now, Mr. Wiggie Coolguy, you and your little world could easily be history by this time tomorrow. Isn't this so very existential, Mr. Biggie Wiggie?" Cute sarcasms filled my mind as I headed straight into the unknown just ahead and foolishly tried to save the dead camper. "In for a dime, in for a dollar..."

A passing semi honked, slowed and pulled to a stop in a turnout ahead, and I ran to the opened passenger door. A voice called out, "Hey, yo'all belons-tat' ol' pickup back'ere gotta blowout? Hop in son. No problem!"

I climbed up into the semi cab and this gracious Southern truck driver delivered me to a service station at the first exit ahead. All the while I'm sitting and chatting with him, I'm also stuffing long strands of hair up underneath my wig. The black-as-night station attendant listened to my sad story, then said, "OK, might take us a coupla hours to get y'all fixed though..." and he motioned me to follow him over to a real tow truck. This guy was incredible, did all of the hard work while I watched, trying to keep him entertained in the afternoon broiling sun, baking everything on the highway, all without a negative word ever being said. I loved him for this simple gesture of our mutual humanity, while at the same time I kept pushing him to hurry up and be done. When he finally finished and I could get back on the road, I was feeling so happy, all of my earlier anger was gone, melted away.

I'd passed some quality time with a real human, with a man who made his living with hand tools working in the brutal sun in Macon, Georgia, the very heart of grits and gravy, redneck racist America. His help and his sweat-soaked effort, made without a complaint, his stepping in when I asked for help and the calmness he brought to bear on my crazy situation, calming my anger, for all these reasons I knew that everything was healed, fixed now and OK. I tipped him well for his work, which made him really happy. Whether he'd known what I was up to or not, it was pretty hard to miss the unmistakable sweet aroma of baking marijuana that oozed from the camper. It just didn't matter. We were each doing our jobs, nothing more to say about it. I bought a good spare tire and heavy-duty jack from him as well, just in case.

Bart the Fart was the brilliant director of this smuggling reality play that I was acting in, a tale that he believed was entirely his own creation, and which unfolded on a public stage in his own crazy, private theater. When problems or tense situations happened out of his sight, like if a driver had a flat or had an accident, none of these were his fault, they were not his to solve or worry about. Bart understood the dangers we all faced, but was too stoned and lazy to give another person's safety his full, conscious attention, which the business always demanded of the manager-director. But Bart was smart enough to maintain his lead role, and I kept working for him no matter his numerous shortcomings. The pay was that good, and I was prepared from that trip on for the unexpected.

After the first flat tire, I never drove another car for Bart that needed repairs, at least not until they'd been fixed. And I refused to let Bart ever ride with me when we were working a load; he was unpredictable at best when things got tense, couldn't stop drawing attention to himself when he should have just melted into the background.

Chapter 37
Awakening 1963

December, 1963. Everything had changed that night. No one survived intact, unbroken, or in one piece. In the blink of an eye, the van we were in shattered into severed flesh, shards of glass, and twisted metal sheets spread across and into the surface of the highway. I pulled my hurting body out from the remains of my VW, which looked like chunks of crinkled tinfoil tossed about on the road, only to step on the soft remains of someone's head. Holy Shit! Someone was calling my name over the drum-like pounding rain and wind. Pain and confusion filled my mind; there was nothing I could do to reach the voice. "Is this a nightmare?" No. "Why not?"

Everything I'd assumed about my life to come, the journey into a worthwhile career and family, the good future, disappeared, just like that, vanished into the night. I even understood that the accident was an accident, nothing more. It just happened. But thinking about philosophies and then experiencing first-hand how quickly my own, anyone's, life could be over at any moment, without explanation or reason, was a shocker, another unplanned twist to an already unusual journey through my short life. It took the jolting shock of a broken back, a brain-damaged wife, and the needless death of a friend to break me out of my meaningless, indifferent life and suddenly imagine, in fact, see, the real possibilities for the first time. I was handed the potential to live in full consciousness, knowing the future was entirely up to me. Life was mine to create, manage, and engage with however I cared to. I could do whatever the fuck I wanted, whatever felt right, and it didn't matter one way or another, as long as I believed in it.

    I had survived to finally wake up, if only ever so slightly, to see, to be aware that I had dreams and desires that were my own, and not the same as everything I'd been told was real before. This realization of my own self worth and value just so happened to coincide with the explosive awakening of a similar new consciousness by my generation, the start of an extraordinary few years in 20th century history, when a cultural revolution burst into life right where I happened to live. I was at the heart of it. Suddenly, self-consciousness was alive and was important, and flew in the face of existing politics and religions and societies we no longer believed in. And this meant great changes were possible and close at hand. I woke up to a new self-confidence, and followed my own desires and creative drive wherever it led. It was the same for the people I knew and the deeds we all were involved in.

Part III:
Boron

After nearly two decades of evading the law, my dad finally found himself in the situation that he had always so meticulously planned to avoid. One evening in 1981, Dean answered a knock at his California residence to find the police there for his arrest. Dean and his two associates, Richard Badolato and Richard Vaughn, were separately arrested and charged with conspiring to import and possess marijuana and interstate transportation in aid of racketeering. Apparently, someone had unknowingly hired undercover cops during the planning of an East Coast smuggle run.

Although Dean denied that he was involved in illicit drug dealing and offered an alternative explanation, the court still found him guilty. He was sent to Boron Federal Prison in the searing heat of the Mojave Desert. At 40, his life took another sudden, unexpected turn. He would sit in a minimum security prison battling an onslaught of emotions, boredom, and resurging past traumas.

Dean's arrest was a sensitive subject. He always maintained his innocence and he never viewed himself as a 'true' criminal. On the contrary, as he says throughout the memoir, he truly believed his drug dealing made him a hero. He was not afraid to allude to his time in prison around me and my siblings, but he always tiptoed around the subject. It wasn't until I was an adult that we ever had a concrete conversation about it. His story, and official defense in court, was that he was wrongly arrested and only present at that particular smuggling operation because he was researching the business for a screenplay he was working on.

However, the circumstantial evidence and Dean's history doing that very thing – smuggling drugs through East Coast corridors – always made me a little wary of his claims of innocence. Some of his letters from prison seem to contradict everything else he wrote about in this memoir. Regardless, you could view it as bad luck or an inevitable outcome for walking such a fine line outside the law for so many years.

The following is a compilation of journal entries that he transcribed, letters to friends, and stories of the characters he met that paint the picture of his time in Boron.

-Evan

Chapter 38
How Did I Ever End Up Here?

27 April 1984

Dear Todd,[1]

This epistle will hopefully explain a little bit about who I am and why I am this very day serving a five-year criminal sentence in a federal prison. I sit incarcerated in this California high desert minimum security camp as a result, in my opinion, of an overzealous government.

Our Justice Department believes that it's possible, in fact, it is its moral obligation, to search out and destroy the biggest, baddest problem facing America next to terrorism, the main 'gateway' substance leading to absolute drug addiction and the enslavement of drug dependence in our country, the nightmare weed, marijuana.

My troubles began when I started to question why forty million Americans have tried, or currently smoke, pot; and I still wonder how our government can so radically disagree with the opinions of so many of its citizens. I decided to write a movie script that would tell it like it is.

The drug culture that came to life in the '60s blossomed and matured in the '70s. The '60s generation would itself become the new leaders, movers, and shakers of our country, and by 1972 the interest in and use of marijuana had penetrated deeply into every corner of America, even into

---

[1] Editor's note: It's unknown who the 'Todd' is to whom Dean sent this letter while in prison.

a college journalism class I taught during the '70s in Santa Cruz, California. My students felt comfortable exhibiting photographs of their favorite, home-grown pot plant, of themselves or their friends smoking the illegal drug; it was a popular topic to explore in my class.

My interest in the widespread use of drugs was further stimulated when I joined the Office of Education's National Drug Abuse Prevention Training Team at the University of California, Santa Cruz, in 1972. I worked with the drug culture for years, with a population from every state in the nation. We planned and executed community drug intervention programs.

And so, when one of my best friends from those days ended up working with the film company that produced the drug cult hit, 'Midnight Express,' we all agreed it was time to do some serious research and begin a film project on the drug culture, focusing on pot. This was one of my bigger mistakes.

In the 1980s I hadn't the slightest idea what would happen once I started to do research for a truthful, insightful, and relevant piece on the subject of drugs. I quickly discovered Uncle Sam's vehemence towards the world of drugs, and towards those who, independent of the government, try to figure it out on their own. As it turned out much later, they had a vested interest in this drug trade, and people like me, trying to open it up to public scrutiny, were a pain in their royal ass.

In 1980, I met and briefly traveled with a variety of pot smugglers in Florida and southern Georgia. I knew people who knew people who accepted my role as a potential big pot buyer from California. I was immediately drawn into a group of very serious and very successful smugglers, who were looking for new markets way out west. The lure of the trade was very tempting, but I was way over my head, and after a few weeks of exploration, I returned to California to begin writing my screenplay. The working title was 'Deep Cover.'

Six months later I answered a knock at my front door one evening. I opened my door to four guns pointed at my chest. I was arrested in California and charged with a number of federal drug violations, including conspiracy to import and distribute marijuana. Jeez. I was the property of the Federal Courts, Southern District of Georgia, and was tried, convicted, and sentenced to three, five-year terms, to run concurrently, in 1981.

The court agreed that indeed, I was a screenwriter, but decided that the constitutional rights covering free speech, and the rights of a free press, did not extend to nor protect screenwriting. I was guilty of not informing on a drug conspiracy when I decided to leave Florida to write a screenplay. The law says, if you leave a conspiracy, you must immediately inform the Feds about the conspiracy, or you are guilty of participating in it. Drop a dime or do the time.

I discovered that when I left the group to return home, I was required by law to turn in the smugglers I had made contact with during my quick trip to Florida, even though we never saw a single leaf of marijuana. If you are ever in a room where some marijuana is being smoked, and you don't immediately phone the authorities when you leave the room to inform them of the crime, you can be found guilty of the crime and can go to jail for quite some time.

The Courts said that I was also guilty of seeking gain or profit from the sale of the movie script, by participating in the conspiracy, even though I had no criminal intentions. I was foolish enough to think that you had to consciously commit a crime in this country to be a criminal. As it turned out, some of the peripheral members of this smuggling crowd were actually DEA agents, and I was just one of many unfortunates rounded up in one fell swoop shortly after Ronald Reagan became the president.

I believe that the experiences of the '60s helped awaken in me a powerful, indelible sense of self-respect, of strong personal values in the face of an ever-changing world, and a deep respect for the importance of one's word. I seek a certain 'quality of being' in my daily life, and try to have a very grand time living it. I know that it is the law in Russia to report all forms of wrongdoing to the government, be it family or friends, but I didn't know that the same law is currently enforced in America.

My style of journalism and writing is a definite 'child of the '60s.' I have heard it called 'Gonzo' journalism. To fully report an honest picture of a happening story, you've got to jump right in, head first, and get your feet wet. Surround yourself in the story to get to the meat, the heart, the bottom of it all. This is what I taught my students. The writer not only tastes the event, but he also merges into the totality of the experience to discover its full significance. Now doesn't that sound like a '60s flower child describing that first big acid trip?

This is a great investigative method, as long as the subject matter isn't on our government's long list of No-No's.

The drug smuggling folk heroes of the '60s and '70s are an enigma to the conservative culture of the '80s. Guilt by association, innuendo, entrapment, or false testimony now seems to be the rule of law. The big business of crime prevention and detention is an economic growth area, and depends largely on rewarding the testimony of one partner in a crime against the other partner...the reward being freedom. Rat on your friends and you won't go to jail. Somehow this system of justice reminds me of a great force that my parents fought so hard to destroy in the last World War.

Hey, by the way, as far as prisons go, this place I now call home is the best. Lots of humorous lines come to mind, but no, not here. It is mildly humane, just kind of dangerous, while having all the rules and restrictions of a full-blown prison – a place for non-violent types to do their time.

So, as far as drugs are concerned, there no longer has to be any actual crime, just the thought of it is enough for a conviction. Tell me something, don't you think that the investigative media might want to look very closely at the court's ruling on my case? It seems that any form of undercover research, or private investigation into criminal activity for personal gain, which isn't immediately reported to the government, can result in a criminal conviction for conspiracy to engage in criminal activity, regardless of intent.

Child of the '60s, branded felon of the '80s. Difficult for me to figure out. But I do have one thing straight, you can bet money that I will think twice about where I put my own two feet once I am free from prison. First time, shame on you, second, shame on me.

Yours truly,

-Dean

Chapter 39
Journaling in Boron

Editor's note: The following is a selection of entries from Dean's prison journal. It includes day-to-day observations of life in Boron, as well as reflections on earlier life events, including times with the Merry Pranksters.

~ ~ ~

14 July 1983

Thursday, my first full day in prison.
    Everyone here has a story, this is Walt's.
    Walt is 42, married, with three kids, and owns a company that makes highly polished, very specialized mirrors needed for larger lasers. In 1976, he was bidding against a military firm to supply the government with his mirrors, and his bid was 10 times cheaper than the other company. But the government awarded the competitor, their 'friend,' the contract, and Walt cried out "CHEAT!" He testified at a congressional hearing that he had been victimized by greed and corruption. Walt is a true, right-wing American patriot, served in the Air Force, wears heavy black-framed glasses, Mr. Nice Guy. And he believed that if he told the truth, he would prevail. He is the high-school volunteer soccer coach and an involved member of his community. He goes to church and doesn't swear, drink, or smoke. (Walt is lying on his bunk beneath me as I write. He just added that his wife is a Sunday school teacher.) He likes to design things, patent

them, and sell them, that's the total guy.

In 1976, he had a West German firm representing and selling his mirrors in Europe, and when the U.S. government decided to hold a trade fair in Moscow, the German firm took his mirrors to the show and sold some to the Russians. Shortly after this show, Walt was indicted for selling parts of a weapons system to the Russians – Star War sorts of mirrors to be used in Russian satellites, with lasers to destroy the U.S.

The government indicted Walt under many strange laws and twisted logic, mainly, he feels because he was so naive as to openly accuse the military of corrupt activity. Then, he hired a lawyer who turned out to care less about his plight. He was so innocent that he openly trusted and believed that if you give a lawyer money, he will give you his best shot. His wife was also indicted, as she is a principal in his company and could also have known he was selling secret stuff to the commies. And that's what's so funny: This little man and his wife hate commies, and would never sell anything to them.

So, through bad counsel, misplaced feelings and papers, filing dates missed, and poor planning by his attorney, he got the royal shaft. Now, seven years later, he gets six months for some obscure law that doesn't, he claims, really even exist.

I sleep just above Walt, and he can't believe what is happening to him. He is outraged and more confused than I could ever be. Checkered cutoff polyester shorts, lime green, a geek in normal life. And the only thing he now really cares about, however long it takes, is proving his innocence and suing the government. He says he won't stop unless he is killed, which he thinks they already tried to do. He is learning the laws so he can file his own suits, and control his own life in the years to come.

For a couple of early morning hours, and then after 6 p.m., the heat is bearable. At night I can't see the stars from the main compound, they are obliterated by the mercury vapor lights that turn even the crickets some strange color. The few trees that survive are filled with animal and insect life, bugs, birds that eat the bugs, and more bugs, and crows that eat anything. A wind blows that takes the moisture out of any container. It cools my shirt, evaporation. I am here, for however long. I am still figuring out the routines, and am just beginning to feel I'm really here.

~ ~ ~

15 July 1983

Day 2 in prison.

There are so many rules to learn, like how important it is to keep privacy and respect always in your mind. You do your own time, listen to advice when you can, and never talk too loud. A new friend told me today that he could hear me talking on the phone because the door wasn't shut (too fucking hot, and they put the phones directly in the sun just to make it that much harder to use them) and I talk loudly. This somehow pisses off some of the other people, it gets into their space. He also told me that knowing people are listening to you on the phone gives the snitches something to think about. I really appreciated this man helping me learn how to behave.

I talked to Don, a man of many talents and grand energy. I don't know how much of what he says is true, but it makes no difference. Don has conceived of and just written a movie script, his first attempt, and it sounds like a fun story. He lives on Mulholland Drive in L.A., seems to know everybody, and has grand plans to produce, write, and direct the whole movie. He claims he has commitments from literally hundreds of people and companies for free stuff and time for his film. His enthusiasm is positive and energizing, and I like the group hovering around him – funny people, each with a story unique and wild. They read and write, exercise, think about nice things, and have a cocktail in the evening. Very scary stuff to a newbie on the cell block just learning the ropes.

One is Willy from Chile, who will be an ongoing 'drama king' and character during my years here...this is a mild introduction to a really weird dude. He's the man with two mouths and one ear, who knows everyone and has been everywhere. Busted for coke. People seem to feel he's a nuisance, a dangerous label, but I see him as a spoiled, very bright kid, used to having his own way, with little patience and a lot of anger and frustration.

Frustration, emptiness, how to keep one's self-respect and still live with and into an emotional, alive mind. Very hard. I know for sure that my years of meditation have given me a sense of calm throughout the storm. I am trying to be invisible.

I walk around the perimeter of this desert camp, right in the middle of nowhere. The Rim Road is 9/10ths of a mile in a circle and climbs up 500 feet at one edge of the camp, where Edwards Air Force Base maintains a giant radar complex...guarded and secured from our entrance. I see the same people walking over and over, and we nod and say hello. I walked four miles today.

Howdy Doody and The Dragon Lady are two hacks, guards, cops that charge through the compound. I sit and look out over the desert, watch the changing colors and mountains expanse move through light and shade.

~ ~ ~

16 July 1983

So today was strange; the inmates' outsider visits seem to leave most of them wasted, and more lonely than before. Consequently, the rooms are filled with sleeping, depressed people after visiting hours.

~ ~ ~

17 July 1983

Mike is one of four roommates. I only know that he has spent four years 'behind the wall,' and now is here on his road from hard time back into society. These camps are used to re-socialize the heavies before they get released, and man, they are heavy and very scary.

Mike is handsome, well-built, and walks through his space with a genuine self-confidence that comes from being with one's self for a long time. He has special knowledge of how to get along and moves like a dancer when he walks. He is also a Hell's Angel. He never talks about the crime that got him in here, only that he was a felon in possession of a firearm and that was enough to get him five years. But I feel he was very big in whatever it was he did.

~ ~ ~

28 July 1983

Now I seem to have my job. I guess I am capable enough to be made warehouse foreman. My routine is taking shape. Don and I are hard at work on re-writing the movie, and I am trying to put together what will come next for me after he leaves. I am getting the 'Rogues Gallery' in focus. The stories are unreal.

Today I met 'Doc,' an M.D. from Pebble Beach. He was busted for prescribing Quaaludes without due cause, a well-known gynecologist for the infamous 'women of the night' in Honolulu. It took one female cop over five years of non-stop, constant badgering to finally get Doc to write her one prescription for the drug to sleep, and then she brought down his medical career.

I live amidst a population of millionaires and sophisticated criminals. Corky, a bartender from Aspen, is a champion rugby player, and his friend, John, is an ex-CIA agent, visiting here in the desert, convicted of stealing $400,000 from the Navy. I mean, we have bank robbers, common thieves, and the 'Mr. Bigs' of every variety. The real Mr. Bigs generally keep to themselves.

My job as warehouse foreman is pretty hard to take seriously. But they tell me I will be responsible for all the coming and going of inventory, keeping the books straight, and there's an audit just around the corner. So, of course,

I have to keep balancing the books to hide all the stealing my fellow inmates brazenly perform on a daily basis: extra sheets here, fresh T-shirts there, and I quickly get with the program. Quikquik takes all the canned fruit he can muster, and has a buddy making 'prune' in one of the dorms...rotgut booze, but it gets them off. Hell, if they had some money they could just hire a runner to bring in whatever they need as Don does.

The camp sits high on a mountain in the high desert, surrounded by miles of emptiness. At night, contraband is unloaded from cars and hidden behind plants and rocks, about a mile from the perimeter of the camp. There is an old fence, with many holes, as this place is minimum security. You can run away once, but if you get caught, you'll never get camp time again. So some inmates earn very good money to help support their families by running out at night to bring back 'the goods'...and you name it, it comes in.

~ ~ ~

2 August 1983

I continue to be amazed, when my eyes are open, at what there is to see around here. I have seen new flora each day. Today a trumpet flower, Datura, and it led to a large pocket of Datura at the end of a drainage pipe for some workshop, sucking up and flourishing in the wastewater. A hawk at sunrise, top of the hill, I have seen it many times now, always flying eastward. A medium-sized rabbit that is confused by my presence, sometimes running towards me, other times into the brush.

New arrivals to Boron Federal Prison Camp are subjected to standard prison intake humiliation and degradation policies and procedures, including strip searches and asshole inspections, and occasionally an asshole finger probe. They write down every visible birthmark, scar, and tattoo to add to your official federal record. New inmates are provided underwear and worn-out Air Force uniform shirts and pants to replace street clothing, always in sizes suitable for

The Substitute Asshole

King Kong.

"Over there for your pictures...we'll let ya know when to pick up your street shit," a pimply-faced prison hack told me with a threatening glare on my first day. He then tossed me a shabby army blanket, a pillow, two stiff sheets, and a white plastic cup with a green lid. "Gotta drink lotsa' water out here. Cup's for coffee too."

And new prisoners arrive daily. They all look just like I must have my first days here, full of fear and confusion. Is eye contact OK? Who is a friend, who to speak to? One man gets off the Bureau of Prison's boiling bus the inmates call the 'Gray Goose,' shackled with chains and cuffs on his wrists and ankles, dressed head to foot in winter army fatigues. It must be 110 degrees. I watch as the hacks remove his cuffs and make him undress right next to the bus. Under many layers of drab olive, worn-out U.S. Army-issue clothing is a final layer of newspaper and strips of cardboard covering his brown skin. He has enemies in the system, is afraid of being stabbed as he steps off the bus, and he's packed his extra t-shirts and shorts, stuffed them into his shirt sleeves and pant legs along with the paper and cardboard, covering all of his body, neck to ankles, with paper and cloth anti-knifing protection armor.

When prisoners arrive they are issued their khaki or olive green, used U.S. Army uniforms, one size to fit all. Nothing fits anyone. Some buy or trade for tailoring services. Steel-toed safety shoes are worn during daily work hours. They are cheaply made and don't fit anyone. They also exacerbate my mild toe fungus that started in the original county lockup after I was arrested, and turned it into a full-blown case of toe rot. Hot, sweaty shoes in the desert.

The different cultures wear different outfits: Mexicans wear perfectly-white t-shirts, levis, and sandals. Blacks wear brand-name gym outfits, nylon pants, and jackets from Nike. Whites wear loud, colorful t-shirts, cut-off levi shorts, the most comfortable, loose fit they can find.

I played my first game of hard basketball tonight, a nasty, sweaty workout. Didn't get hurt, but once was almost enough. Don and I are now known as 'the producers.' We hang around and talk about the script. It is coming together. Don leaves in three weeks.

I have a good job but don't like to work so much. The warehouse is hot, although I do get to drive the Dodge van around the camp, delivering supplies. I want more time to myself to write and dream. I am putting out the vibe to work in the garage as clerk. There is a desk in an air-conditioned room, with a typewriter. The job is high on many seekers' lists, and the competition is fierce whenever a good job opens up. Don has it now, and he says he's putting in the good word for me. What will be will be.

~ ~ ~

Undated entry

Once a week, if an inmate has established a cash account, or wants to spend his weekly earnings, a store is available with fresh fruit, vitamins, ice cream, soft drinks, avocados, and hot sauce. And cigarettes.

The line forms as soon as the evening count is finished and the loudspeakers announce it. Inmates are forbidden to run in the camp, and guards watch the compound to catch runners to the line and give them shots.[1]

If you don't get there towards the opening, all the good stuff is gone: stamps for letters, ice cream, fruit, so many inmates develop their scam to get a position closer to the front.

A long line forms in the hot summer sun or the freezing wind of the winter desert. It can easily take an hour to get to the front, and certain people hustle the line for loans and favors. Some rich inmates hire runners to save their spot. Some con men just work the line to keep their talents in shape. They don't want to lose street skills.

Some people eat entirely from the commissary, junk foodies to vegetarians. Some buy hair spray. Some get head bandanas. A quart of ice cream is devoured in two minutes.

---

1   A mark on your prison record.

Lots of guac parties revolve around this night, fresh supplies that rot quickly in the heat.

~ ~ ~

12 August 1983

My handwriting size changes with the intensity of my thoughts, gets smaller the harder I think. I sense a need for a focus to point my energies towards, someone, something. Is it possible that I might find some point worth focusing on inside of my own being?

I see my hands aging quickly, the air is so dry and I am using my hands like I haven't in years. I sometimes feel a power creeping in that scares me, that part of being that knows no bounds and fears the unknown. I could break something inside of me, even as I sit here. I feel it when I walk or wake up while I am walking in a daze.

The light, the shades of light to dark, clouds to sun, heat waves to desert hues, that is what is happening in the desert. That, I can get behind. I need to touch the colors. I need so much, even though I know I need nothing.

~ ~ ~

26 August 1983

'Lizard Man' raises a lizard, feeds it, and then turns it into a belt buckle, does the same thing with chipmunks if he can trick them. Another guy carries a lizard around to show whomever how it bites him, "Here, look, it really bites," and the little beast nails his finger. He jumps, and then tries to do it again. "Hey, look, this fucker can bite!"

It looks like I am going to experience how prisoners are forced to continually harass and petition the prison system. The 'system' seems to arbitrarily change its mind whenever it chooses, regardless of whatever has been said, implied, or previously agreed to. This has a tremendous effect on the lives of its prisoners, usually for the worse. My new roommate is an aggressor and likes to confront the system, sue it, and make it adhere to some predictable body of rules. I will get involved because he will get the three other people in his room involved, either actively or after the fact.

My other roommate, J.C., is a stand-up bank robber, using a real gun, pointing it at the bank teller. He's not a wimpy junkie handing someone a note. He usually gets everyone's attention by shooting once into the ceiling. He's spent eight hard-time years in Lompoc, most of them as a junkie. Finally getting close to release, they are using the camp life so he can re-socialize. J.C. studies astrophysics in prison. He's a very smart but uneducated mathematician. He hangs in the pottery shop and smokes dope whenever possible, which keeps his mind from the heavier drugs. I've had interesting conversations with him, getting inside the mind of a real criminal.

Then he gets his first furlough in eight years, with only three months left to go on his sentence. He heads to a casino just across the Nevada border, holds it up with a bomb threat using a bag filled with rocks, and takes a lady hostage. He rapes her shortly thereafter along the bank of the Colorado River, and somehow gets caught right after this event. He'll spend the rest of his life in jail.

I walked four miles around the hill today, named 'the Gibson Mile,' after a previous inmate, and friend of my walking partner, 'H&R,' a tax crook who walks 20 miles a day and swims one nautical mile when the pool is functional. He's 60 years old. He's in Boron for "doing taxes for the mob," and has lost 57 pounds "doing the Gibson."

~ ~ ~

5 September 1983

The visitors room, minimum security.

A community of misfits, from inside and outside, meet as friends and relatives in the visitors room. The visitors must arrive by car. We inside watch our friends and family get all lined up in the wind-blown, sand-covered parking lot, waiting for the 8 a.m. visiting hour to arrive. There are fancy cars, limos, junk heaps, all lined up in single file down the only road in or out, waiting to visit us prisoners, everyone in the very hot or very cold desert sun.

The process of getting in for a visit is demeaning, hot, takes way too long, and is nerve-racking for everyone. And what goes on once everyone finally gets inside, is truly strange: love, sadness, loss, sex, touching, bible-reading, petting, kissing, eating, crying, noisy running kids, board games, families, revealing dresses, open blouses, uptight wives watching another's love-action two feet away.

Drugs are used, passed, and smuggled inside. Vodka pumped into oranges is consumed, money gets passed and hidden in shoes. Deals are made, marriages are dissolved, and younger girls and daughters are ogled over by older inmates. Gamblers from Vegas set the football spread for next week's games. Hired lawyers confer with clients while inmate lawyers try to console wives.

The room is hot, everyone is packed together, and they keep it that way. No room for intimacy, except when Quikquik jams his current squeeze in behind the Coke machine for a quick fuck.

The visitors get searched when they enter, the inmates get searched when they leave. At the designated time, all visitors get up and leave, and the collection of cars melts in unison into the undulating heat waves and dust that someone's beat-up, old Plymouth raises on the way out, filled with a Mexican family. It's a long drive back to anywhere from this place. All that's left is the garbage, which is carefully and systematically packed up and out of the visiting room by the guards, no chance of anyone leaving an extra 'gift' in the greasy mess that way.

~ ~ ~

19 September 1983

One inmate who has a litigation mind goes after the opportunity to harass the system whenever possible. Prison officials delight in withholding or giving wrong information. This guy is into his own case so heavily that he has to take care to stay on top of what is really happening and make sure something unnecessary doesn't happen to him. They have already rolled him up a number of times, just ahead of some important court document being delivered, and more often than not, he has missed some important filing date or didn't have the right information, because he is fucking with the system and they are fucking with him. He found that a secretary had stupidly added 10 days to his sentence and that another angry official had changed the official crime level of his particular case to a much worse numeric level in the system computer, which then added months to his sentence. He is very busy trying to sort it all out, and they make it very hard for him. This prisoner feels the prison officials do it all on purpose, because they love their work, dealing with human suffering, and making it happen.

There exists a procedural administrational remedy to problems in prison. But to file for remedy and then stick to it to see something happen requires strong conviction and strength. Because once one begins to question the system, it can strike back in any number of ways: strip searches, room checks, threats or loss of privileges, loss of good time served, or loss of a decent job while in the system. This one inmate is prepared to stand up and fight, armed with Bureau of Prison policies and a quick, even mind. A weaker person would cave in after the first threats to the daily routine and privilege of being housed in a camp environment.

A Hell's Angel likes to lie back and make fun of everyone. He gives everyone a sarcastic nickname and tries to incite other inmates to respond to his dark humor. He hangs out alone in his room, shades drawn, staring at the ceiling... doing hard time in a soft camp.

One guy is always brewing something to drink, yeast from the kitchen bakery, sugar, water, and whatever canned fruit he can throw in. Another man has to steal something wherever he is, part of his human nature. One older man is actually enjoying his two-year sentence in jail, a rest from a hard life outside. He is reading all the books he nev-

The Substitute Asshole

er had time for before, has slowed his life down, regained his health, and finished re-writing a book on scuba diving. He has read over 190 books and keeps a running list with a two-sentence review of each one. He has also learned to read and write Japanese, all this while working seven hours a day as a clerk. He finds time to swim, sunbathe, and jog around the hill every day as well.

~ ~ ~

10 October 1983

How to describe what it means to wait in line for the telephone? Sit patiently while one man screams at his wife, another tells his woman on the outside how to do this and do that like she doesn't have the ability to have one thought of her own. Endless drivel, endless pain. How can a phone call from here bring anyone closer to reality? Mainly I see the pain, the rejection, and the sorrow of suffering lives and souls. But the phone is one of the only ways to reach out and feel, to receive warmth and satisfaction, and we all keep standing or sitting, waiting in line for our turn.

~ ~ ~

November 1984[2]

Wind. It comes in around the windows, blasting anything that dares rise off the bed. Oh, we do have beds. Dust-covered from the fine sandy powder, everything in the room is sand-blasted by the wind. Most of it seems to land on my bed. They can keep you locked up for 180 extra days for a dusty bed.

I have two pictures on this platform, 12 inches from my pillow, and I talk to them. They won't talk back, at least

---

[2] There is a large gap in Dean's prison journal from January 1984 to November 1984. We don't know if these writings were lost or if he simply didn't write during this time.

not while I'm awake. But if I roll over to talk to them at the wrong time, like early in the morning, my bed roars, ancient, rusty springs, and my hard-timing, heavy roommate gets real pissed at me for making noise. So I don't move around too much when he's in the room.

The choicest bed is the one that's hidden behind the door when it's opened. I'm in it now. No one gets many visitors in my room, so when the door is suddenly thrown open, we know it is the cops, doing a random search, or making their appointed room checks. They need to know what we are up to all the time. They come in anytime, many times throughout the day and night. At night, they make sure they wake you up, just for the fun of it.

Every once in a while they actually catch some dimwit doing a criminal act, like smoking a joint, or in the act of hiding a stinky can of prison-brewed 'pruno' under the bed. And then he immediately loses his minimum-security privilege and is transferred to a lower level in Hell. Everyone knows this is the risk run for breaking any rule. I don't want to spend one minute longer here than I have to, and can't imagine living in a steel cage, so I am such a good boy now, it is sickening.

The real, been-down-a-long-time convicts just stay in their rooms and stare at the ceiling, something that can't get you in any trouble as far as I can tell. It's what they learned locked inside the bad places with steel bars, metal walls, and razor-wire fences, filled with some bad people.

The prison walls here are invisible, but they exist. Everyone knows exactly where the perimeter lines are. One step over, you're rolled up and shipped outta here. They change the line and move it closer without telling us.

There was a 7 a.m. fire drill this morning, with a special lock-down headcount…meaning freeze in place, stand absolutely still wherever you happen to be. What they maybe forgot is that many inmates leave our rooms at 6 a.m. to exercise in the cooler morning air. So when they counted the various units at 7 a.m., some souls were missing. Just before the shit hit the fan, real alarms going off, some half-naked, shivering cold inmate somehow turned on a piece of the dormant brain of the drill lieutenant with an insightful remark that shed light on the situation. "The seven missing from the count are in the exercise area." Why would any hack know that?

When there are surprise inmate counts it's always a wild scramble for safety as the cops run around trying to catch campers out of assigned areas. They often do this when they suspect someone has just escaped camp or is running in the desert for contraband. The runners and spotters have elaborate ruses in place in case a count happens during a run. There are many routes to take back into camp.

~ ~ ~

Undated entry

I do have to describe Thanksgiving dinner...beyond the realm of the twilight zone. The visiting room by itself is worth an attempt at description. Add the thrill of a real holiday, crowded and very close quarters, and something unworldly happens.

Giant piles of food, lines in the small TV room, where they placed the microwave oven to warm up the goodies. Those waiting to warm up their holiday dinners are fighting for space with those sports fans who just sit and watch football with their visitors. Combine this with no ventilation, cigarette smoke, and screaming kids mingling with the food smells of various ethnic holiday feastings...and the event starts to take shape.

Turn one way too quickly and dripping, greasy brown gravy will cover your shoes. Then, just there, a lady keeps looking in her small cosmetic mirror, adjusting her wig while the two inmates she is visiting wolf down handfuls of her feast. Something brushes my leg, it's a child covered in mashed potatoes. Give it a swift, firm push to move it along its way. Over there a woman is jacking off her man, while both are pretending to eat some goop she brought. Will he come in her napkin? How can he stand that fat, greasy hand jerking on his dick in this hot, smelly, thick crowd? Beats me. But I love it. Good, sweet, illicit sex. And this goes on and on, then a whistle blows to bring an end to all the fun. "Visiting is over."

Visits still seem to be basically depressing. The men I see after a visit are usually withdrawn and quiet, then try to sleep off the memories.

~ ~ ~

9 January 1984[3]

The Pranksters

Faye, Kesey's wife, was a true earth momma, not in a happy, psychedelic sense, but as a center of strength, the calm center in a raging storm. She would always feed the hordes, smiling, rounding up her kids, and never seemed affected by the madness or gladness around her.

My brother had a short affair with her, right after George Walker's, and I never did quite understand the Prankster's sexual experiments. They were quite convoluted, many people got upset, rejected, or just freaked out as a result. But if Kesey thought it was OK, the rest of the pack did their best to follow suit. Fuck and be fucked. Take what you can get, and try for it all. I was always worried about VD or crabs: The downside of sex was always a side topic of discussion when I went one on one with different Pranksters outside of the group mind.

Faye would be cooking or washing dishes, a smile on her face, while seven Hell's Angels chug-a-lugged beer, Pranksters madly speed-rapping, 10 feet away. She was the provider, the link to some real, concrete sense around the insanity. I always wondered how someone could get her alone long enough to have an affair. Probably when Kesey was away adventuring.

---

[3] For organizational purposes, a few of these journal entries are out of chronological order, particularly to group together the entries when Dean reminisces about Kesey and the Pranksters.

The Substitute Asshole

Her kids mixed with everyone and she was there changing diapers on Jed, making sure they were always fueled and clothed. I don't know if she and Kesey ever discussed relationships, but they sure seemed to have some unspoken agreement that allowed each to find their own level of fun. Then again, Ken was the 'chief,' and no one really even tried to question anything he was doing, except some of us who weren't in the inner circle.

The inner circle was a sore point with me, and I never did come to terms with the hypocrisy I experienced being around the Pranksters. They were somehow "more hip" than us poor day visitors, who hadn't shared in all of their historical, social experiments. They weren't sharing the great learnings, only trying to reproduce them for the public at large. And when Kesey wasn't around to provide the vision, there was no central theme guiding the trips.

The Pranksters were horrible sponges and liars. "Hey, man, loan me 10 until tonight." Once I loaned my brother a truck to drive to Chicago. He, Hassler, and Zonker were delivering some pot to the Midwest. They were going to pay me later. Sure. Next thing I knew, Hassler had torn out the dashboard, leaving just the steering wheel poking through the floorboards, and removed the bench front seat. Babs fiberglassed the firewall in Day-Glo pink and green, added two, side-by-side, small, antique wooden school chairs for driver and passenger, and then claimed the truck as his own. Fuck Dean and the $50 we owe him. I mean, it was only fifty bucks, but they burned me. I would have been made to feel like a complete, cheap-skate asshole if I ever dared ask for the money. That is if I wanted to continue to play with the gang.

Never trust a Prankster was their motto, and it applied to friend or foe. They called their lifestyle 'Rat,' and would consume anything put in front of them: people, wives, cars, drugs. If they wanted something you had they would ask for it, and if you refused, they would make you feel like shit.

So all the excitement and great moments in Wolfe's

book[4] were true, but they were rare, and on many days the Pranksters were hungover, coming down, freaked out, and sick. I figured out in a flash never to carry more than a couple of dollars, and a rationed supply of drugs to offer up for consumption when I visited. I was confused about my own selfishness, my not surrendering to the higher consciousness of their vigorously pursued communal effort. Use versus abuse. Bottom line, they were sponges with rare moments of gut-wrenching insight.

If you loaned a Prankster your car, it would be returned broken, out of gas, and filled with McDonald's wrappings. And the radio wouldn't work. I was both attracted by the 'here and now'-ness of the scene and repelled by the way they used things up, spit them out, and then forgot them. But the high times were really high.

Ideas: The Pranksters used the 'I Ching' many times a day for spiritual guidance. They needed to trust in something. The night of the first Hell's Angels party, it was Cassady's old lady and June the Goon who were fucked by all the Angels and many of the Pranksters. Cassady's old lady went willingly, but June the Goon was so flipped out by way too much acid that she couldn't resist. You could see it in her eyes, but they dragged her into the mess. I was pissed that night when Kesey didn't step up and protect that crazy, screwed-up girl. She couldn't say no, or yes, and wasn't even given a choice. I watched as they all raped her and the other lady, hooting and hollering until one of the Angels asked if I was gonna jump in. When I said no, he told me to get the fuck outta there, which I did.

~ ~ ~

---

4   'The Electric Kool-Aid Acid Test,' a 1968 nonfiction book by Tom Wolfe.

10 January 1984

Cassady

Cassady[5] was there for everyone, beyond anyone's wildest imagination or ability to understand. He would always be talking and moving, usually flipping a small sledgehammer into the air and catching it without skipping a beat, or looking at it. If you followed and listened, you would realize he had worked you too into his incredible rap and unfolding story.

At first, I thought he was looney-tunes, but I wasn't paying close enough attention. He could easily take an hour to make a point. And if you got it, understood how he had arrived at the point, and how he had evolved a cosmic line connecting himself, you, and everyone else in the room with everything that had ever happened on Earth and in heaven, for eternity, you stopped and stared at him in awe. It was pure, never-ending consciousness.

I loved to hang around him, and understood that was why I kept coming back for more. The Pranksters worshiped Cassady, and he loved their attention. Cassady always let me into his world and would try to explain it all while doing a hundred other things. When he was around, I felt part of a larger group of minds.

He remembered me by my 1947 Oldsmobile coupe, and he would work the car into his streaming rap as soon as I appeared on the scene. He loved certain parts of the car, and could describe them in detail, like the feel of the large steering wheel and the weakness of the front, swing-arm shock absorbers. I frequently asked him to take me for a drive, and finally, at a Homer Lane party, everyone on acid, he accepted. No sooner had we rolled onto Alpine Road and reached the Olds' maximum speed when he looked at me like I was a stranger and said, "This is the first time in my

---

5   Neal Cassady – a major figure of the '50s Beat Generation (Dean Morriarty character in Jack Kerouac's 'On the Road') and the counterculture of the '60s, including the Merry Pranksters.

life I've never had a destination," and then hit the brakes, pulling hard left on the steering wheel, and we did a 180 degree spin and drift down Alpine, ending with Neal taking us right back to the party we had just left.

A couple of months before he died, Cassady told me that Owsley's new drug, STP, had destroyed his memory, leaving him very depressed. I also had a very bad experience with STP and quit working with Owsley because this new drug we were making had made me crazy too.

Kesey's downside

Kesey was invited to speak at the anti-Vietnam War day at U.C. Berkeley. I drove to La Honda to help the Pranksters prepare to pull off their next major put-on. They were painting the bus in someone's idea of psychedelic camouflage, building swiveling gun turrets on the roof, dressing up in faux, outrageous army outfits, and generally getting themselves worked into a merry mood. You could say they were drinking a new batch of Owsley's Kool-Aid. They were going to prank the very anti-war people who had invited Kesey to speak. Pull up shooting and raising hell, bringing a little humor and light to the politicos. Vietnam was very serious business, and a good dose of merriment just might do more to stop the war than a thousand speeches.

But when I got to Kesey's, the 'inner group' had closed up around the wonderment of their own genius and made me feel instantly like some unwanted piece of a shit outsider. They were going on with all the preparations but ignoring the few of us that didn't live in or near 'The Bus.'[6] My brother was involved in the importance of doing Kesey's bidding. He was trying to round up Day-Glo vests like the ones California highway workers wore. Very important work. He successfully made me aware I wasn't part of the real Prankster crowd, and that I wouldn't be allowed to ride with them on the bus to Berkeley.

This was a perfect example to me of the problem one

---

6 'Further,' the Pranksters' psychedelic-painted bus.

faced in the Kesey scene. I had to agree that his ideas for the Berkeley anti-war day were inspired, and brilliant, but I also realized that he cared not for the individual over the group. I drove to Berkeley by myself.

As things turned out, I was happy I didn't have my drug-crazed picture on the front page of the S.F. Chronicle the next morning like my brother did. He was pointing a toy gun at the camera. Their anti-war humor and theater were misunderstood and rejected by the East Bay politicos but scored big with the local, stoned hippies.

Being seen, being highly visible, and being a living statement were important trips for the Pranksters. I had already realized that The Man was dangerous, and safety came with anonymity. But thinking I was less obvious and therefore further from the reach of the law was totally confused thinking. A straight could spot a hippie a mile away. It was so easy.

~ ~ ~

17 January 1984

Homer Lane

In 1965, I moved from Hayes Valley in S.F. to Homer Lane, just behind the Stanford campus. The crowd living there had decided not to follow Kesey to La Honda, but were keeping the movement alive and well in Menlo Park. I got a house next to Vic Lovell, to whom Kesey had dedicated 'One Flew Over the Cuckoo's Nest.'

Homer Lane was a dirt road, lined with cabins built years before the area had become famous because of Sunset Magazine. Expensive homes were being built all around, but this little area was perfect for students and hippies seeking the perfection of nature and a good place to get high. There were 10 little houses built in a row in the cul-de-sac at the end of this dirt road. A stream flowed just next to my cabin, and across from it, I could see the Stanford golf course. The idea of playing golf on acid was beyond the beyond, as the golf culture represented everything we were trying to shed from our minds. But that life was right next to our life, and that made for very interesting interactions.

Many Stanford students lived on Homer Lane and were the earliest LSD pioneers. While Kesey was pushing the edges of the envelope out in the woods, we instead focused on getting high and living on the inside of the moving picture. There was a grad student in economics, a number of psychology students and Skinnerian researchers, two M.D.s, a child psychologist, and artists, like myself. We started taking acid almost every day, and spent more and more time together, playing music, painting, talking, and soon everyone in school had dropped out to stay with our experiment. The liquid light show was invented one night in The Shack, by R.S., and he quickly shared it with the Pranksters over the hill.

The Shack was an abandoned shed that backed up to the creek where we would gather to trip. It was the farthest from any neighbors and the safest gathering spot. Every cabin's inhabitants were involved in the LSD craziness, and our little village became a stopover between the City, Palo Alto, and La Honda. It was a non-stop party, but we were streetwise kids from back east and knew enough to keep our noises inside at night. No sense getting the cops interested. Kesey had a much different approach and seemed to be so outrageous that he was inviting the law to jump in and lick his stamp. We didn't wear 'Take That In Your Face' clothing and didn't paint our cars in Day-Glo pinks and orange colors. We were the hipsters, not the Pranksters. And we shared stuff, money, and cars, but took care of business too. The group was as important as any one individual.

The real problem was electric music sounded better than acoustic music, and electric music needed lots of space between neighbors so as not to attract attention. Eventually many of us decided to move from Homer Lane to a safer spot, and live communally. We rented a remote Spanish-style mansion, Rancho Diablo, on top of the mountains behind Palo Alto. 75 acres, with a view over La Honda to the ocean and enough bedrooms for everyone or every couple to have their own private space. Things just fell into place in those days. If you needed a car, something would just appear that was cheap enough. The list of miracles is endless.

We had found our common crazy home ground, very high, in our own emerging style, not the Kesey style. A rock band grew out of the acid trips and time spent together, the Anonymous Artists of America. The six-car garage became the music practice room, and the giant living room in the house became the performance arena. We bought the first music synthesizer on the planet, a Buchla Box, that looked like an IBM mainframe computer. Len Fraser played at its keyboard when he could get it in focus.

Michael played guitar, Trixie the bass, and Lars sang and worked the harmonica. Norman the Foreman played lead guitar and Manny Meyer kept the rhythm guitar licks on time and in tune. The only trouble was, Manny was the only musician, the rest were rank amateurs, and the band never sounded much better than beginning child's play. But it was fun, and many members stayed with it for years. We all knew that the Beatles had had a similar beginning, and the Grateful Dead were playing the same Acid Tests as we were.

I was the group facilitator, and the communicator, and kept Rancho Diablo in touch with my outside world. I would drop by La Honda at Kesey's, then drive up to Berkeley to drop in at Owsley's, and be back at the Triple A's on the mountain before dawn, sharing information, money, and drugs. I was a good source of rent money too, as I wasn't becoming a musician, but rather an enthusiastic and successful acid and pot entrepreneur. Buy some here and sell some there, with everyone very happy with the work I was doing.

~ ~ ~

19 January 1985

I hate to say it
but it's true

and I don't know
what else I can do,
I'm paranoid, Jack,
and I'm singin' those blues.

I have decided to try and keep some kind of daily chronicle of the rest of my stay here in Boron. I feel very self-conscious about doing it, as it seems there is really nothing much to write about other than myself. That bothers me. I am sick and tired of just staring off. It used to work when I had my mind under stronger control. Now I am thinking, thinking all the time. And consequently, torn apart by my lack of any power to move the world.

I think if I start writing, it will help me to get moving creatively, but I am not sure. I have a hard time holding a plan or dream in my mind for very long because it just starts to hurt. Plots have no ending, and no resolution; scenes have no beginning.

I worry if my pillow sits just right on my perfectly-made bed, or if there is any obvious dust on my floor or dresser. I would be lost now without my single room and I could lose it for just some small infraction.

My temper seems short. I am not very forgiving of others' shortcomings, which everyone has, some so blatant that I have to hide in my room to keep myself out of trouble. I have a big mouth, and it could get me in trouble. I now ask my Muses to bring my world to life on these pages so that I can know who it was that passed through this real prison.

~ ~ ~

25 January 1985

I think about my future work, and how I want to be part of a system that grows and evolves around talent and performance. So naive a desire, fulfilling employment. Isn't that how all this got started, I was disillusioned with the straight world of meaningless work?

13 February 1985

A day of surreal changes. My friends/neighbors of many months are moved to other dorms, for no reason, just a way to keep the folk unbalanced and paranoia levels high.

They use lots of techniques here to keep things unstable. It's hard to believe that they go so far out of their way to cause inmates trouble, but they do. As soon as the camp seems to be feeling on course, even keel, something gets taken away, things get stirred up, and more punishment is meted out. They set new off-limit perimeter lines, and take away some rights they call a privilege. Or change the dress code, so what's OK today will cause pain tomorrow. Everyone gets upset, people get pissed, and tempers flare, for no other reason than the loss of another small chunk of self-respect.

When this is over, everything I ever knew or did will be completely changed – my life, my friends and lovers, my home, and what I do, all different. What a chance for me, and I plan to go for it.

~ ~ ~

21 February 1985

"Mean Dean's under the weather," shouts The Lizard, my Hell's Angel buddy. He's hurrying by to watch the evening's TV special. He drags one leg with a little hop, damaged from a bike accident. Nobody fucks with his TV, but it's the TV for him every night, nothing more. There's a big fight looming on my floor over the TV. I can sense it coming.

Two new redneck boys on my floor have decided they can do whatever they like, which is fine. They succeeded in getting the black domino players out of the TV room, which made for one less source of unending yelling and noise. The domino players slam their pieces hard on whatever surface they're playing on, which is way too much racket when the

TV's going, loud jive talk is flowing back and forth, and different radios are blasting their competing songs.

The same people sit and watch TV every night, and it depends on which group in which dorm will watch which show. The rednecks are spitting their gobs of chewing tobacco into big metal cans...an awful, sloppy sound. They get off on all the game shows, reruns of Three's Company, cartoons, and westerns; nothing more mature than that, or it's a yelling match escalating to a fight.

I can feel fists being thrown any second now. I'm on my bed, hidden in my room, sick as a dog. The door's closed. I'm sitting up, reading, and watching my curtain move to the cool air blowing in from the industrial swamp cooler outside. Either that, or I listen to my radio or sleep. Very little sleep, just hanging around on the edges in a hazy daze.

I hope and pray I've learned enough about patience and discrimination to make my new future unfold as smoothly as possible.

~ ~ ~

22 February 1985

I know that if I read these pages someday, I will wonder if I really felt that bad back then. It seems to be one bad day after another; I even know to expect the darkness, and when it takes over, it still seems so unreal.

Uncle Lew, the hack boss dying of lung cancer, told me over a month ago he'd explain to me how the prison now views me and my case. I've asked once, given him the official, 'cop-out' form request once, asked again, and then today I went by his office and asked, "Sir, do you have time now to explain what my Central Monitoring means?"

He raised his head, glared at me, then said only "No." I just turned and walked away. Everything that happens here comes like that. I learned that I've been under some recent special observation, for what or why I don't know, and there's no way to find out. No help, no explanations, and it leaves me feeling very alone. Sure, all I'll ever have is myself, I know, but I'm really lonely here.

I don't play cards or board games, too competitive. I do very little team sports. I am expecting mail that doesn't come, but have no way to find out, no one to call who can help me learn why. I asked yesterday to have two pages of paper photo-copied for a legal matter, and the uniformed office guy was sitting right next to the copier. It's my legal right to get legal papers copied. He looked at me like I didn't exist, held out his hand, and told me to come back tomorrow. I didn't leave the papers with him. I still have a tiny bit of self-respect left.

~ ~ ~

23 February 1985

I remember one night 20 years ago when I decided deep in my heart and soul that what I wanted was to be with Terry.[7] I felt that I really did love her, and my soul jumped out in bliss. As it turned out, she rejected my total surrender to her right then and there. I didn't understand this immediately, but I was there, ready for the total commitment to a deep, bigger-than-life-itself love I felt we shared.

She didn't feel that way about me ever, but it took her a few months to let me know. I woke up to our reality when I got home one day to find she'd just run off with a friend of mine. I was totally devoted to her and wanted nothing more than to bathe in the pureness of a love that I'd only imagined we shared. I don't think I've recovered from that deep hurt to this day. It makes the past hit-and-runs that I've done with different lovers seem even worse than my own experience of rejection. Somehow I should have known better. I'm not a substitute asshole, but rather a real one.

I've no doubt that my life will be meaningless without the intensity and commitment of a deep and reciprocal love. But I have rejected those lovers since Terry, or have not understood how deeply hurt I am and how little I really

---

7   Dean's second wife.

know about how to be in love.

It's hard for me to believe how much I think about this problem; in fact, it's the only real thing I know. I've got to have it, sink into it and soar with it, and be completely true to it, without the fear and hurt I've kept so close, so well hidden all these years. And even now the anger.

~ ~ ~

26 February 1985

I called mom and dad tonight, checking on the status of any letters about my halfway house. That was all it took to get them jumping all over each other. It would be humorous if it wasn't so real. How is it that two intelligent people can carry on like that for thirty years or more? It's way beyond me, but I'm probably just like them. One more link in the chain of my weird life.

I am unsure of how to act these days. Should I just forget about all the things I carry around? My bed is too uncomfortable to lie down on. I have been on hold for too long now. The shadows of my past are haunting me.

~ ~ ~

27 February 1985

Nothing to write about, and then I thought of sounds. Now, at 9:20 p.m., I hear the very loud soundtrack to Dynasty down the hall, even though my door is closed. Then, the vibrating, high-pitched rattling water cooler starts up, and goes for about 60 seconds, reminding me of a train somewhere in my childhood. Two different guitar players strum, one singing Rolling Stones music; the other, heavy into Mexican folk. An ascending roar from a water pump, buried somewhere under the building, comes on every 10 minutes or so, 24 hours a day. It reaches a crescendo and stops. There are hacking coughs; the flu found fertile ground here this season.

The wind: The bathroom door, down the hall, slams shut again and again. Someone's left the bathroom window open and no one will get up and close it. Dominoes slam down, and card players argue back and forth. Some nights the rotating floor-buffer machine swirls its high-pitched whine into the cacophony; someone's polishing the worn-out linoleum in their room for inspection. We have to polish to protect our sanitation, they say. There's an orange fungus growing on the walls of the shower.

The cops wandering through the dorms laugh and talk loudly all night every night. I'm able to recognize certain people by the sound of their shoes, slippers, or coughs, their shuffling walk, and a certain pitch of laughter or swearing, all with my door shut. The cops open my door a number of times during the night and shine bright flashlights into my face.

~ ~ ~

12 March 1985

I am now the co-purchasing agent at the Officers' Club. I sit at a desk, have my own phone, and write reports on everything coming into the restaurant. I've learned all the ins and outs of the official government paper shuffle, and I am good at it. The job is intense, busy, and so much better than bussing tables. I buy food stuff from the big camp food store, sign receipts, and deal with salesmen. What a strange way to be in jail, doing a job for 15 cents an hour that normally pays at least $25,000 a year. The bad part is coming back here at night.

Coming into the camp is like descending into Hell. We get off the bus, line up to be searched, and pass through the portals of paranoia to be back where we sleep. I eat dinner before I leave the base, so after we go to our dorms to be counted, I stay in my room when everyone else runs to dinner. The clientele here has again taken a turn downhill, with more and more inmates with an attitude, heavy cons, and hard timers. You can see it in their eyes, their clothes, and the way they carry their bodies. Hunched over for protection, never appearing outgoing or standing upright. Keep it all inside, look at the ground, and keep moving.

~ ~ ~

Undated entry

I had a custom desk built, with a drawer for pencils and paper. It was designed for easy installation and removal; you never knew when they would just up and change your room. I moved it three times, leaving small holes in the wall when I unscrewed it.

The desk became a trusted friend, encouraging me to write letters.

I got access to the old typewriter for the first year, but they figured out that we were filing petitions to the courts with it, and took it away. The only workable typewriter was in the law library, a small room open for a few hours.

Some of the guys also built shower boxes, wooden containers for soap, shampoo, and toiletries that many inmates would carry to the bathroom. I ended up with a box with a false bottom, opened by sticking a nail in a small hole, releasing a spring-loaded lock. A great stash place that I never used. I passed it on to a major crook before I left, and I'm sure he enjoyed it.

All the private work was done for trade. I got two joints from another guy to pass to the carpenter for the desk. The work was all illegal, so moving stuff from the shop to the room, and from room to room, required help and subterfuge. We would all share in this activity; when something was being moved, lookouts would watch for the hacks, and engage them or distract them if they got too close to the action. As long as the desk was mounted on the wall, it was legal. Just don't get caught moving it between walls.

~ ~ ~

19 March 1985

So free
to be
a man of substance.
No rejection now acceptance,
just eyes for hints of
the truth.
Patience is my guide.

~ ~ ~

24 March 1985

Another long weekend. I have been thinking about the beneficial sides of this whole experience, and it has many good effects. Time will tell if they hold, but now I feel like I have a new chance to get things straight in my life. So many easy delusions to pull over the eyes.

I know I will need to adjust gradually to the pressures of real-time, so that I won't fall into any old patterns to relieve pressure, etc. Sometimes I can feel the tension I know awaits me, and my head hurts from it. But even the flow of my time through here has its interesting sides. The lessons in patience, boredom, and dealing with people, and now all I am learning about restaurant management. Nothing mysterious, just a lot of hard work.

My jailhouse attorney, Kevin, is another amazing story. He just stopped by with his arms full of paperwork. He claims he gets real joy, and makes his jail time meaningful, by helping inmates get their legal problems ironed out. His work is almost full-time. It is like he has two full-time lives, one for the camp, and one for us.

~ ~ ~

7 April 1985

I called mom last night. It was the required 'Easter' call, and I found out the warden has sent my mother a letter, letting her know that I am getting a six-month halfway house. I was really excited last night; at last, I knew when I was getting out of here, in exactly three months. The weird part is that they told my mother about my release, but not me. Now I just have to wait and see if they will tell me to make it real.

~ ~ ~

10 April 1985

Stayed in from work at the base today with some injury complaint, so that I could see Ms. Lyttle. My excuse to go to her office was some paperwork that needed to be notarized, but my real purpose was to talk with her about my early release. She said she hadn't heard from Danny yet. I left her office and went to call Danny. Surprise, I even reached him. He told me he'd just finished talking with Ms. Lyttle, confirming the job offer for me to work on his film. Twenty minutes later, Ms. Lyttle is telling me she's now going to try to get me released in time for the job. I wanted to cry, the first time in two years someone has offered to do something for me.

I heard my name announced over the camp PA system, paging me to report to Ms. Lyttle's office a couple of hours later. She told me she'd started my release paperwork. She should get me out of here in June to Los Angeles. Well, it has been a big, small day. Something happened, a change in my life, but nothing's for sure yet. I feel like the movement has been in my favor today, and I'm almost giddy. I walk the hill, laughing, and have to struggle, climbing into the stiff, brisk wind to make it to the top. My emotions are strung out like a tight wire, for the smallest hint of positive events evokes such a response!

~ ~ ~

17 April 1985

Woke up this morning at about 3:30 a.m., drifted in and out until six. Hard to sleep, I am losing my passivity, anxious to get on with whatever is coming. I am having the classic short-time blues, like what really will happen? Will I be a complete failure, with no friends, and unable to be around people?

How strange, I still wonder who I am and when I will find out.

~ ~ ~

25 April 1985

Take a short walk around the hill with an inmate walking buddy, everything comes spilling out. Maybe there's a humorous twist to it when all is said and done. We're all such loose screws, bad seeds, gathered here for 'the duration.'

Perhaps there's no meaning beyond the fear you feel. React, be strong, and don't look back.

Was I always an existentialist? Why take pictures when you create them with the eye? That one hung me up for years, taking, holding, and owning the result, versus direct perception.

~ ~ ~

29 April 1985

It's night, late, and my grief is under control. I got my last letter from Cleve[8] today. He wrote half and Gwen had to finish it. She said he has only a short time left. He has been fighting death, to stay alive, I guess, forever. It is the saddest day I've had in a long time, the worst I've felt that I remember. Cleve is one of a very few people I've known who treated me respectfully, even while speaking the harsh truths of an enlightened being. Roland Hammond, my first wife's father, spoke the truth with respect, too.

Cleve the yogi changed my life. I often think about those

---

8   Cleve the Apache man who cured Dean after he had lost his mind in Owsley's Denver lab.

days when I first met him. He forced his way through my ego and into my deeper mind, forcing me to look at myself without the guilt and stupidity caused by the ego's mind. Yamananda, Bliss of Death. I've died again tonight. I've been able to turn to Cleve when in need while in prison. He's been here with me, and now he's soon to be gone. I feel more loss than I can express. He told me all the time that he is a god, a realized being. He showed me more than I now comprehend, and I wonder if I ever will. It's as if a large, very colorful piece of the scenery I live with just lost its brilliance.

Cleve spoke of always going for grandness, no matter whether biological life is only about survival, with fear and competition as life's driving forces. I'm crying and afraid to cry. I'm in prison and displays of emotions from the heart are not allowed, someone'll jump all over you if you show vulnerability. I'll try to speak to Cleve next week on my furlough.

Gwen, Cleve's friend whom I've never met, wrote that love was filling their home, and I can sense it, or my lack of it, in here. It's love I'm longing to have. Cleve offered me such a special kind of love, he told me so many things. I feel empty and drained. I wrote to him that I should be getting out just about the same time he is leaving for good. It is all too weird.

~ ~ ~

Undated entry

I remember the day of my physical exam for the Vietnam-bound draft in 1965. It shook my body. Somehow this place drags up old visions. I was standing in a room of faceless, hopeless baby men, waiting to bend over for the asshole examination. Only I refused to pull off my pants, as I wasn't wearing underwear. And I couldn't bend over anyway, the rigid back brace strapped from my hips to my neck made that impossible.

"Ho Ho," said the Sergeant. "What have we got here, a

mommy's boy drag queen?"

Not far from what I wanted him to think. I had written down on the application form that I was a homosexual, heroin-addicted communist, with conscientious objections, and severe physical and emotional problems, including a recently broken back and a wife whose mind had been completely rearranged in a car accident.

I wore my pants all day, as we passed through different testing stations. I refused to pee in a room full of men wearing only underpants. I refused to allow any blood to be drawn from my veins. I had such an amphetamine-pumped heart rate that I almost broke their machine, and had to balance myself against a wall all the time, as I was holding my breath until I almost passed out.

At one point, the real moment of truth appeared. "Boy, if you don't let me take your blood right this minute, I will see to it that you are the first person to be put on that draft bus outside the door, today!" But I stood my ground, I was committed to staying in the U.S.

Fortunately, the next step was the psychiatrist interviewing possible mental cases, and he had only one question for me. "Are you truly a homosexual?" I looked him right in his eyes and answered, "Yeah, I am." He decided right then and there that the Army had no use for a "butt-fucking faggot" and with three giant steps, cranked up and moving fast, I was out of there. I had failed!

~ ~ ~

1 May 1985

May Day.

May Day feels good. I got another piece of official mail that says the paperwork is on the way. I am starting to get some ideas about movies, but have no idea what to expect.

My progress report from Boron describes me as a "very mature" individual. That means I haven't caused any trouble in the desert, little do they know.

I noticed some more new people doing what all new

people do: Walk slowly around the hill, sit and stare at the distant desert from the top, and worry about the danger of snakes, especially the Mojave Green rattlesnake, a few of which I have encountered. Walk, walk. How many hundreds or thousands of miles have I put in on that trip around the hill? Hot asphalt and loose rocks.

I know I am very lucky to look as good as I do at 42, and soon I am going to become 34 or 35 again, for Hollywood. Why not? Feels right for my new life.

~ ~ ~

2 May 1985

Out of my window, 200 feet above, 600 feet away, is the chapel, a rocky slope from here to it, covered now with yellow-flowering creosote or greasewood, now bending in the evening wind. Also, this late in the season, there are some purple asters still blooming, closed up for the night.

The ground is rocky, glowing in sunset colors, pinkish. Dull gold or plain brown under the glare of the daytime sun. The chapel is window height, and a ridge leads left for a few hundred feet, and I can see the joggers and walkers on the ridge. In fact, I can tell who most of them are from just their particular style of movement.

There is a barbed-wire fence 75 feet from the window, but it is a remnant from the Air Force camp days. The prison hasn't kept the perimeter fencing in repair, and if you want to run away from this camp, it is pretty easy. Some of the holes on the backside allow the smugglers easy out-and-back-in access for their nightly deeds. Often the point where the chapel is built serves as the lookout for the smugglers' helpers, who can black out the chapel light to warn the desert runner if they see trouble coming towards the area.

A telephone pole frames the right side of the window, and thick wires run across my field of view. Sparrows and starlings fly across it when the sun is out. Beneath my window is the main path to the gym and weight pile. All the noises, grunts, cheers, and effort from the gym and the horseshoe pit come through my window when opened for the breeze.

I have spent many hours gazing out of this window, and almost always I can find something alive moving through my vision in this god-awful, desolate place. Now I always look for some animal or bird, be it rabbits, coyotes, ravens, nighthawks, owls, bats, a road runner, or other bird. And the chipmunks. I am amazed at how long I can look out of the window. I know that soon I won't have the 'luxury' of this kind of free time. I used to leave my windows open at night to look up at the hillside, but I guess too many campers were running out for goodies, sex, and contraband at night, and they put in some very bright orange lights which shine through my window and light up my bedroom wall. So I pull the curtains shut now, one more little freedom lost.

~ ~ ~

12 May 1985

Just returned from a five-day furlough. Chelsea[9] and I split up the stuff we own. I got some help from Joseph C. to move my pile into the garage next door. Still more to go. Chelsea is convinced the house we shared is hers, it doesn't occur to her that it might not be.

I lined up a divorce attorney and had to scramble to get the money. Stanley literally had to run to catch me just before I entered the no-man's land at the gate to hand me an envelope with $1,000 for the lawyer. Then off to L.A., a quick trip before returning here. It seems like something is waiting for me there.

My attitude here is changing. I don't feel so under their control, the victim with no power. Bad things could still happen, but I don't feel so vulnerable.

I had a great night with Daisy. She fired up my libido once again as if awakened from a deep sleep. It wasn't so

---

9 Dean's fourth wife whom he met rafting in the Grand Canyon. They divorced while Dean was in prison.

much the act of sex but the sharing of energy, laughing, and tasting the juices. I need it more, you bet.

I don't like getting divorced. It doesn't seem to have any good sides. I must take care not to fall too quickly into another relationship. There is a part of me just looking for a cure. And kids.

A child held my hand and it was such a nice feeling. Feelings, I crave more and take them in whenever they are offered. I am strong in my body and I want to say my mind, and will keep this positive attitude now no matter what. And keep trying to understand what it is all about.

I sent off my movie idea to Peggy today, and I think maybe I have a winner on my hands. It is a perfect story about this whole experience without having to deal too closely with the real terror. A comedy of substance. And now, what's next?

~ ~ ~

19 May 1985

What a long day, one of the more depressing for me recently. It is only 7:30 p.m., but I can't remember a much longer day. Actually, I do remember one, when the walls of my room wouldn't stop, just sat there looking at me, cold and white, forever.

I watched a baseball game tonight, and if there is ever going to be physical violence in here on a group level, it will be over something happening during a game. Lots of name-calling, and running into opposing team members with intent to do harm. Very strange, much better to be a spectator. I can't wait to be out of here. It is too much to think about, so I have quit thinking, which is pretty dull.

Reading is hard, being friendly is hard, getting out of my room is hard, taking a long shower is hard, and listening to the radio, to the general mayhem of the dorm, is hard, too. I want to hear some good, loud sounds that will shake my bones. I am getting anxious for a companion, all kinds of feelings about having and holding, but I don't want to get into it too heavily because I can't have it yet.

We have a three-day weekend now, and I won't get any news about my halfway house for another week. Today they brought in the Air Force sniffing dogs and searched another dorm and many buildings. Nothing was found. It was quite a scene, all the cops getting to play 'serious business,' a favorite game.

All important announcements like count buzzers, random drug tests, and visitor call-outs come from this mirrored-window office at the main entrance to camp. They are old speakers, mounted inside the buildings and outside on poles. They can barely be heard. If you miss your name called, and they have to come looking for you, they are pissed.

Noise echoes from these speakers in the surrounding hills, but actual words can't be understood most of the time. One of the hacks, Bullock, makes microphone sounds like he has marbles and a filter over his mouth. He is completely impossible to understand.

Inmates with a drug problem start scrambling when called. The rule goes, they try to find you immediately, but if you can hide from them and try to get something into your system to block the test, go for it. The rule says they can give you a shot if you don't report for the drug test within three hours after being called. Salt can confuse a marijuana test, and the guilty first go to ground, then start drinking gallons of salted water, often throwing up numerous times before taking the piss test. Many discussions revolve around how to switch piss, dirty for clean, during a test. But it's hard, as a hack stands right there watching while you piss in the bottle.

~ ~ ~

28 May 1985

It's Tuesday, sun going down, and I've just got to say it again here so that I'll read it later. This is a completely miserable, horrible way to live, and as close as I am to being out, I am going nuts just with the total picture, with my inability to do anything, with the level of ignorance and suffering that surrounds me, with my lack of a friend, or anything that has to do with being close to someone. The wind is driving me nuts too, constantly fierce enough to keep me out of it. Enough! I ride the elevator and am hanging around for my up button to get answered.

~ ~ ~

31 May 1985

Yesterday they told me 31 more days, "firm," so now I believe them, I guess.

I am going to spend the next month practicing being open, friendly, and helpful, while also watching closely my aggressive sense of humor. There is no sense driving anyone away from me. I am a bit short on conversational skills, but hope they will be renewed in a more gentle, loving style.

Thirty days now, and I am thinking about packing my stuff already, how many boxes it will all fit in. And then how to get them on the bus into L.A. The small things loom so large. The process feels good, and now my last act in here is to try and arrange a good halfway house.

~ ~ ~

9 June 1985

Too hot to walk, I am thinking about a couple of friends here who have to stay for a couple more years, on top of a couple already.

I want to cry for my failures, they seem so stupid and such a waste of time. It gets right down to "Who am I?" and I haven't the slightest. I think about love and relationships all the time now. And I am afraid I will rush into something too quickly.

~ ~ ~

16 June 1985

I have a blazing frontal, left eye headache, the first since being here. Must be anxiety over what happens next. It is almost overwhelming, on the verge of physical sickness, so much to get straight, so few resources. So many, many questions, from such an insecure base.

I used to think about this time when I first got here, and saw the anxiety that leaving here produced. Told myself I wouldn't be like the other people I knew who were leaving. They all got twisted as the fateful day arrived. But lo and behold, it's happening to me. And it blows my mind.

~ ~ ~

23 June 1985

Single-digit midget, one week to go. The good feelings are rising. I found myself going through papers to throw away today. Did a quick line drawing, something I have wanted to do. I will spend three days this coming week with my pens and drawing paper. Something...something.

And the rush of short time plans; what to do? I am floating, very surreal and I love the feelings. Having had this single room has saved me from so much negativity. I can be alone with my growing high.

Chapter 40
Boron Stories

Johnnie Dimes

Johnnie Dimes was a short, stocky, aging Italian mobster, rumored to have been a West Coast official mob debt collector before I met him in Boron. Johnnie's thick fists were like wooden mallets, his stubby fingers too short to hold a roll of quarters; but when wrapped around a roll of dimes, that was another story. A hand-held roll of 50 dimes made the smacking around of deadbeat gamblers much more effective than just fists, hence, his nickname. Johnnie was someone you didn't ever fuck with. In fact, once you'd somehow encountered the man, from that moment on, you tried your best to avoid him whenever possible. Dimes was hardcore, a different sort of criminal than the hip L.A. crowd I'd chosen to run with at Boron. To Johnnie, everyone was a mark to be taken advantage of, every social interaction some competitive hustle where only Johnnie knew what to expect.

My first prison job was in the warehouse where all prison-issued clothing was stored and doled out as needed. Johnnie only wore the used Air Force garb. I never saw him sporting street clothing, but his khakis always looked brand-new and freshly ironed. So before I understood what Dimes had in mind, I was agreeing to supply him with a few new t-shirts, taken unnoticed from the warehouse where I worked as manager. It was impossible to say no to Johnnie. What self-respecting criminal couldn't steal t-shirts or socks from The Man? I learned later that Johnnie never washed his dirty clothing while at Boron. He always had fresh supplies on hand to replace what he discarded regularly, all a part of his intended image to anyone who looked carefully at him. And he never varied in how he looked, which made him close to invisible in a group of prisoners while running whatever scams he was pulling off. He was a truly-serious master of intimidation.

If by chance you were standing in a line near Johnnie, and you stupidly made eye contact with this guy, it meant that Johnnie was looking your way because he wanted something you had or could supply, even if only a better spot in the line. Johnnie would sink his hooks into you in ways you'd never experienced before, and you'd end up doing whatever for the guy because he'd convince you, and everyone else standing around listening, that you owed him a favor. Johnnie could turn any situation to his favor, and every contact always ended up with you being the big loser.

The handful of mobbed-up criminals at Boron mostly kept to themselves, and hung out together playing cards or watching TV. The small community room in a dorm where they gathered was off-limits to other prisoners not housed on the same floor. Passing through, it was obvious you were never to stop and try to socialize with them, and all non-whites would usually take a longer detour to get somewhere rather than walk by these guys. There was a good reason for their anti-social behavior: Boron, like most minimum security federal prisons, housed a percentage of federal snitches, imprisoned for crimes but held in less-confined settings so they could easily be taken far away to testify in some trial and then returned with little notice or fanfare, to serve out their reduced sentences. Every new arrival at Boron was treated badly at first, assumed to be a snitch, a rat, until the details of his case became common knowledge.

My first few days were pure hell, as one Hell's Angel who lived on my dorm floor decided that I was a rat, and every time he saw me, he snarled that he was going to kill me. No matter that another Angel I was rooming with decided I was cool after an intense grilling session, his partner wouldn't change his mind. Fortunately, the angry Hell's Angel was paroled within a week of my arrival. It took a few weeks of peer scrutiny before any seasoned criminal would talk to me, having learned or decided that I wasn't a snitch and wouldn't do them harm.

So the mobsters mostly kept to themselves and went about handling their lives in quiet privacy. They were professionals about the whole affair and were never a bother to the prison officials. An actual snitch usually acted pretty much like Johnnie, always looking to take advantage of a weakness in others, always trying to get the upper hand in every social interaction. And they had no problem with using physical violence to settle a score.

~ ~ ~

Doc

Doc, a 60-year-old gynecologist from Honolulu, was in jail for prescribing Quaaludes to his Waikiki prostitute clientele. He told me that "ludes" were the finest sleeping pill ever invented, and his hard-working streetwalkers needed something that really worked for them. At his trial, Doc wouldn't plea bargain away his medical rights and belief in the illegal drug, and in retaliation, the courts came down hard on him, sentencing him to 10 years in jail and permanently terminating his license to practice medicine.

Doc arrived at Boron with a plan for the coming three years he'd be living in the desert: His first few years in a hard-core, steel-barred jail were difficult, and to avoid serious prison conflicts, he'd withdrawn, retreated into a private, inner world in order to keep his sanity in prison. He'd spent quiet years researching scientific journals and focused studies in preparation. A complicated, intelligent, and formerly-engaging person, he preferred the privacy of locked-down cells to avoid the dangers of being in the general population. He had been preparing for his future transfer to the camp in the Mojave Desert, where they sent all white-collar, non-violent offenders for the last three years of their sentence.

He got himself assigned to the prison's ground maintenance crew as a skilled carpenter and project manager, as his long-term ant project needed special materials that were only found in the maintenance shop in the prison.

The key component Doc used to implement his plan was his sturdy nylon cup, which he used to smuggle out a wide variety of building materials each day from the maintenance warehouse; small quantities of dry cement, rolled wire, pieces of white kitchen and bathroom ceramic wall and floor tiles, short lengths of metal rebar retrieved from the trash cans, all items forbidden to the prisoners. Doc located two different species of desert ants on the steep, rocky hillsides inside the camp's boundaries, hid the stolen materials in small piles in the rocks close to his secret desert construction site, and very quietly, slowly started working on his project for a few hours every evening after dinner. If anyone needed to speak with Doc, you'd look for him somewhere hard to reach. He always appeared to be deeply absorbed with whatever he was doing, most likely reading and not wanting to be interrupted in some place few wanted to climb to. Most prisoners respected his quirkiness and rarely bothered him, and most campers and guards assumed Doc was another harmless nut case, by himself, maybe doing yoga, definitely not wanting to be social, up on some steep, hard-to-reach hillside for some strange reason. But, in fact, something much different was going on with Doc; he was engaged in his own weird scientific research.

Doc was a principled intellectual, in prison for all the wrong reasons, and prison life was especially difficult for any thinking, eccentric man. To keep his mind occupied, Doc was interested in desert ants and spent most of his daylight free time performing various studies on the ants' habits and rituals. He observed and documented the ants' visible life, their feeding, fighting, territorial defenses and warfare, care of their colonies, and all the above-ground activities they performed in an extreme physical desert world. A few of us prisoners were aware of his work, and I knew that this strange character, through his observations, had become an expert on two specific ant sub-species that inhabited the prison's terrain. To facilitate his careful study of the two groups, one red and the other black, he first identified colonies that were very difficult to reach. Using the building materials, Doc constructed intricate, reinforced steel and concrete structures directly over an ant colony's main entrance, each new building a work of art itself. One had Grecian columns supporting graceful arches, the other tiny towers overlooking open galleries and tiled courtyards, all in miniature scale and built below ground level, hidden from sight. When ready, after the ants were used to their new environment, Doc would drop scraps of specific food groups into his creation, then sit and study the ant colony's eating/fighting habits, etc. He built his living ant research sites to outlast an atomic bomb, reinforced buildings made of steel and cement, colored to look like the surrounding rock and dirt.

Doc chose his anthill structure locations with great care, as each had to be difficult to reach and built over the main entrance to the underground colony. He had to be visible to the roving guards constantly patrolling the area, yet keep the ant structures and his activity as camouflaged and invisible as possible. The safest places were on the prison's rocky, steeper hillsides. He meticulously sculpted intricate, futuristic shapes from cement, mortar, and wire that blended perfectly into the stark desert landscape. Seen from above, each structure was almost invisible. But if you sat down and looked into one from the side, a strange alien world appeared, filled with arches, and flat eating spaces on different levels. Doc carried water, cement, food, pieces of cement reinforcing metal, maybe nails, screws, and lengths of wire to each site, all hidden in his white nylon coffee mug. This smooth, rugged cup was his cement mixer, finishing/sculpting tool, and a great hole digger. The man's plan was to build a work of art that could last forever, and blow someone's mind if stumbled upon a few hundred years in the future.

One evening a patrolling guard, nicknamed 'Howdy Doody,' decided to make the difficult, uphill climb over the loose rocks, most likely just to see what trouble he could cause for the criminal doctor. It was the same for every inmate. Howdy Doody tried his best to inflict pain and suffering whenever the opportunity appeared, his insidious, obvious game always in play, the lesser mind trying to exert control over the 'elite,' minimum security prisoners surrounding him in the desert. This overweight, splay-footed, cartoon puppet of a man especially liked to hassle the brilliant Doc. The mostly-illiterate prison guards obviously enjoyed using their real, visceral power over the inmates. After tripping and stumbling up the unstable hillside to reach the doctor, he finally saw what Doc was doing, studying this strange, miniature tiered platform, like something he'd probably seen in a King Kong movie, but never before in the desert. The structure seemed carved into the rocks and covered in earth, somehow cleverly terraced into the hillside. The whole thing reeked of criminal behavior, was hard to spot from even a few feet away, and was definitely of interest to the convict he'd often seen sitting there. It had to be against some law.

In typical hack behavior, instead of simply asking Doc what he was looking at, Howdy Doody burst out laughing, overcome with pleasure as he considered his next action: the damage he was about to inflict on Doc's obviously illegal structure.

The overweight Howdy Doody stepped forward, forcing Doc out of his path, and, without warning, kicked the hidden structure with all the power he could bring to his steel-toed boot. Howdy Doody recoiled, gasping for breath, in great pain, then limped quickly down the rocky slope to find relief. The structure remained.

Doc's miniature fantasy world was carefully crafted into the rocks, secured with rebar and cement on steep hills, invisible from the road, and inaccessible to any vehicle that might hope to run over and destroy it. This guy built three or four ant palaces while I was there, and he'd rotate his ongoing research so as not to draw attention to any one structure...all made possible by his ubiquitous nylon coffee cup.

Chapter 41
Hollywood Halfway House

The day I'd dreamed of, waited for, and badly needed finally arrived. After 24 months of incarceration, Boron Federal Prison, at last, paroled me to spend the coming six months remaining on my sentence in a federally-approved half-way house in Hollywood, California. It was such an unlikely area of L.A. to warehouse ex-cons while they transitioned back into society, and the group living facility had a bad reputation for helping ex-cons overcome the lifestyles and pressures that had steered them to crime in the first place. This was the word coming to Boron via the prison grapevine.

At dawn, the prison van was waiting for the few of us leaving Boron, and it dropped me off four miles downhill at Kramer's Junction, a desolate, windy desert bus and re-fueling intersection on Highway 58 and Highway 395. The few possessions I'd kept fit into the paper grocery bag I carried: clothes, letters, and paperwork. Most of my possessions I'd passed along to friends still inside. I departed Boron a very different person than the man my now ex-wife had dropped off there two years earlier, a time far back in the distant past.

I'd certainly learned the prison lesson; the secret to never returning to prison is "If it smells even slightly like it's a crime, don't say a word, just walk away. And trust no one." I'd have to completely reinvent myself and was eagerly anticipating whatever challenges I'd soon confront. Prison churns out fierce gladiators; a few, me for one, planned to never return, but most parolees were ill-prepared to survive, let alone thrive, in the civilized society outside the walls, and many were back inside within a few months of freedom.

I was as physically fit as I'd ever been, mentally capable of taking care of myself, but unprepared for the looming emotional pressures that I'd soon be facing in the real world. A much stronger, self-contained person emerged than the Dean I'd known before. As I boarded the Greyhound bus my eyes swept front to rear for an empty seat. I didn't miss that the seated passengers avoided any eye contact with me, all surely sensing the primal, raw energy emanating from my physical presence.

I felt like an alien in an unfamiliar world, a being just cut loose from two years of tempered paranoia, anxiety, and restrained violence. My mind and body were substance-free for the first time in forever. I was alive in each new moment, a stripped-down version of my former fairly-complicated, convoluted self. I understood immediately that my physical presence, simply standing there in the aisle, told the whole story. The vibe I was emitting to the world needed some calming re-adjustment.

I had eight hours to present myself in person to the residential parolee house and program in Los Angeles, July 1985. My former writing partner, Big Ben, met my bus at the Greyhound depot near Chinatown and delivered me to my new home. Big Ben was scrambling himself to stay above water by writing screenplays, had a family, and was unable to open any doors for my future in film. But I understood. He was struggling in the industry's dog-fighting trenches just to stay sane. He'd been there for me as a friend and had only one bit of advice for me about my future in film.

"Man, good-fucking-luck. I mean it. Don't let it get you down on yourself when they fuck with you and your work, OK?" Encouraging words of wisdom from his personal screenwriting experiences. On a brighter side, he owned a two-flat building below Pico Blvd. and south of Hancock Park, with Leonard Cohen, the poet and musician, who was living in Europe at the time. Big Ben offered me the no-cost use of Cohen's empty upstairs apartment for as long as I needed, or until Leonard returned to L.A. Very cool, I now had a refuge and a place to work on my writing.

Touring the neighborhood surrounding the halfway house before I actually appeared inside, I discovered that the area was even lower-rent than described by former inmate residents. This was a decaying, 1950s James-Ellroy-Hollywood-noir seedy section of L.A., with no specific ethnic or racial identity other than simply 'the forgotten.' It had the essential crack-house and hooker hotbed sort of curb appeal – attractive to addicts and degenerates cruising by day and night, looking for some action in this run-down, inner-city, open-air realm of sadness. It also felt a bit edgy and exciting to this desert survivor.

The facility for paroled federal prisoners lived up to its reputation as well. It had a pathetic, stucco crash pad look meant for losers and junkies. I was assigned to spend my nights on a worn-out, lower bunk mattress, in an airless bedroom filled with four bunk beds. At eye level with my pillow was the lower third of a filthy glass window, painted permanently one-inch open; must be someone's sick excuse for providing fresh air ventilation to the stuffy, rank-smelling room, or whole house.

My first night of freedom came straight out of a pulp fiction novel; buzzing, biting attack mosquitoes and a late-night hooker plying her trade not one foot from my face, at my sleeping eye-level, keeping me awake most of the first night. The woman had squeezed her wide butt into the narrow space between my window and the cement-brick wall maybe 24 inches away, giving blowjobs out of sight from the passing street traffic, and just a few inches from my face. The whispered negotiations, then desperate slurping, sucking moans and groans, and occasional cries of momentary release no longer fazed me after the first few nights; everything about my new home became the inspiration for my next screenplay. After one week of nights in this place, I'd gathered enough material to begin writing 'Hollywood Halfway House.'™

I was up and out the front door by 6:15 a.m. each morning and signed myself back in there each night just before the mandatory midnight witching hour. I tried to entertain the night door guard with tasty movie-star stories, or bits of insider Hollywood gossip that I'd make up or overheard earlier in the day. Hopefully, I would divert his thoughts from drug testing me. In 1985, if you worked in film in L.A., you drank, smoked pot, and most likely used a variety of other mind-fucking drugs as well; a few drinks were allowed, but returning drunk or loaded at midnight while on parole was a bad idea.

Late one steamy hot night, a fellow resident stuck his head into the bedroom, taking orders for new floor fans, 10 bucks each, to be delivered within the hour. The bedroom was always too hot to sleep well during warmer months, as we were located too far inland to benefit from any cooling ocean breezes. The fan I ordered arrived 15 minutes later; the paroled burglar made frequent, rooftop forays into the adjacent Lowe's store, whose wall was just outside my window, stealing to support his drug habit. Junkies are unstoppably creative, clever, and industrious when supplying their never-ending, daily needs.

I had to ask him that night, "Hey, dude, it's a razor-wired jungle 'n shit all over that wall, how the fuck you manage that?"

I got a big smile in response: "You lookin' at one badass mutherfucka, y'know, wurkin' hard not 'ta jones, y'unnerstan. Yo, dude, gots my dime now?"

I gladly paid him 10 bucks for a new, kickass fan. From that night on, all sleep issues disappeared. The fan quickly replaced the stale air and its whirring blades blocked out the penetrating late-night street chatter from outside my window. After a few nights of solid sleep, the first I'd had in a long time, I was more than ready to get work making movies.

Peggy had praised and encouraged my writing skills long before my incarceration, and frequently mentioned the "production" opportunities she'd have waiting for me after prison, expressed during her visits to see me in Boron, during phone conversations, and in letters she'd written to me in jail. I'd mentioned these job offers to my parole advisor, who seemed impressed with my contacts and glowing future in Hollywood. Peggy's husband, Danny, had even spoken to my warden early in 1985, telling him I was needed on his just greenlit project about to begin shooting.

Peggy and Danny's support was instrumental in my being released from Boron six months ahead of schedule. The only problem was I believed everything they'd said or promised about the opportunities waiting for me. Even after learning that Danny's story to my warden was pure fiction, he'd never had any work in Hollywood, let alone a movie close to production, and that Peggy's job offers existed only in her mind, I couldn't really believe that both friends had been deceiving me all along. Was I naive or just dumb? How little I understood about this film world I'd chosen to live in.

I'd had enough foresight to store my Cadillac in L.A., so it was waiting for me upon my release. During my first week of freedom, I'd slowly cruise west in the warm dawn over the still-quiet, peaceful streets, through neighborhoods poor to wealthy. I'd head to Peggy's rented mansion high above the Roxy Club, cruising along on Sunset Blvd., one of life's simpler pleasures I'd missed in recent years. I'd arrive long before Peggy was up or awake, spread myself out on her comfortable living room couch, and take a nap in the quiet of her morning neighborhood. I'd often try to visualize Peggy flying down the wide staircase one morning with glorious news for me about my future career.

Peggy issued my marching orders one morning exactly as I'd imagined she would. Only, though delivered during a very dramatic morning entrance coming down her staircase, it had a different ending for me.

"T-W-D (my nom de plume for a piece I'd written for her Rolling Stone 'History of the Sixties' collection of stories, Teenie Weenie Deenie), what great luck! We've got something and a huge favor you can do for me, too. It's brilliant, an interim bit until something better appears! You're the perfect sweetheart to manage my home reconstruction, don't you agree?"

She needed a trusted worker to oversee the interior remodeling of her recent Baja Hancock Park real estate purchase, and she knew I had to demonstrate job-searching progress to my parole officer each month.

"Peggy, that's brilliant! There's no one better suited, I'm perfect for the job, what a great idea!" I enthusiastically lied to my new boss as she swept by my resting body on her way to the kitchen.

"No way, control yourself!" I'm thinking it's not the right time to ask. She'll be offended, very uncool to discuss the important details, questions like, what's the wage for a 10-hour day?

I'd first met Peggy through my Berkeley/New York friend and lover, Franny. They'd been roommates at Pomona College. Peggy employed Franny's artistic and creative vision for costuming and set design in a few of her early films. When Peggy lived in Manhattan, she was an editor at the New York Times Magazine. Her husband, Danny, had agented the publishing of the Pentagon Papers, and ran with a heavy politico-literary crowd; interesting friends for a pirate pot smuggler, and I felt a deep respect for Peggy's and Danny's risk-taking and edge-balancing efforts to save the world. Peggy and I flirted in muted, subtle exchanges and eye contact, all in great fun. When Peggy headed to L.A. to work for Peter Gruber, then David Geffen, I'd drop by her Sunset Blvd. offices with gifts of great weed and she relished listening to insider tales of my smuggling escapades.

The following morning I was still enjoying Peggy's couch in the cool morning comfort, maybe for the last time, when Franny appeared in the living room. She was in L.A. working on a Peggy film. Peggy hadn't mentioned that my former lover was working for her, or that Franny was in town. After inquiring about Peggy's whereabouts, Franny whispered, "Shuush," holding a finger to her lips, and beckoned me to follow her into an adjoining room. I quietly shut the door behind me as Franny produced a letter from her shoulder bag.

"It's a letter from Peggy. She wrote to me a few months ago, while you were still in prison," Franny revealed. "Read it quickly, and don't dare tell Peggy I showed it to you."

In the letter, Peggy explained to Franny how they could

leverage my post-prison situation to their mutual benefit. Peggy had no plans to find work for me in film, but they could hire me for less than $3 an hour to manage the remodel project, and Dean would do whatever else was needed doing to get the house finished ASAP.

"Dean's such a faithful puppy dog, he'll do whatever we want without a complaint," concluded Peggy.

Well, thank you, Peggy! Stunning! Another WHAM! BAM! body slam, wake-the-fuck-up jolt, felt in the pit of my stomach, real information that hurt me badly from head to toe; just what the struggling convict needed to know to get back in the groove.

Franny was doing me a real favor, forcing me to realize the true nature of my current relationship with Peggy. I returned the letter to Franny and she left, having her own personal demons to deal with. She'd known for a while that my friendship with Peggy had only been about what I could do for Peggy. The veil had been lifted and the truth left me feeling like shit.

With no other employment options in sight, I jumped into the remodeling project; I needed spending money. Still believing I had cash coming from my divorce settlement with Chelsea, I'd been living on a stash of credit cards I'd kept for just such a time in my life. As far as anyone knew, I had savings to last a lifetime, when, in fact, the exact opposite was my real situation. If I was patient, if I could hold on for a while longer, something to do with film might still appear, maybe through Peggy or Julie, an agent I had reconnected with and who I'd been seriously dating, seeing every day. But Peggy's lying abuse had already begun. I was forewarned and unconfused when, not long after jumping into the remodel, Peggy started issuing me new orders.

We were discussing some aspect of the construction project when Peggy, out of the blue, let loose her new power and control over me: "By the way, you need to stop seeing Julie, I have a big problem with her."

That was it, nothing more, Peggy had a problem with the woman I'd been seeing every night for weeks, and was surely falling in love with. Peggy's direct order wasn't up for discussion; I'd been instructed and that was that.

Without thinking, and almost laughing out loud, I said, "Jesus, Peggy! Cut it out! You can't be serious. Please, tell me you're only fucking with me."

But was I ever wrong. My little outburst fell flat on the floor as the now pissed-off Peggy turned and stormed out of the house.

Peggy's lack of empathy was profound. Her need to wield absolute control over her workers was beyond anything I'd ever experienced, or considered possible from her before. Her normally narcissistic behavior was fairly predictable and even insightful and humorous. What had occurred between us was too weird right then to understand. Surely I'd misinterpreted her intentions, or had it really just happened?

The repercussions were immediate, a stern lesson in my former friend's quirky moods and underlying motivations. Peggy's bottom line was absolute: subservient obedience and nothing less. I showed up for work the following day, prepared to apologize immediately for my behavior and any silly misunderstandings if this still seemed necessary.

When Peggy appeared later in the day, not only did she fire me on the spot, but she also accused me of stealing money from her petty cash remodeling fund. In one fell swoop, Peggy eliminated me entirely from her life and left me with no possibility for redemption in the future.

It's hard to imagine how many abandoned souls' careers and ruined, forgotten fellow human dreams she's left in the wake of her relentless pursuit of success. Peggy comes off as being so confident of her abilities and insights, and also, so self-absorbed, that she had the balls to write an 'insider's' expose of some of the film industry's worst behaviors, revelations, and tales about her most ambitious, deluded colleagues and deceitful lovers, a look at everyone she experienced but herself. Peggy's first published novel, is, in fact, the actual story of her own twisted life and world, and her compulsive drive to find and gain ultimate control and power over her associates, at any cost.

So, OK then, regarding my career in film? Hey, like everything else happening in my life, I knew enough to stand back, take a deep breath, and try to stay cool. I'd just have to play it by ear. And if Peggy didn't get back to me, well, I was already on top of my backup plan.

My go-to backup plan was another film industry insider and friend, Kenneth: an unpretentious, hip contemporary who I'd been told was from very old East Coast large green. We'd connected easily when Franny introduced us during an earlier New York smuggling caper. Kenneth had written to me in prison that he'd moved west, his passion had turned to film, and he planned to open a production company in L.A., "and be sure to look me up if you get to L.A."

I'd contacted Kenneth after settling in at the halfway house and was invited to "come by, I'm having a few friends over..." at his home in West Hollywood. "Can't wait to see you, Teenie Weenie, lots to catch up on...introduce you to some interesting folks...must be ready for some fun..."

Ready? Shit, just to be invited to a real party was more fun than I'd had in years. I hadn't a clue what to expect. I'd never been to a real Hollywood salon before.

Kenneth's modest bungalow was standing room only, packed with friendly, animated faces. Kenneth saw me as I entered and beckoned me over. He's a tall man, at least as tall as my own six feet, and one observation I've made about the film world is that it is strangely over-populated with short people. So it was easy for Kenneth to catch my entrance. The mood was brilliant and boisterous. While threading my way through the party-goers to greet him, I had a whips-and-jingles, spine-shivering moment, realizing that, for the first time in years, I was happy and, in fact, a free man. I had to squeeze back an urge to burst into tears in front of so many strangers. Yes, I was really fucking free and it felt good to be alive! "This is it," a voice in my head whispered. "You've hit the jackpot." I was more than ready, willing, and able to have some fun that night.

Kenneth welcomed me with a hearty hug and caught me up on his life as we walked through his home, stopping frequently to introduce me to the actors, artists, writers, musicians, studio executives, producers, gaffers, audio engineers, and friends who gathered regularly at his place after work. He bragged to everyone that I was fresh out of prison, a survivor with a wild, mysterious history, and a writer with amazing tales to tell; I achieved instant party status, certified A-OK as a cool guy to know.

I'd arrived in Los Angeles believing I had allies in Hollywood, and Kenneth's nightly gathering of creative minds was the big boost that my self-respect desperately needed. Kenneth's salon embraced me as a celebrity, a hero returning from war. The stress from my recent confrontation with Peggy had been stronger than I'd wanted to believe, and being at Kenneth's that night lifted pounds of dead weight from my body, and my spirits rose without effort.

I was hanging with industry insiders: David from L.A.'s popular punk band, 'X,' and Hudson M., a co-creator of 'Cadillac Ranch.'[1] I met Margie, one of the first rock video producers, from a well-known, old East Coast banking family, and the first in her family to sport tattoos, and Kevin Jarre, one of my favorite screenwriters. Has-been, current, and budding actors, screen-writers, agents, underground directors, studio executives, and film producers, above-the-line staff, and below-the-line workers, all mingled, drank, got stoned, and treated Kenneth's old friend like a welcome breath of fresh air.

It was one of these evenings that Kenneth asked me if I remembered Julie, his ex-girlfriend, the one I'd met years before in New York.

"How could I ever forget her," I replied.

Kenneth, chuckling, said, "Let me re-introduce you, Julie's a big-time agent now, she's single, you should really get to know her, Teenie Weenie." He led me to the spot where Julie was sitting, smiling and very relaxed in a decorator chair, a tall glass that looked like bourbon in her hand, almost as if she was waiting for us to come to her.

"Of course, the dashing smuggler, I remember you well," she greeted me. With an even more inviting smile,

---

1   Doug Michels did the installation of 10 Cadillacs buried nose-first in the ground in Amarillo, Texas, 1974.

gazing deeply into my eyes, "Your time in prison has served you well, at least in the 'looking-good' department."

I blushed, realizing I had taken her proffered hand in mine to shake, and I hadn't let go. My god, she was beautiful, now a full-grown woman, no longer the precocious, impudent teenage Yale student I'd met back in Kenneth's penthouse apartment.

"Doing splendidly yourself, if I may say so," I replied, and relaxed my hold on her petite hand and dainty fingers.

Julie listened to my stories, seemed fascinated by tales of my life behind bars, and said there was at least one, maybe more, great prison stories that would work as screenplays.

"So, Dean, sweet-cakes, write the good one," she said. "Write the goddamn screenplay and I'll sell it for you."

What? Someone thinks my story is sellable? Someone who I'm going to sleep with tonight? Her words and feelings were exciting, like sweet icing on a delicious cake; my first real taste of possibility after incarceration.

How quickly we hit it off, and how quickly this very personable, seductive Julie reeled me into her soft, unattached, well-endowed world that first balmy Hollywood evening at Kenneth's.

OK, I wasn't stupid; I understood some of this game. No matter that I was falling head over heels for Julie, most likely our relationship would be short-term, only about the immediate pleasures we could provide one another. To be (was this really happening?) pursued on all fronts by a so-young, so-smart beauty who understood the sensuous, with the added bonus of very inviting, very large, creamy-white breasts as part of the deal, this worked for me. Julie pulled me in under her stunning umbrella of tricks, then directly into her bed.

That's what Hollywood agents do: Identify new talent, do whatever it takes to sign them up, and then quickly get them started on a project. In my case, everything moved at the speed of light after that first mutual attraction at Kenneth's. Those initial magical explorations, intensified moments of mutual lust, were working their best on both of us. Julie seemed to enjoy my company and the intimate hours we'd spend together each morning before she'd leave for work. The sex was as much fun as I'd remembered. She brought me back into my body. Perhaps we'd eat a tasty breakfast somewhere nice before she was off for the day.

We'd meet for drinks after work, occasionally just the two of us, but more often for her personal networking. If I was invited, I always enjoyed the company and introductions to her world of movers and shakers. These daily social hours could be followed by an intimate dinner, or a working dinner, then later a party, a visit to Kenneth's, or to a pre-release screening, where every interaction was connected to her work. I enjoyed every opportunity to be included in Julie's world and to hang out with her friends and associates.

In no time at all, it felt like we'd progressed from the initial infatuation to a much deeper connection, with possibilities for the future. I certainly felt that way. I was being opened and lifted emotionally in ways I'd forgotten were possible, emerging from a soulless desert world of lost dreams, expanding into a state of grace and love that included a fountain of youth. When Julie was up to making the extra effort, she could turn her normal, physical being into a raven-haired, Memphis-bred southern beauty, packaged in a striking, voluptuous, alabaster-skinned gift of pure, unblemished femininity. I loved the tiny pirate's sword blades piercing her ear lobes that she'd choose for special occasions.

I imagined that Julie's attraction to me was due in part to my edgy background, unspoken experiences, and she enjoyed being seen with ("Do you think? Is he…?") a potentially dangerous ex-con.

Julie was immersed on all fronts in the industry that I hoped to break into. She represented a wide range of industry talent including very bankable actors, musical artists, directors, and screenwriters. It felt like I was covered, and moving forward.

Dating a person positioned higher up the food chain than yourself, a person who can potentially make or break your future in Hollywood, I quickly learned, was to become skilled in anticipating the exact moment to reach for, grab, or pick up the bar-dinner-breakfast-theater check/tab and then pay for it. It was an industry-wide practice and expectation, an investment in your own success, a small token of your appreciation for the tremendous effort your guest(s) made each day on your behalf, working to ensure your future livelihood.

I had that stack of credit cards I'd collected to use for situations exactly like this, to invest in opportunities that could enhance my future in film, and my financial security. Another dumb shit Hollywood dream, for sure, a rationalization justified by the bigger picture. One always had to consider the bigger picture. For instance, if I ever did hit the jackpot with a killer screenplay, the money invested now would come back in aces.

Passing time again felt almost dream-like. Was I really coming back to a new and better life? Driving west with the rising sun each morning, waving to the same blond-wigged hooker working the same block of Fountain Ave. on the edge of West Hollywood, was as real to me as my new life with Julie. To hell with Peggy, I was a player now in this incredible dream world, with a completely new life beyond my wildest expectations. My path seemed laid out in front of me, waiting to be embraced and made my own. Julie and her lover were an 'item' around town, and we were seen at many A-/B+ level events and parties. Julie never argued when I paid for dinner and drinks. It was the price of admission, and well worth the cost. She knew everyone and took me inside her close-knit piece of Hollywood, the just-out-of-prison edgy screenwriter working on a great story, a man to watch for. You bet!

I learned that Julie represented a successful screenwriter, Dao, who'd hit gold with his screenplay for an animated film of a popular children's fantasy. No shit, this was the very same witty Dao I'd worked with 25 years before on our high school newspaper. Having history with one of Julie's favorite clients felt very cool, very karmic. A childhood friend, with big-time Hollywood credits. Julie immediately arranged to partner me with him to co-author 'Hollywood

The Substitute Asshole

Half-Way House.' I'd write the story, and Dao would step in to clean up my screen-writing ignorance.

Very cool. I was writing each day in the Baja-Hancock upstairs flat. I'd drive once a week to Dao's Malibu hillside spread for his input, which usually meant waiting for hours before being granted a few minutes of his precious time for a brief conversation.

Dao had been aloof in high school, brilliant but uninterested in sharing anything he deemed too personal. We were never really friends, so I'd appreciated his keen wit and intelligence from afar. I learned that he struggled constantly to fulfill a studio contract that paid him to deliver a screenplay a year to the buyer. The buyers rarely turned his work into films but could claim ownership of important new work from a well-known screenwriter. The concept of paying a good writer just to keep his writing unavailable to all competitors was a new twist on earning a meaningful living. Each year Dao delivered a script for a fee, which was possibly the best deal a Hollywood writer could ever hope to achieve.

We worked on the screenplay for three months. The project moved along at a nice pace and it felt like the effort might really turn out well. Hey, Dao and I had found a creative groove, my evening life with Julie was exciting and fun. I was meeting and being seen and partying with the right people. One might think I was on an upward trajectory to newfound fame and fortune. There was one slight downside that I faced daily: I had to be in bed at the halfway house by midnight sharp, and then wake up at 5:45 a.m. to drive back to Julie's bed each morning. I needed to be the first person she'd wake up to before leaving for work. Out of sight, out of mind.

I used credit to participate in this costly game. Either a writer is so incredibly talented that he gets a deal the first week in town, or he slowly networks (buys or assumes debt) his way into a deal, just like I was doing, which only made sense if the writer could actually deliver on all his personal hype and promises. The deal game begins with buying dinners and drinks for new group of industry friends, anyone who might help get a deal secured. I understood the routine and knew that I was a 'pay-as-you-go' deal-seeker; good enough to hang out and see what developed, but not necessarily a sure thing.

After six months of good times with Julie and associates, I realized one night while trying to pay for dinner with her at Musso and Frank's that I was totally broke. Duh! My last good credit card was rejected. Embarrassed, I mentioned my financial crisis to my friend, agent, and lover.

"Julie, I can't cover our dinner tonight. Do you..." That was enough information for Julie to reply, "That's all right, Dean. I'll pay. I don't ever want to see you again, OK?"

And with that, she got up and left me sitting at the table.

"That's it? That was funny. I mean, what just happened? Was she for real? Nah, she's just goofing with me." I was in shock, and total denial, believing everything would be back on track in a minute or two. "Hello, Julie, please pick up the phone..." No way, dude! I left her a hopeful message.

In Hollywood, when two phone messages go unreturned, you know something really bad has happened, that you've been removed from at least one person's 'must return' caller list. My slippery agent lady lover had vanished from my life, for real, just like that. Wham Bam, it's over big guy!

Well, at least my old buddy Dao still existed, but again, I only reached his answering machine. "Hey, Dao, it's Dean, are you home? – you'll never guess what happened last night – hey, have you heard from Julie? Please give me a call when you get this, OK?"

I waited for two days for Dao to return my calls before driving to Malibu for a face-to-face with him. Both cars were in the driveway, meaning someone was home. No one answered my knocking on the front door, no one opened it to welcome me inside. Julie had cut me off from everyone, it was really over. Cold.

I understood that my high school buddy was just another one of Hollywood's paid-to-remain-a-loser and a complete fucking asshole. And I saw in a flash the common theme that had been woven through most of my relationships for a very long time: I alone had chosen to associate with, to work and try to be friends with, some real fucking assholes, for as long as I could remember.

The intense pain and suffering I felt at that moment morphed into a milder sort of manageable PTSD over the next few days, and my conscious, be-here-now life became easier to deal with on a day-to-day basis.

A week later I completed my allotted parole term in the half-way house, and I just packed up and left Hollywood. It was spring, 1986, and I was able to see the wild opportunities for a seasoned sales guy like myself bursting open in Silicon Valley, just a short commute from the shitty house I still owned back in Santa Cruz. It was time, and I was still young enough to try to get real for once. I borrowed $3,000 from Ben and Sandra (saved my ass they did), packed up, and moved back to the house I was awarded in the divorce in Soquel.

Part IV:
A Fresh Start

After considering his post-prison attempt at Hollywood to be an utter failure, my dad returned to Northern California without many prospects and completely out of money. He decided to restart life in the familiar area of Santa Cruz County. He reconnected with an old friend, my mother, and they got married in 1988. They had their first daughter, my sister, Anne, in 1989, and later twins, me and Nik, in 1992.

While Dean was struggling to find direction in life after prison, having children gave him a whole new purpose. He discovered a new depth of what it means to love another human. However, divorce and a shared custody arrangement of every other weekend created a new set of problems. He tried to make the most of the diminished role that he would play in our lives.

Dean did not get around to writing extensively about the final decades of his life, but it does not lessen the importance of these years to him. Like the rest of his life, they were complicated – full of thoughts about existentialism, legacy, family, love, and mortality. These were topics that were difficult for us to talk about, but working on this memoir certainly helped us begin to broach them.

The following includes stories Dean wrote about this time in his life, but I have also inserted a couple of letters and emails that he wrote to his children towards the end of his life to help the reader understand the relationship he had with us.

-Evan

Chapter 42
Mary's Gifts

Circa 1987

I used to talk to Mary Bridges – although we'd never met in person – while slowly wandering through her former estate, now my new home. I'd pick up an object like a heavy crystal jar and wonder what on earth she'd used it for. I liked this lady and spoke with her as if she stood next to me and she always replied. "Candy, I filled that one with jelly beans, silly boy."

Buying Mary Bridges' home and complete estate on Hugus Ave. was a welcome surprise. The house was lovely from the outside, all redwood unpainted board and bat construction, real wooden window frames and sashes, hidden away at the end of a short, dead-end street, overlooking Branciforte Creek below from a forested bluff. The house was surrounded by tall eucalyptus and mature fir trees, all alive with monarch butterflies and migrating birds.

The warm, weathered wood house felt like paradise to me, a refuge for this abandoned, worn-down, recently freed felon. It was a safe, protected space to regroup, re-design myself; a place to contemplate the meaning of it all, and to consider the 'here and now,' and my life from here on out. It was the perfectly hidden-in-plain-sight dwelling for a suffering veteran of the '60s Revolution to recover and then reinvent himself.

I hadn't yet settled into accepting or even understanding much of this new reality with its rejection from so many friends and lovers and the loss of any meaningful income. I was never quite sure why everything had turned out this way. I had lots of suspicions and theories to consider, which so far led nowhere. I'd found no substantiated proof to explain or even help me understand what had gone on to make me such an outcast, and it was still coming down all around me. All that remained, all that could be salvaged from my mini-empire, was enough cash for the down payment on Mary Bridges' estate.

I'd been kept from inspecting the inside of the house by the probate executor, some distant relative of the recently deceased Mary, and I only figured out why she wouldn't let me in much later. She was searching high and low for some hidden treasure that Mary must have squirreled away amidst her incredible collections of exotic furniture, marble chests and table tops, large oil paintings, and complete sets of everything a new homeowner might need in the way of pots, pans, beds, sheets, and any other furnishing one could imagine.

I had purchased Mary's estate lock, stock, and barrel, and finally took possession when the relative decided to leave the premises. I understood that this relative must have found whatever it was she was looking for, but there was so much minor and major treasure to examine that it had taken her quite a few weeks of assured privacy to do so.

All the time I was settling into my new house, I was wondering just what the treasure was that the executor finally found. What valuable prize – or prizes – had Mary squirreled away in my house? It was a game I started playing with her, asking her out loud as I sorted through her old things, tossing out a lot of useless junk. "Yo, Mary, am I getting closer to your hidden treasures?"

The light switch cover plates had all been unscrewed from the walls. The furnace vent covers had been unscrewed and left lying on the floor throughout the house. There was food going rotten in the fridge, balls of string and rubber bands stuffed into kitchen drawers, a complete set of cast iron cookware, and a wonderful variety of crystal wine glasses. Mary had been a collector of the unusual, and when she died, it all was included in the sale of her house. There were at least a dozen fine Oriental rugs that covered the wall-to-wall carpeting, and there were dozens of small to large oil paintings and prints purchased during her world travels, along with rows and rows of bookshelves filled with leather-bound collections of the world's greatest writers. No obvious treasures were left for me to find in that vast collection of strange stuff.

I began by throwing out the top shelf of old vitamin pill bottles stored in the fridge. Poor old Mary had died from some form of cancer, and had mounted a valiant attempt to stop the disease with vitamin therapy. Jars filled with pickles and beets, all kinds of old health foods, went directly into the garbage.

After throwing out 30 half-filled, brown glass jars of old vitamins from the 40 or so jars stuffed into the freezer compartment, I finally opened a large bottle only to discover it was filled with folded five and ten-dollar bills, as were another five of the remaining 10 jars in the freezer. I had to laugh, for I'd never know how much money I'd already thrown out, already moved to the local garbage dump. I'd probably thrown away a small fortune, but no one will ever know if Mary had left me a fortune, or not. What a trip, money stored in the freezer, hard, cold cash. I had to thank Mary for the few hundred bucks that I did accidentally stumble upon. "Mary, you are one tricky little thing, you sure are. I want to thank you for all the stuff you left me. I've used it all, having moved in owning nothing, so it was all put to good use."

Mary was good to me at a time when everything else in my life had turned pretty grim. Her gifts, her possessions, inspired me to start moving forward once again. She's an impetus that still affects everything I've done in the last 30 years, and she was behind my making some life-altering moves and decisions that still drive me forward into action, even to write this letter.

Chapter 43
Victims by Our Own Hands

24 July 1996

Visited with a therapist, Elaine, tonight, 9 p.m. This is the only time I have been able to find someone to see me. It was the first meeting and I want to go back for more. I haven't talked to a soul on a personal level for so long. I need it.

She suggested I find an expert in "eye movement" therapy for PTSD, something new that seems to break through ingrained barriers and effect change in a very short time, compared to months with traditional talk therapy, and then continue seeing her.

PTSD, she got it, what has been knotted up in me for so many years now. And the outcome is a complete lack of empowerment. She thinks both Stella, my current wife, and I are totally at the mercy of this lack of control over our lives, and that both of us need to discover how we each create our own worlds as victims, but victims by our own hands.

So far, Stella and I seem to keep from taking any responsibility for ourselves; we keep blaming the other one for the terrible feelings and situations we get into. I can go with this, and explore my own miserable outlook because at some time I lost control of my situation, and when I lost the attention I craved from Stella, things just went downhill.

The prison experience, coupled with the internalizing of the suffering and losing any power to make things better, has stressed me out. And now, when something brings to mind my lack of power, I am overrun by the stress, and I react.

I need to gain some understanding of this problem so that I can go forward without its crushing pressure always guiding my emotions.

~ ~ ~

31 July 1996

I spent 45 minutes with Elaine tonight and went over the brief history of my life. Seems like I was on a pretty good roll until 1981, and suddenly everything stopped, changed direction, and things continually went downhill for many years.

There was a previous life of great excitement, travel, good times, and good friends that was suddenly turned completely inside out when I was sent to prison – post traumatic stress. I'm a perfect candidate.

Elaine says she was amazed that both Stella and I thought we could handle having two more children and me starting out in a new business, all the pressures and problems. Well, I guess it turned out she knew something we didn't know, and we can't handle it. She said she spoke with Stella about this, and that was pretty much when Stella and she stopped being as close as they had been before. I don't know, where do I fit in?

This life is a little too reminiscent of Boron. I put in my hours at the job then come back to my cell. This room is bigger, and I can do many things now that I couldn't then, but the emotional landscape is pretty bleak for me these days.

Chapter 44
Tales to Tell You

To My Children:
Seven years ago I decided to pull these stories together into a letter I'd written to the three of you. But I had some common sense parenting questions, like should I tell my kids these perhaps too-personal adventures and stories? When younger, you all were fascinated by pirate tales and fantasy cartoons. Well, now you're my three adult children, and I hope you'll enjoy knowing some stories about the days when Daddy was a modern-day sort of outcast or pirate, maybe 'outlaw' better describes my lifestyle. I was partially that, with touches of Robin Hood and Jodorowski's 'El Topo' added to the mix.

My stories tell of real people I knew, the crazy-dangerous things we did, the intimate love I pursued, the moments of pure pleasure, and the pain often too difficult to avoid. There isn't a simple plot or thread that binds them all into one clear lifeline. My tales are of the intimate depths of pure love and the ease with which I could thumb my nose at having a normal life. I'm describing my life so you'll know who I was, and who I am. A letter won't do it. I'll just let the separate stories stand on their own.

My generation was the first to travel without a plan or care, on big, fast airplanes, to every corner of the world. Some stories I've never told another soul will be exposed to public viewing here. I pursued my outlaw life and sources of income around the globe and was at the head of the line of hippie entrepreneurs building fortunes through international smuggling, where each new connection must be kept separate and safe from any others. Some work I did felt bigger than life, tied to my desire to find and lead a spiritual existence; my efforts had a huge effect on the society I rejected and the generation I identified with. Other stories I held close to my heart to avoid the pain of conflict and jealousy, or because I didn't want to give them up. They are mostly unconnected tales without a thread to tie them into a story that makes any sense, but they all happened to me during an incredibly magical few years of my strange, exciting, and real personal history. I was there, living in the center of a worldwide revolution, and I want you to know about your father, so, hey, enjoy my stories, if you can. There is one major point to remember: The outlaw life I led doesn't exist today. Times have changed since back in the day. The Man is much better at doing his job today. Be smarter, know this, and don't do like your Daddy did. OK?

What do I mean when I say I was an outlaw? My god, how presumptuous of me, putting such dangerous stories into my own kids' heads! God forbid. But by the time you might read this, you'll all be adults, so fuck it, let's go for it.

The '60s outlaws, pranksters, actors, entertainers, masters of the put-on, and righteous criminals were rewarded for creative risks – like importing, producing, and delivering consistently high-quality illegal products with only the most trustworthy customer service. We were all the time searching for some kind of pure freedom and the next promising illegal venture to invest our illegal gains in. One former outlaw friend named me 'Rockets' – in and out of sight, always on the move; others called me 'TWD,' short for Teenie Weenie Deenie, in and out of your heart and soul before you could say anything.

Some outlaws didn't know my real name or my role in different transactions, and that's the way I liked it best. I did most of my work behind the scenes, arranging for shit to happen and staying out of the limelight when everything happened as planned. I never went into the biz for fame or glory; no, in fact, I went to great lengths to remain anonymous, out of the public eye. I've mentioned to you guys that

I took thousands of photographs of the '60s subculture, my world travels, and the people I knew along the way; great pictures too. Yet I've never shown them publicly, had a gallery exhibit, or tried to sell them, always working to maintain my privacy. They go hand-in-hand with the stories I'm writing for you. In fact, they are a part of the same story, but created by me as an artist rather than an outlaw. My photos document many of the people and friends I'm writing about, and maybe I should use them to illustrate the stories.

So, what am I writing about? What does all this mean? Is this outlaw fantasy bullshit flying outta my brain? The outlaws I knew and traveled with rode the first waves of a psychedelic tsunami that quickly covered the whole country. We shared a camaraderie, a revived sense of the potential of a family, of a humanity that I believed (at the beginning) might change and heal America's selfish goals and the destructive products it delivered to the rest of the world. The '60s wave I rode grew out of the minds and hearts of a generation that felt lost. Yet we were hopeful souls, searching for ways to create a better life for everyone on this planet. We dispensed powerful new visions of world insight that offered a renewed spiritual faith in mankind, and did so with an openness that filled many seekers with immediate awe, love, and respect for our efforts. Our work also generated tremendous fear and bad reactions from those still rooted in America's racist beliefs and laws, leading to negative responses to our work by our government and established religions, both milking this fear to grow stronger and more powerful in a very short time. They initiated new laws and rules to control and limit the '60s effect on our nation.

Even with the onslaught of new drug restrictions in the '60s, the waves we rode continued to push inland from both coasts, covering the land, driven forward by the incredible power and energy generated by new ideas and imagined possibilities, converging everywhere with a force so powerful that it changed the consciousness of the land. This wave of a new consciousness continued flowing in all directions, reaching into the smallest nooks and crannies, into every community and back-roads village. Acid and pot temporarily replaced the popular alcohol culture. New music styles, ageless spiritual practices, and meditation were embraced by the youthful generation. What began in California and New York combined into a perfectly unbalanced, unstable fuel that, once ignited, changed everything in its unstoppable path. Today it's called 'The Sixties.'

Chapter 45
Letters to Big Ben

Big Ben,[1]

It's been seven years since our last sighting, here in sunny Santa Cruz. Man, I don't believe it but zooooom the time just flew by. Are you moving into a purchased home in Newton? Are you the same Big Ben of old? I've attached a photo of my kids, taken before the boys' senior prom last Friday, and they are, left to right, Evan, Anne, and Nik. Nik is about 6'5", 200 lbs.

I'm gonna miss my kids pretty soon, as their mother is taking them to Europe in three weeks, and they'll stay for the summer after she returns, traveling with friends from high school until it's time to head off to college in the fall. They like Europe, who doesn't? I'm driving a limo from Santa Cruz to different airports a few times a week, kinda fun sometimes, interesting folk that tell me what the world looks like, if I ask. It's pocket money, since I'm not getting enough from Social Security to make any real difference. Good thing Jeanie and I are close because she's got a little fund that lets us manage without too much extra work being needed. Without that, I'd be on your doorstep for sure.

Not that I'd expect to be let inside, but it's something to know there are a couple of people I still call 'friends' roaming about here and there. I'm starting my own income mill, bought the web URL 'hippie-dippie.com,' and want to sell

---

1   Dean's friend and former writing partner who helped him get on his feet when he arrived in Hollywood after release from prison.

my historical photos as humorous greeting cards. I'll make a million. Then I'll probably die. Mainly though, I've got some great photos from 'the day,' as in 'back in'...that even make me laugh, so why not publish them as cards? I just started thinking about this recently.

I have some nice photos from when you had the greasy spoon joint, and many shots of your former, closest associates and, now, non-existent friends and family. I won't use any photos on greeting cards taken in Boron though, knowing about the current, litigation-happy generation.

Anne works in a bakery selling cakes and coffee, where she gets stacks of dimes in tips, and even rolls them up sometimes. I found a roll of dimes in the car today, reminding me of one 'Johnnie Dimes' I knew at Boron, a mob collector, quite short and muscular. His hands were small and he could only wrap them around a roll of dimes (a roll of quarters would've been the tool of choice) when he needed to enforce physical sanctions on a debtor. I guess it helped the effectiveness of each punch when he smacked them around until they paid up, hence the nickname. He is funny to think about only in hindsight, for sure.

I still think 'Hollywood Halfway House' would be a funny flick, now more than ever with the youth. At Boron, every new arrival was first strip-searched, the standard humiliation and degradation procedure, including body cavity probes, given used Kong-sized Air Force khakis to replace street clothes, a blanket, a sheet, and lastly, handed a sturdy, nylon coffee/drinking cup with a removable lid. You need to drink lots of liquids in the Mojave Desert. I came across my old cup recently, 25 years later, and was flooded with memories of all the variety of uses the prisoners found for their cups – a story in itself.

But what about yourself, Big Ben? How's your back, R U doing the BB playoffs this year? I sorta follow who's on top. The name 'Magic' always reminds me of the highly refined, pure freebase a former associate was loving 30 years back. I mainly read a lot of crime fiction from everywhere for entertainment, most recently with detectives from France, Norway, and Bangkok. Are you working on writing?

My left hand goes to sleep when I type for more than 10 minutes. That, and not being able to walk for very long, are my only bad body complaints…in that the high blood pressure meds removed much of the ol' libido. I find it truly liberating to live with a lessened sex drive protruding into my daily life. Freedom from desire it is, at least from the one desire I held so closely, and so loved for so long. I have no problem dealing with a lack of desires and ongoing dramas. Mind you, every once in a while, we get moved into action, and that too is wonderful, but it's really about the intimacy.

I've been scanning and then photoshopping my 5,000 color slides from the '60s and working on the related memoir story, the same story I've been working on for 20 years… there's plenty of spiritual angst that today I find humorous. Another interesting change is the unexpected deaths recently in my aging '60s friends, so 'Here We Go!'…it's now a race to the finish line.

It seems like a long time, but also an even shorter time as my mind flies, since your visit a few years ago, and I hope we'll get to hang for a while again sometime soon. I think that after my kids are out of the house, Jeanie and I'll do some road touring here and there, including back your way, and why not? What's it like for you to be this far removed from the daily kid-raising experience? I miss them already, and I hardly know them. I see that Sara is doing something in L.A., can't tell exactly what from her Facebook story.

I think about you frequently, it's all good from where I sit, and I hope all is still another mystery, as usual, in your latest world.

-Big Dean

~ ~ ~

13 January 2014

So the reason I've been so quiet the past few months is that I am really starting to feel my age, a senseless excuse, of course, but reasonable in light of what this aging brings into play. It's certainly not because I never think about you. In fact, I think about you, talk to you, just about every day in my own way, and always when I open the Kindle to pick up where I last left off.

So I learned in late October that I now must go toe to toe with a new challenge (on top of the scumbags Scoliosis, Lumbar Stenosis, Spondylosis, and the brutal Facet Arthropathy). It has been lurking in the shadows, unseen, for a long time now. It's a sneaky bastard, a dark, insidious boogie-man. For a while I knew something was moving into my territory, like a cat on its belly creeping into the backyard: the infamous piece of shit, Parkinson's Disease.

I've been wanting to write to you for a few months now, but just couldn't bring myself to the task...and I didn't understand why it was so hard...and since I've seen what the problem is, I still am having difficulty actually sitting down here to put words together in an email...now it's the meds, which are very strange and debilitating, but supposed to settle in soon so I will regain some of what is lacking, mainly in fine muscle control and balance and processing systems.

Today is my 71st birthday, and already my brain wants to stop me from writing any more. It's not so bad now that I put a name to it. So, from one kind of crip to another, Happy New Year!

~ ~ ~

13 February 2014

Hey, sorry I'm late getting back to you. Happy Valentine's Day.

Two weeks ago I met with the head of UCSF's Parkinson's Clinic, and he told me it's pretty clear that I have Parkinson's. DUH! He was a nice guy, tested me for over an hour, recommended I skip experimenting with different PD drugs, each with its own negative side effects, and just get down with Sinemet, the one that usually works for 10 years until it doesn't work anymore. He asked, "So you're 71 now...Do you think you'll live longer than 10 more years?" I doubt it, so now that's what I'm doing, and I'm getting better movement-wise, bit by bit.

I also was introduced by a local M.D. to a friend of his with Parkinson's and we had a wonderful face to face, two guys sitting frozen in their chairs, eyes rarely blinking, talking about what we've got. His name is Howard. He says he knew you a while ago, he's a friend of Tom H. (who apparently also now has Parkinson's, but Howard doesn't ever hear from him much anymore since Tom found out). Anyway, Howard teaches Public Speaking at Cabrillo College, and sits on many non-profit boards, and owns a marketing company. So Howard and I hit it off pretty well, and plan to see more of one another as we keep moving on down the line.

I've been busy with Evan, and Nik and Anne are here this weekend to see him and his mother off to South America. And then I'm wiped out by late afternoon.

My back just hurts all the time, going to have the test steroid injection in three weeks to see if it helps, and if it does, then a Rhizotomy to the little fuck Facet nerves shortly afterwards. I'll let you know. But the Sinemet is looming large in my brain until I'm acclimated. It overshadows even the back pain for weirdness each day. And the local company still wants me to work for them, even after I asked for another month's delay before starting, and also knowing I have PD...so I may start there just for more weirdness in a week or so...can't decide if it's worth it to make $250 for 20 hours a week...not much to get excited about in the way of income.

Chapter 46
Hey Nik, Let's Talk About Money

Hey Nik,[1]

I missed hearing your voice the last two Wednesdays on the radio, you've got a great radio sound that suits on-air talking. I hope your back is getting better and you're not in so much pain.

I wish we could talk a little more openly about money, so I could rant and rave without it upsetting you...but it could get a bit testy for you when the $5,000 college fund runs out real soon, and you won't have any savings or more money from us to carry on. You've got some important choices to make about choosing to work instead of playing during the coming season of senior year parties and your social nightlife.

You've got to save for rent and school. It's that simple. And about the PARKING TICKETS; the bottom line is really simple. Don't get any more tickets. We (you and I) can't afford to pay them...and I'm the responsible party in the eyes of the law.

I'm not telling you anything you don't already know and I'm trying not to preach. I'm not pissed off or mad, and wish both of our financial situations were different, but it is what it is. I could get into talking about what it costs to get old and have some health issues, but I won't.

I'm worried about what's coming up financially for you in May, when the $5,000 is spent and you're low on cash,

---

1   One of Dean's two sons.

and I don't have any cash left to help you out.

I know it's always difficult for parents and children to talk seriously about most things and stay even-headed. So, I'm just letting you know how it's going to be, there's nothing we can do to change our finances. Costco said the check was mailed on March 11, a week later than I thought, and I'll get it to you as soon as it arrives.

Chapter 47

Worlds Away

The following emails are the last that Dean exchanged with me three months before he passed.

~ ~ ~

13 May 2021

Thanks, I'm trying to get a few chapters together to send to you...soon, love, Dad.

Some may be needing a little help, some won't need much, other than fitting one with another when the story in one differs from the next. I've tried to indicate where a new chapter and idea begins, but you can change anything you want to...like the order of the chapters.

~ ~ ~

10 June 2021

Subject line: Worlds Away[1]

Should be an amazing trip...I'll have some memoir pages ready as well, for your reading pleasure. I have a question for you, too. I want to gather about 20 pdf images from my hard disk and copy or change the .pdf's into .jpg's and then send them to Keith, and I've forgotten how to do this, if I

---

1 Last email Evan ever received from Dean.

ever knew. But I've tried and nothing seems to happen. Any ideas? When I try to think about it, a dark hole opens before me, and I go blank and can't remember even if this is possible. Any ideas? And suggestions on what to do or what I could read and easily follow will be greatly appreciated. Have a safe time in The Far East. Love you, Dad

Obituary

13 January 1943 - 13 August 2021

By Evan Quarnstrom

At age 78, Dean Quarnstrom passed away in the comfort of his home in Santa Cruz, California surrounded by his loving family.

Dean is survived by his three children, Anne, Evan, and Nik, his wife, Jeanie, his brother, Lee, and sister-in-law, Chris.

Born to Gordon and Leonore Quarnstrom in Longview, Washington, the Quarnstrom family relocated to Wilmette, Illinois in the early 1950s where Dean attended grade school and New Trier Township High School. It was as a teenager in Illinois where he would first meet the later love of his life, and his future wife, Jeanie Elliott. After four decades of friendship, Dean and Jeanie fell in love and married in 2000. They lived out their 20 years together in the coastal community of Santa Cruz, California.

From a young age, Dean always had a sense of adventure and an unmatched energy that earned him the nickname 'Rockets' among his peers. From his childhood attempt to run away and join a traveling circus, to embarking on numerous road trips across the country, Dean was always looking ahead to the horizon for his next adventure.

Dean's travels eventually landed him in the San Francisco Bay Area, where he found a sense of community among the counterculture 'hippie' subgroups.

At 24, Dean found himself a participant in the midst of the historic 1967 'Summer of Love' in San Francisco, contributing to the cultural and sexual movement that would revolutionize the country. Through his aviator sunglasses and thick mustache, Dean always joked (with a simultaneous hint of sarcasm and truth) that he was, in fact, the *first* hippie.

It was in San Francisco that Dean began to hone his love of photography, taking distinctive images of a generation that would define the era. Having studied photography at the San Francisco Art Institute, Dean eventually passed his passion for photos down to others, becoming a photography teacher at Cabrillo College in Santa Cruz County.

Film cameras accompanied Dean wherever he went, documenting trips that he took around the world to destinations such as Nepal, Morocco, Spain, Switzerland, the Grand Canyon, and Mexico, to name a few.

Dean's proudest accomplishment didn't come until 1989, when at 46 years of age, he finally became a father when his wife gave birth to their first child, Anne. In 1992 Dean received a welcome shock when he was informed they would have not one more kid, but two, with the birth of twins, Evan and Nik. Dean lived for his children and always went above and beyond to assure that they were able to pursue their interests and passions in life.

Dean crammed several lifetimes' worth of experiences into one, and was admirably stubborn in pursuing his own path in life, never succumbing to the status quo. He had a unique, wacky sense of humor that may have been hard to understand, but it made all those within his circle of family and friends always feel welcome and accepted.

Dean's presence will be greatly missed by his friends and family. It was always his dream to get the 'grandchildren experience,' which, unfortunately he passed too soon to see through. His legacy continues through the lives of his three children who will carry his lineage, values, and passion for life into the future.

Epilogue

"I now see the world that I'd lived in before with such clarity, and wonder if my vision is a side effect of my Parkinson's illness. I understand my past life with a lucidity that's blowing my mind. I can taste and sense so many subtle changes that I'd missed before, in the feelings and the beliefs that I'd held so firmly so long ago. I know with certainty what actually happened, what I've experienced and learned from having had so many wild and strange adventures. The memories are almost as vivid and strong as if I'm there in person again."

-Dean Quarnstrom

~ ~ ~

My dad suffered through pain for many years towards the end of his life, but his departure was still abrupt for us. Everything unraveled so fast that I had to wonder how it all happened. As I read through my last emails with him, I could hear him reading out the letters, clear as day in that voice that I know to be uniquely his. In his last email to me, the subject line 'Worlds Away' caught my eye. I couldn't help but notice the foreshadowing in hindsight. It's as if he knew something that I didn't realize, or didn't want to realize, but he didn't want to say. Perhaps he was preparing me for a life without him in the not-so-distant future. It's clear that he knew this memoir would never be completed in his lifetime, something that never consciously occurred to me until his final months.

Epilogue

Dean started penning this memoir with a goal in mind: to show me and my siblings who he really was and to help us understand where we come from. I would say that he was even more successful in accomplishing that goal than he ever could have imagined. Through helping him craft this memoir and the process of turning it into a final product after his death, I've gotten to know my father more intimately. Suddenly all his quirks make sense to me.

All those tidbits of stories that I heard on road trips and over family dinners as a child have unfolded into harrowing, sometimes colorful tales – discovering mysticism in Native American sweat lodges, rubbing shoulders with cultural icons like Ken Kesey and the Grateful Dead, travels to exotic lands like Morocco and Nepal, the harsh reality of going to prison, etc. For example, when I was little, Dean used to tell me and my siblings about how prison inmates were paid pennies to manufacture California's vehicle license plates. He would often reference otherworldly experiences with a mystical sadhu who blacked out Dean's camera film with his mind. He'd tell us that he has "photos of the '60s that will be worth a million dollars someday." Now I get it.

I never thought too hard about his younger days, when he would have had these experiences. I would roll my eyes and nod my head incredulously, unaware of who my father really was or the things he had done. But now it makes so much sense. I now better understand his motives, his passions, his path, his conflictions, his imperfections, his contradictions, and his character. I have a better perspective of the high points in his life and his sources of happiness. I can also piece together his complexities and his flaws as he himself admits that he perhaps held onto immature beliefs for too long to avoid the full reality of adulthood. As Dean recounts the trials and turning points of his life I can't help but notice bits of him in me. I've gotten to know myself better.

When I listen to him pour out his heart about his past failed relationships, I smirk and then realize that perhaps the apple didn't fall so far from the tree. When I truly understood Dean's propensity to run as far away from the status-quo as possible, it made me think about my own somewhat parallel journey of leaving my 'dream job' for a life on the road of travel, new experiences, financial instability, and uncertainty. At the same time, this is ironic because Dean always encouraged me and my siblings to take a more conservative career path that guarantees a financially stable future – something his life choices did not provide him.

When Dean died at home in August of 2021, we were lucky to all be there for that moment. His three children and wife, Jeanie, were holding his hands as he took his last breath. Watching my father pass into the next realm changed me. Seeing someone you love slip away in your hands is something you never forget. But at that moment, I realized that it is an experience that is so innately human. It's as if there is a before and an after in life once you lose a parent, once you watch someone die. You take everything you've learned from them, the good and the bad, and forge ahead as the bearer of your lineage.

Finishing this memoir is closure to a chapter of my life. Dean's project is done. His story is told. It's out there for those who want to read it, especially for the intended audience: his children. It's been fascinating for me to read through this book. Still, I often wonder how intriguing it will be to an outsider who is less emotionally connected to the material. Dean may not have been famous, but he chose an interesting route in life that epitomized and aligned with several wider cultural trends like the 'Summer of Love' and the 1980s 'War on Drugs.' It also strikes relatable undertones that are familiar to many of us, like yearning for more meaning to life than what the status quo provides, the constant search for balance among the everpresent influence of our vices, and pondering what legacy we'll leave when we die.

This project has been decades in the making and well over two years since I got my hands on it. Even in the week after he passed I started putting this book together. I dove headfirst into a dozen or so external harddrives harboring hidden jewels of stories that are now included in the book. I read, edited, and pieced together dozens of loose writings,

Epilogue

and then repeated the process again and again. Most of this project happened while I was embarking on a personal adventure of my own, a 20-month journey that traversed 12 countries and four continents. I mulled over these words on my laptop in cafes in the Indian Himalayas, in musty apartments on the shores of Brazil, and in palapa-roofed cabins in the desert of Madagascar. My step mother, Jeanie, was instrumental in helping me through this process. Her years of teaching English, intimate knowledge of Dean, and level-headed, practical approach to problem solving were a welcomed relief after I had had my head stuck in dozens of Dean's old Word documents for over a year.

Today, Jeanie still lives in Santa Cruz in the house that she lived in for more than 20 years with Dean. His children, me and my siblings, Anne and Nik, are all healthy and well, living around California, and in my case, around the world. In late 2023 we got the entire family together for the first time in two years since celebrating Dean's life in 2021. The weight of his passing has gotten lighter with time. We still share our fondest or quirkiest memories that we have of our dad. One of Dean's realizations towards the end of life was that he would never get to have the "grandparent experience." He passed before any of his children had kids. However, now my brother, Nik, is due to have a daughter with his fiancée, Carli, in April of 2024. Dean's legacy lives on. Wherever it is that he may be now, surely he will be smiling down when the newest addition to his family joins this world.

-*Evan*

www.ingramcontent.com/pod-product-compliance
Lightning Source LLC
Chambersburg PA
CBHW021143160426
43194CB00007B/671